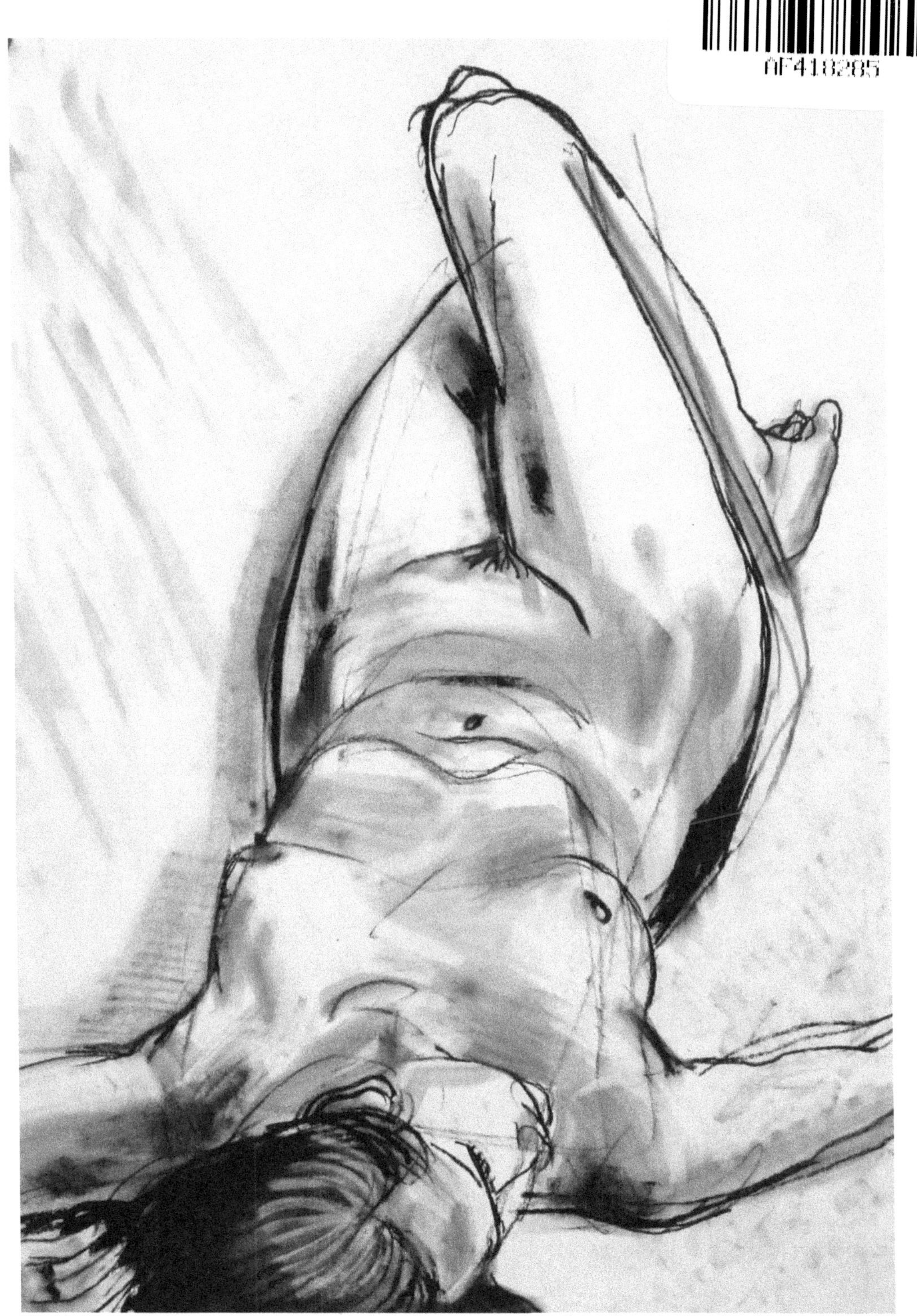

Figures

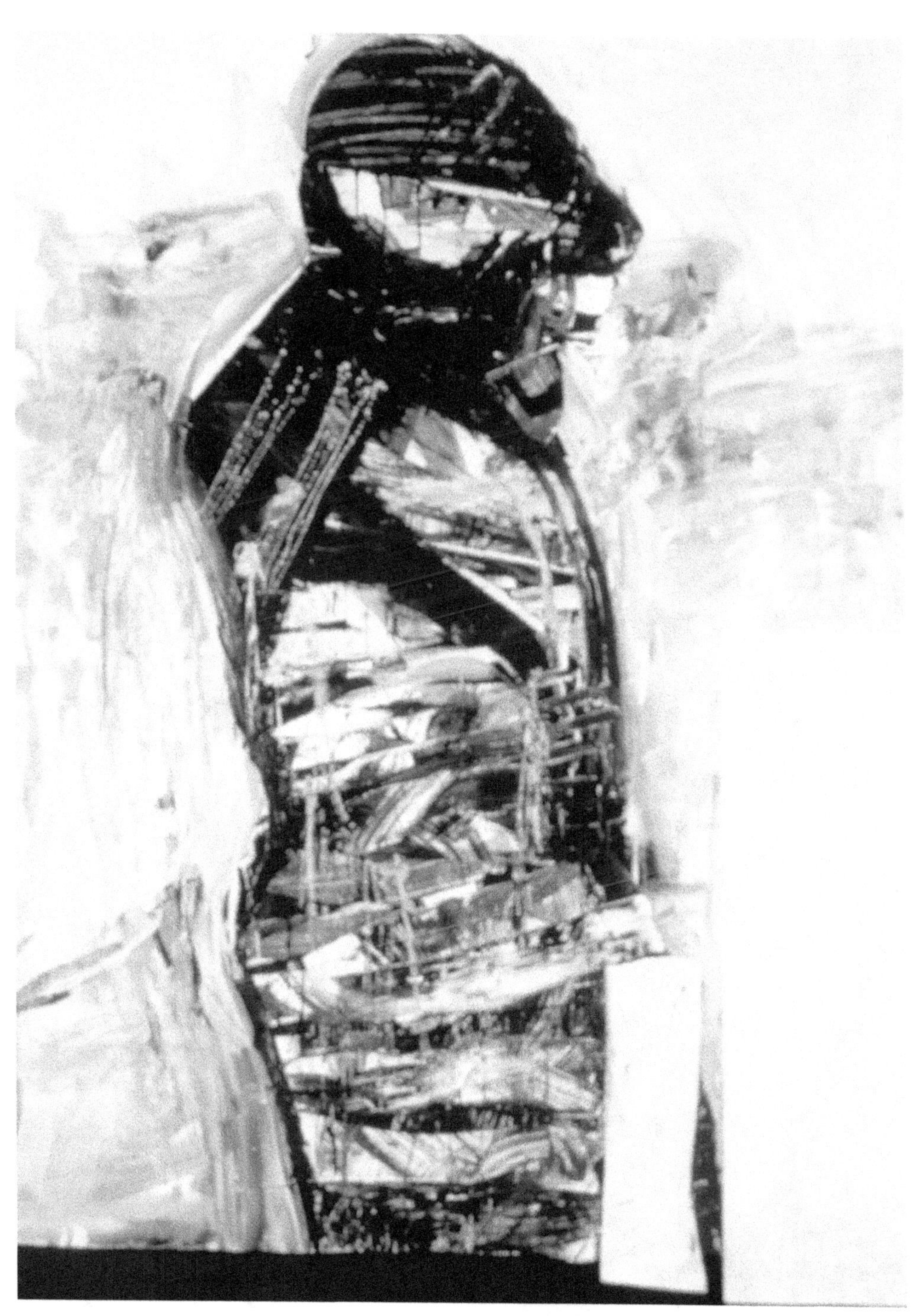

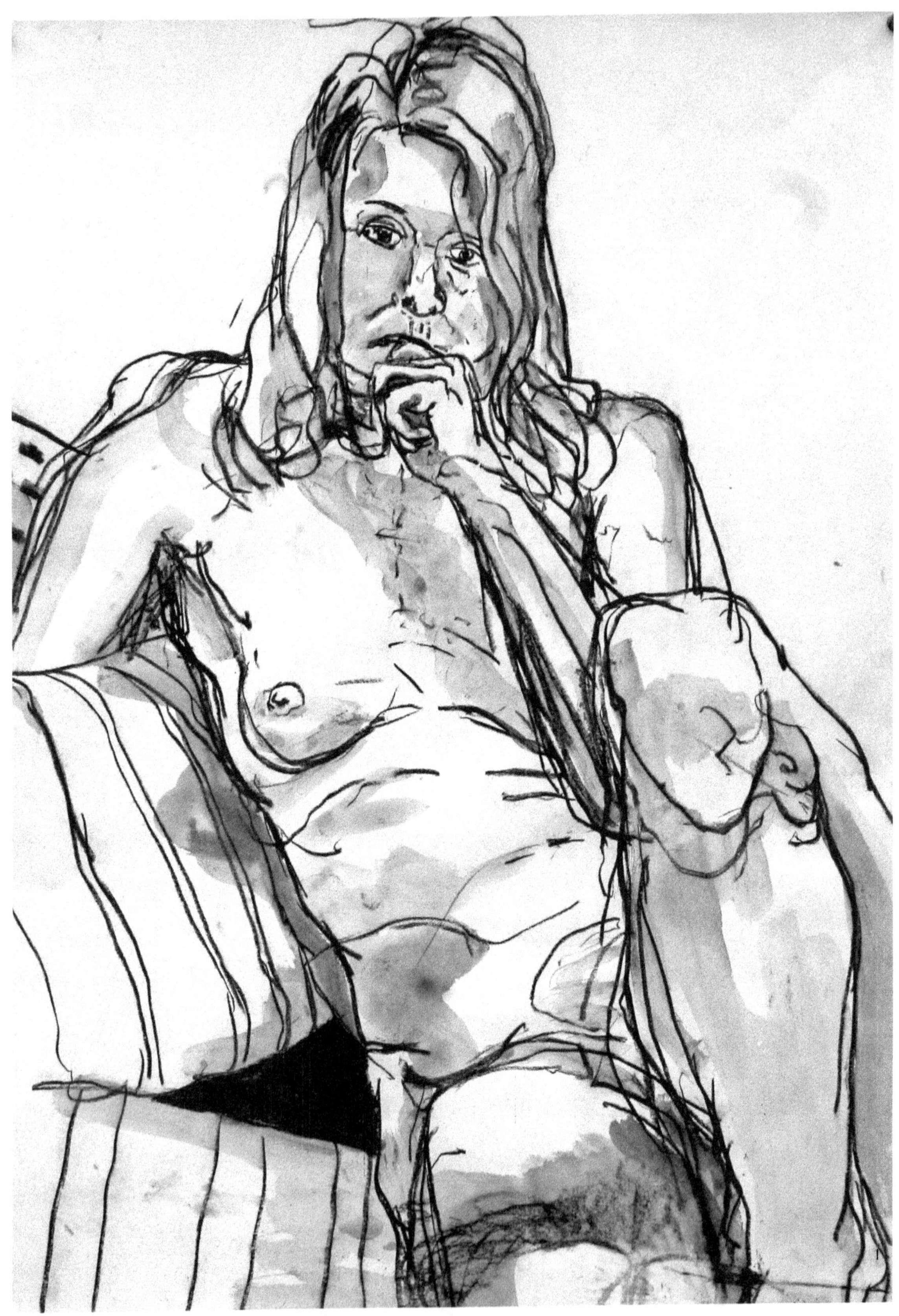

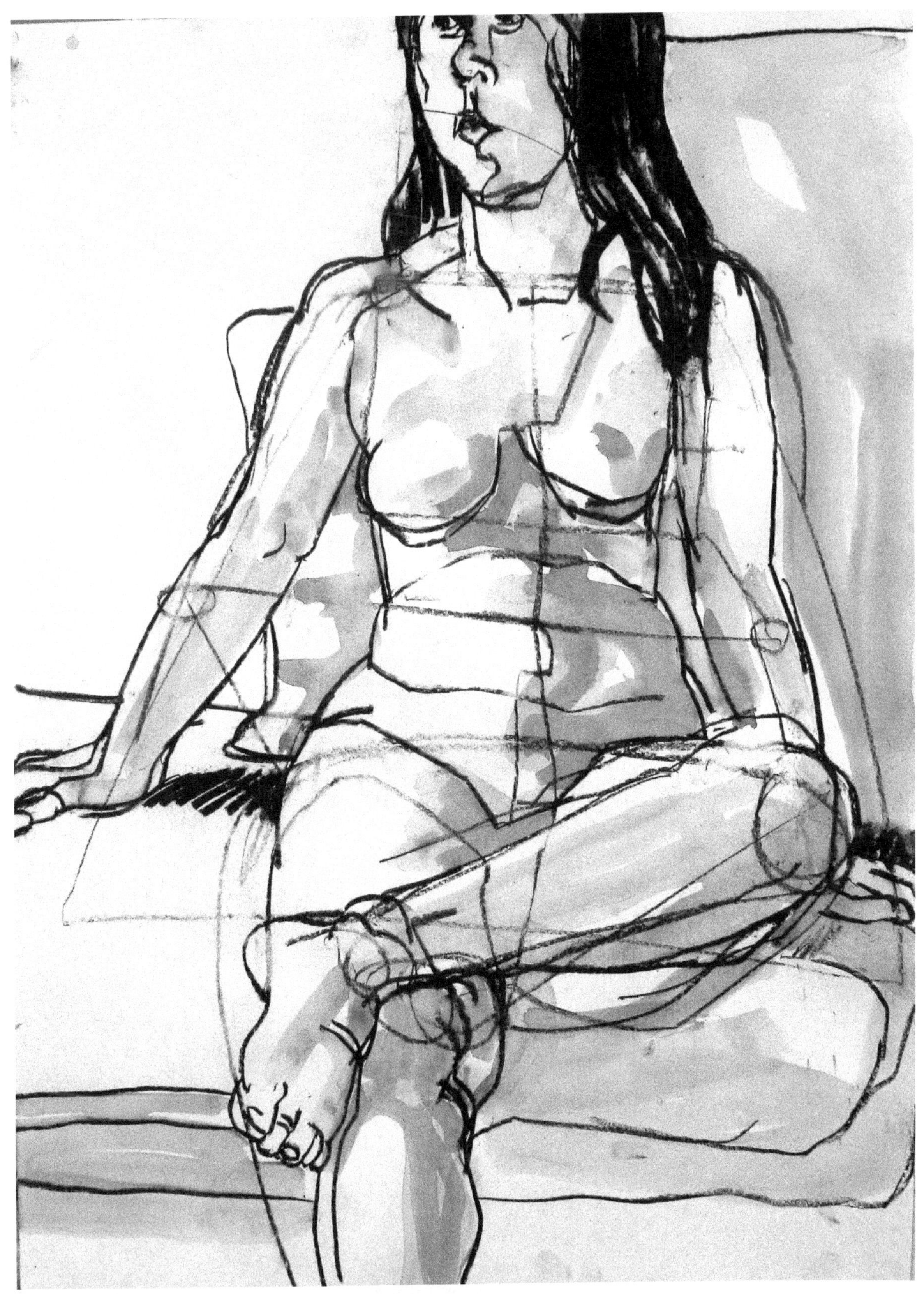

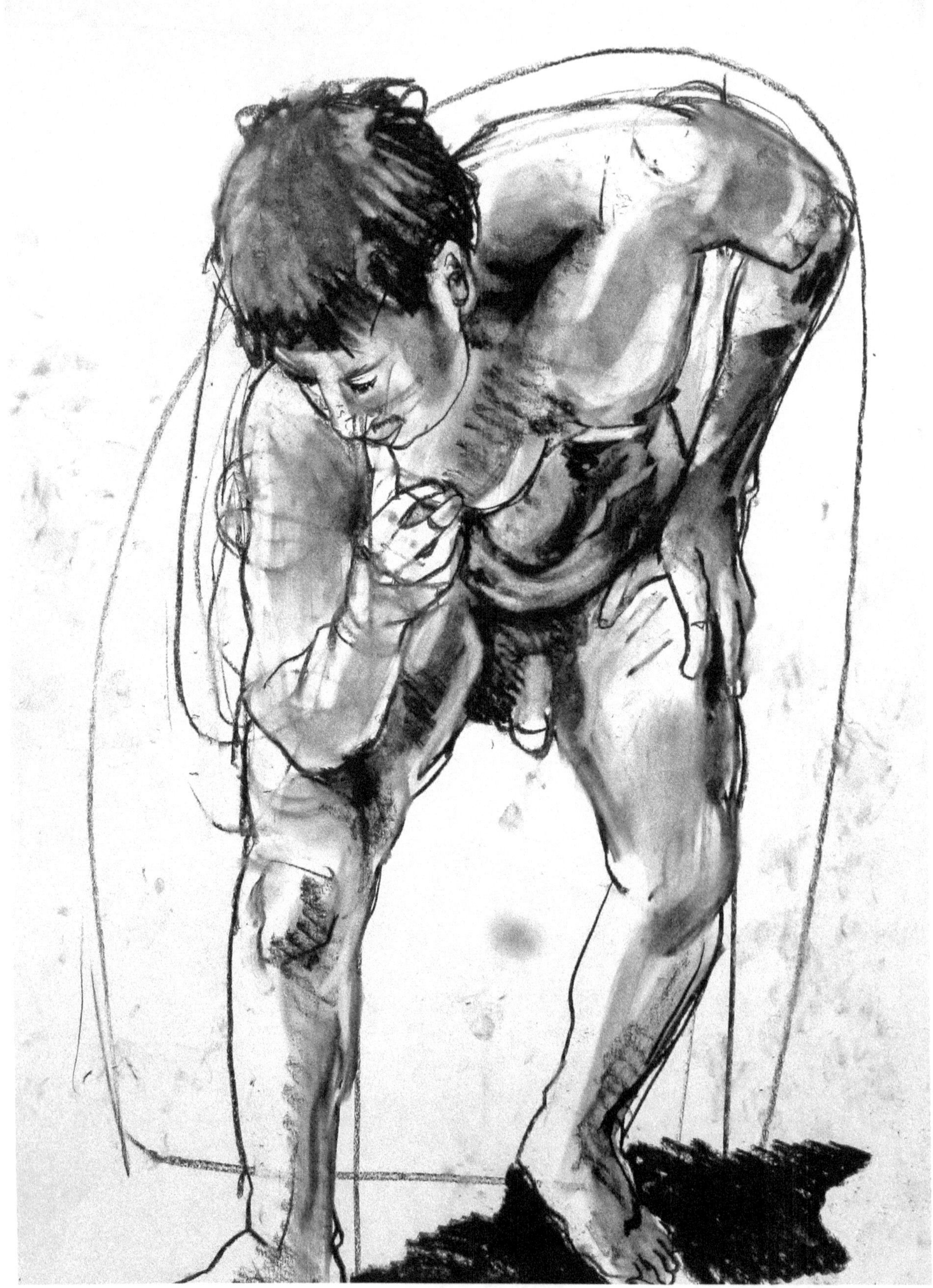

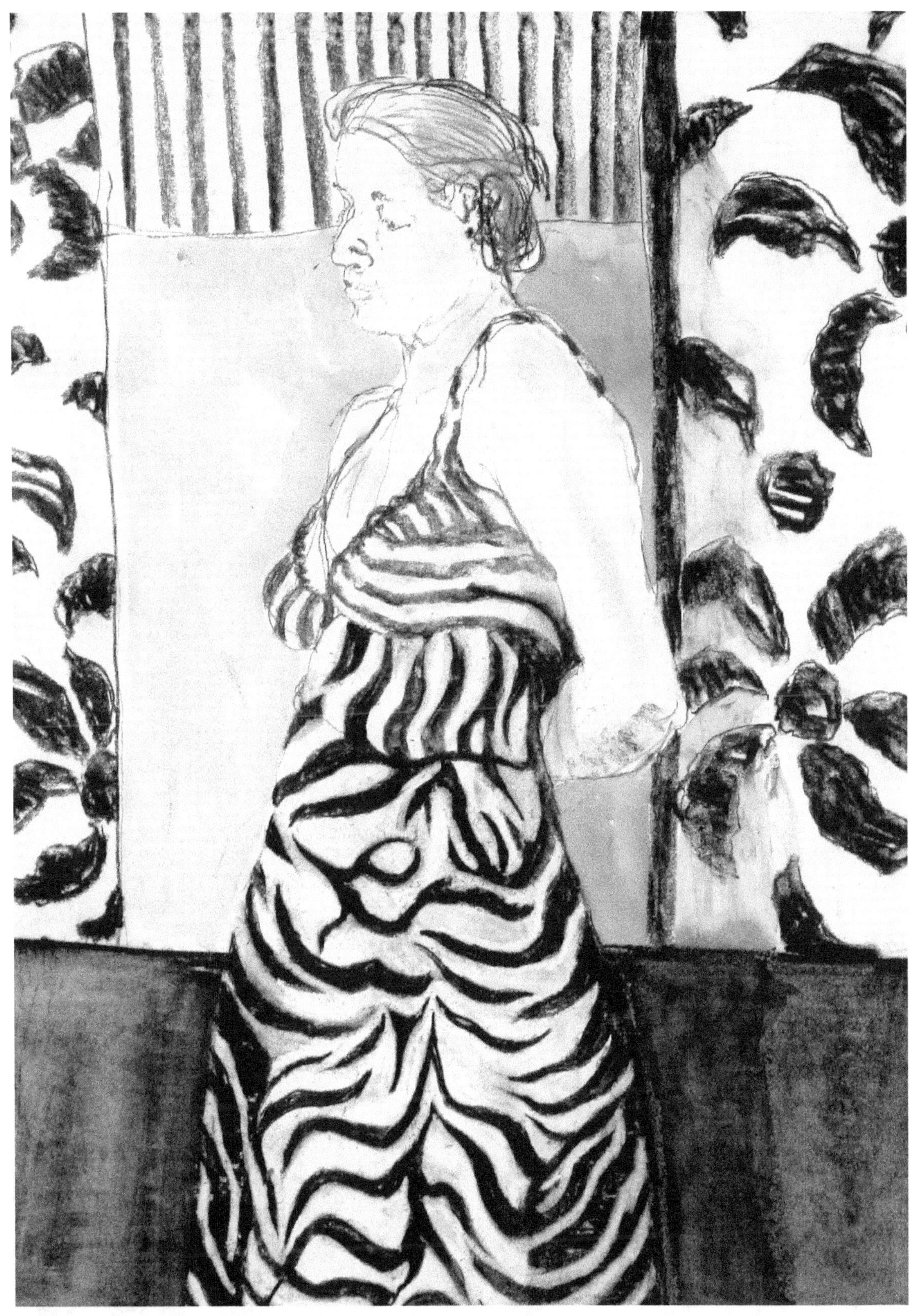

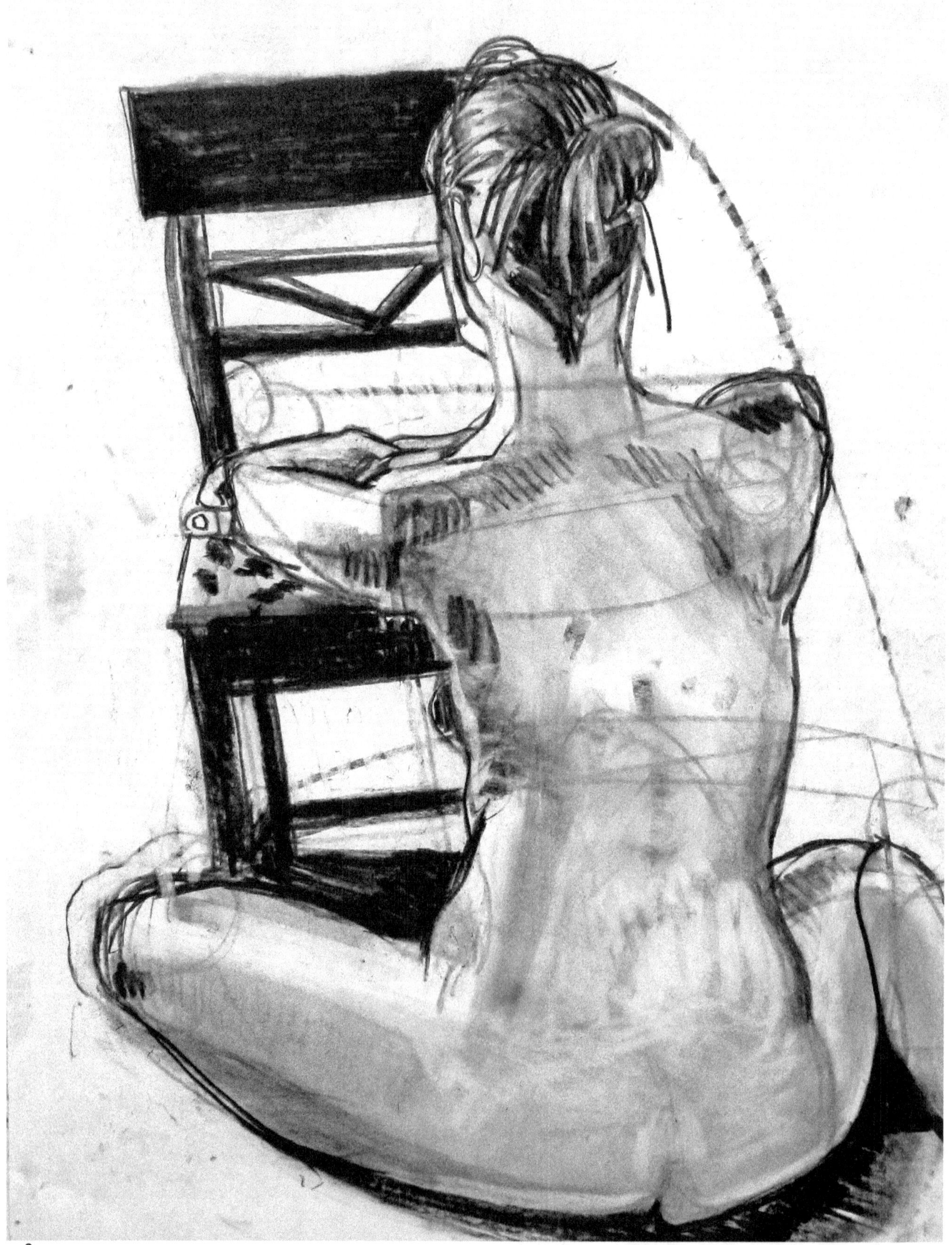

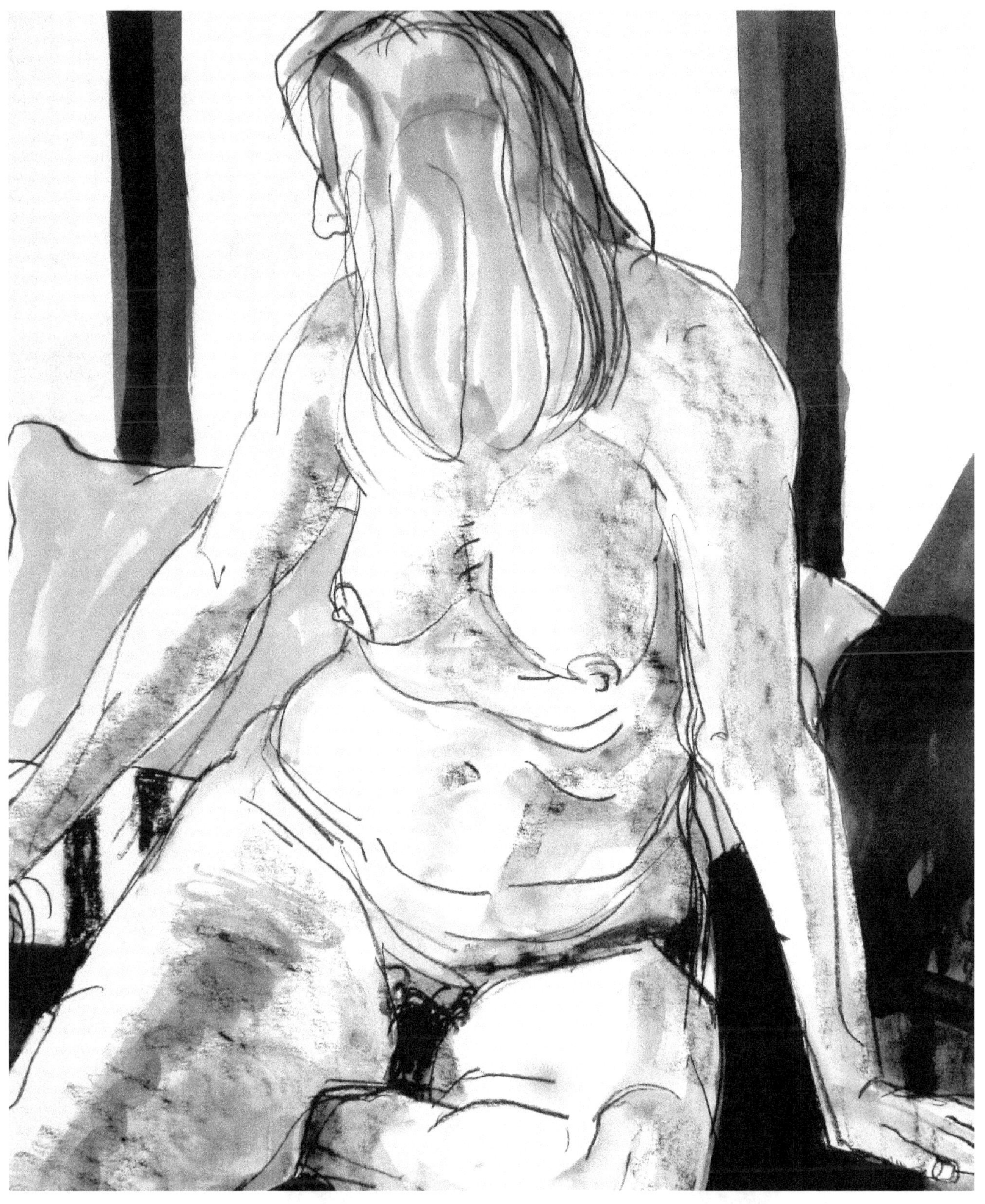

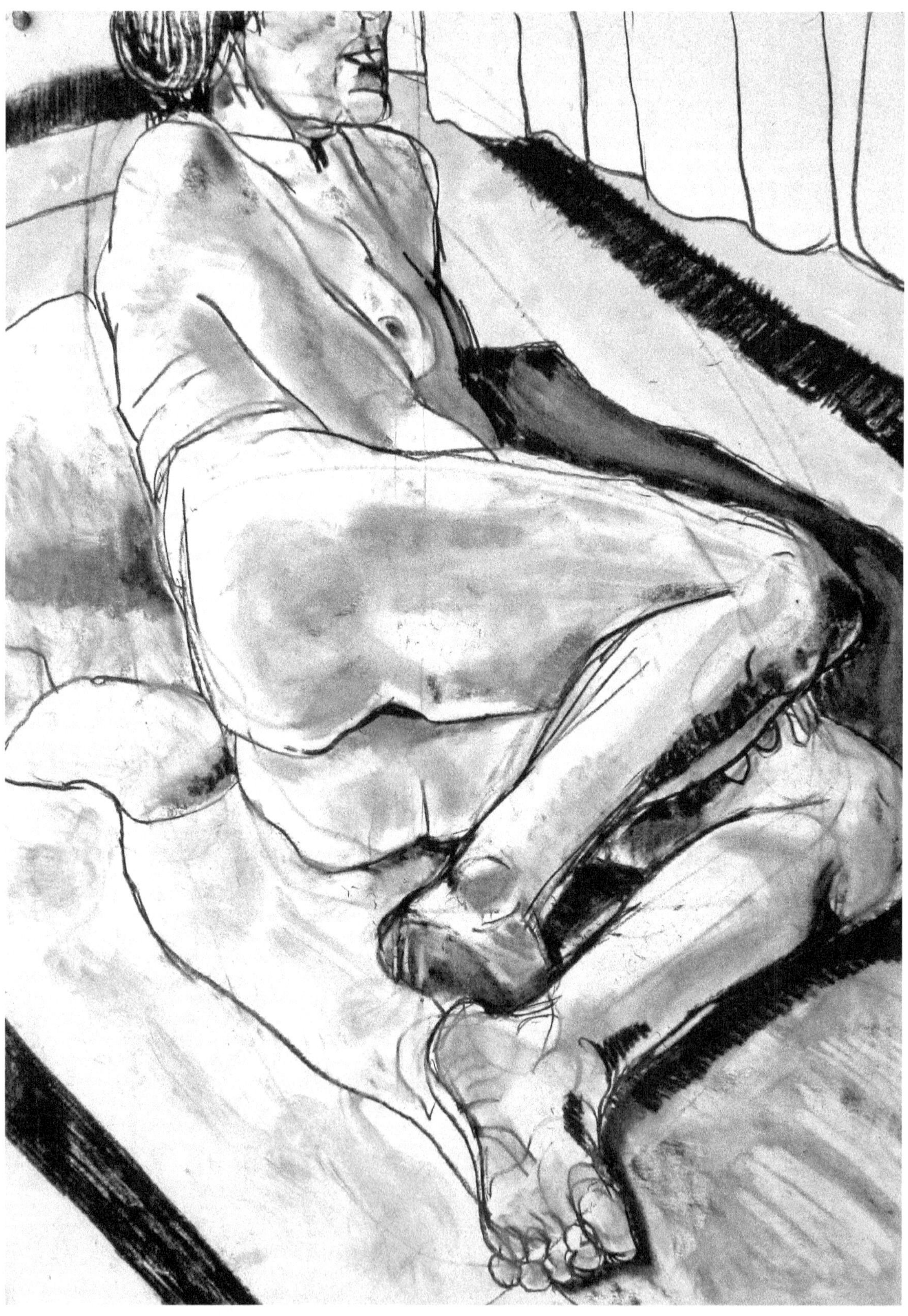

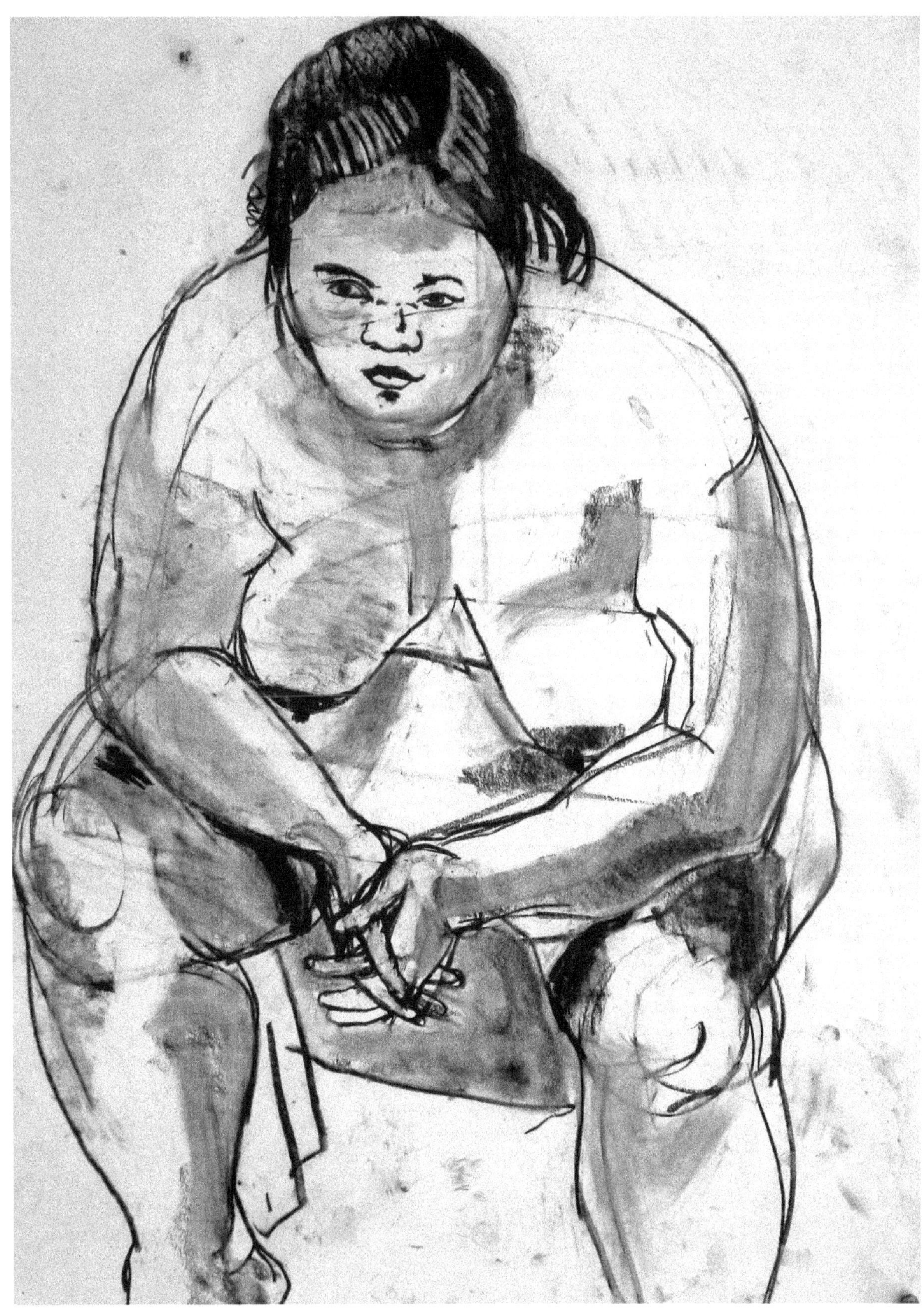

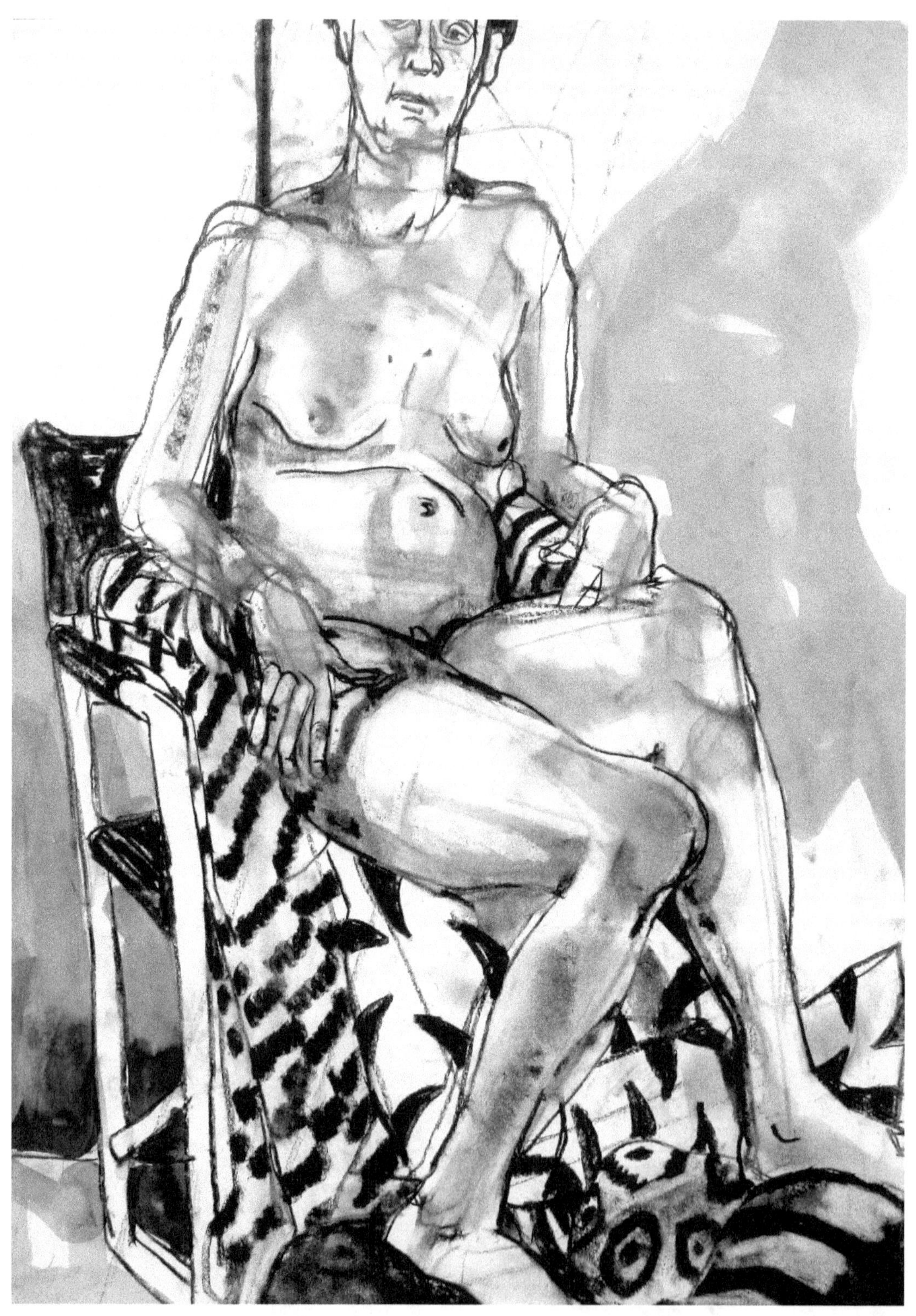

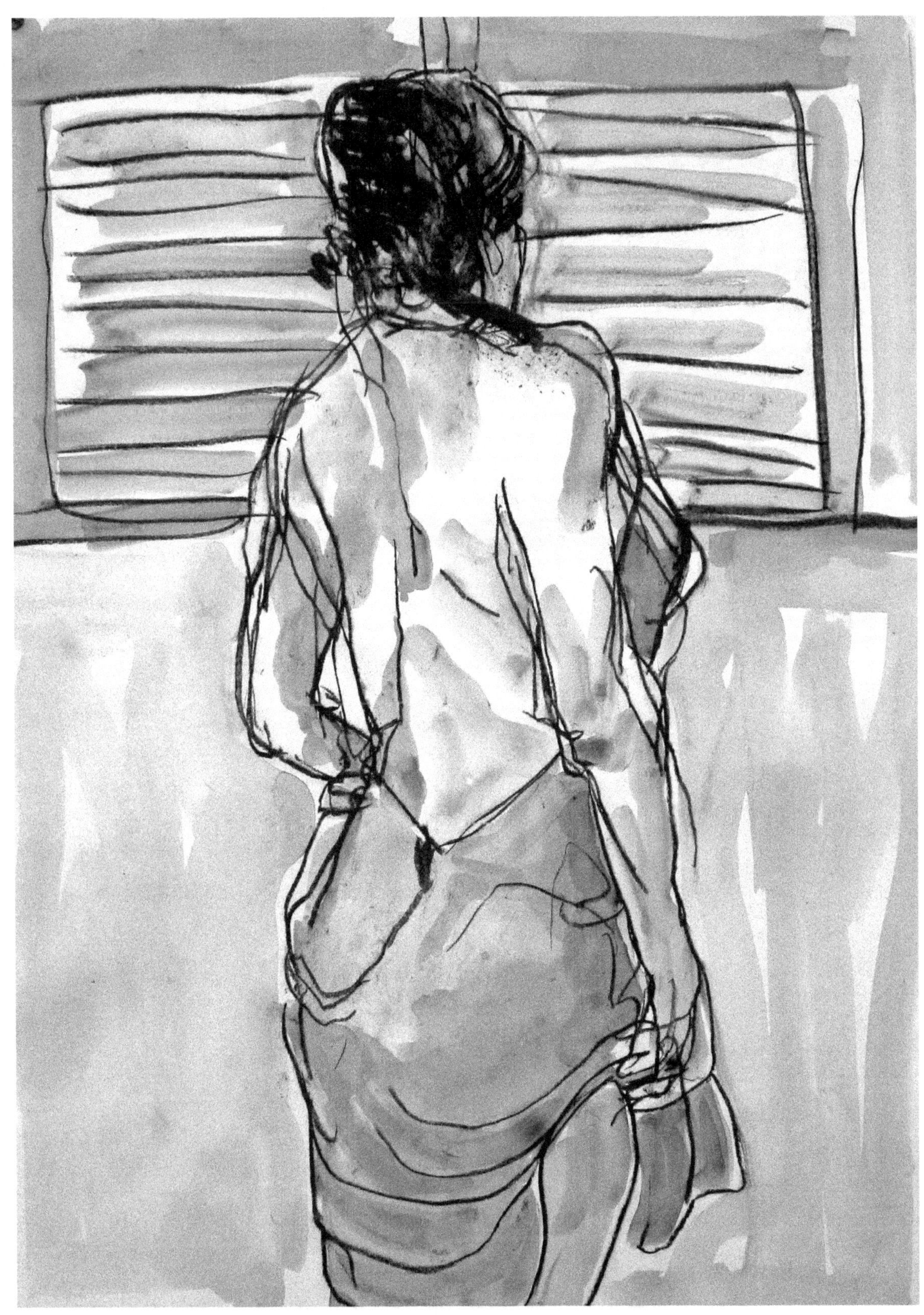

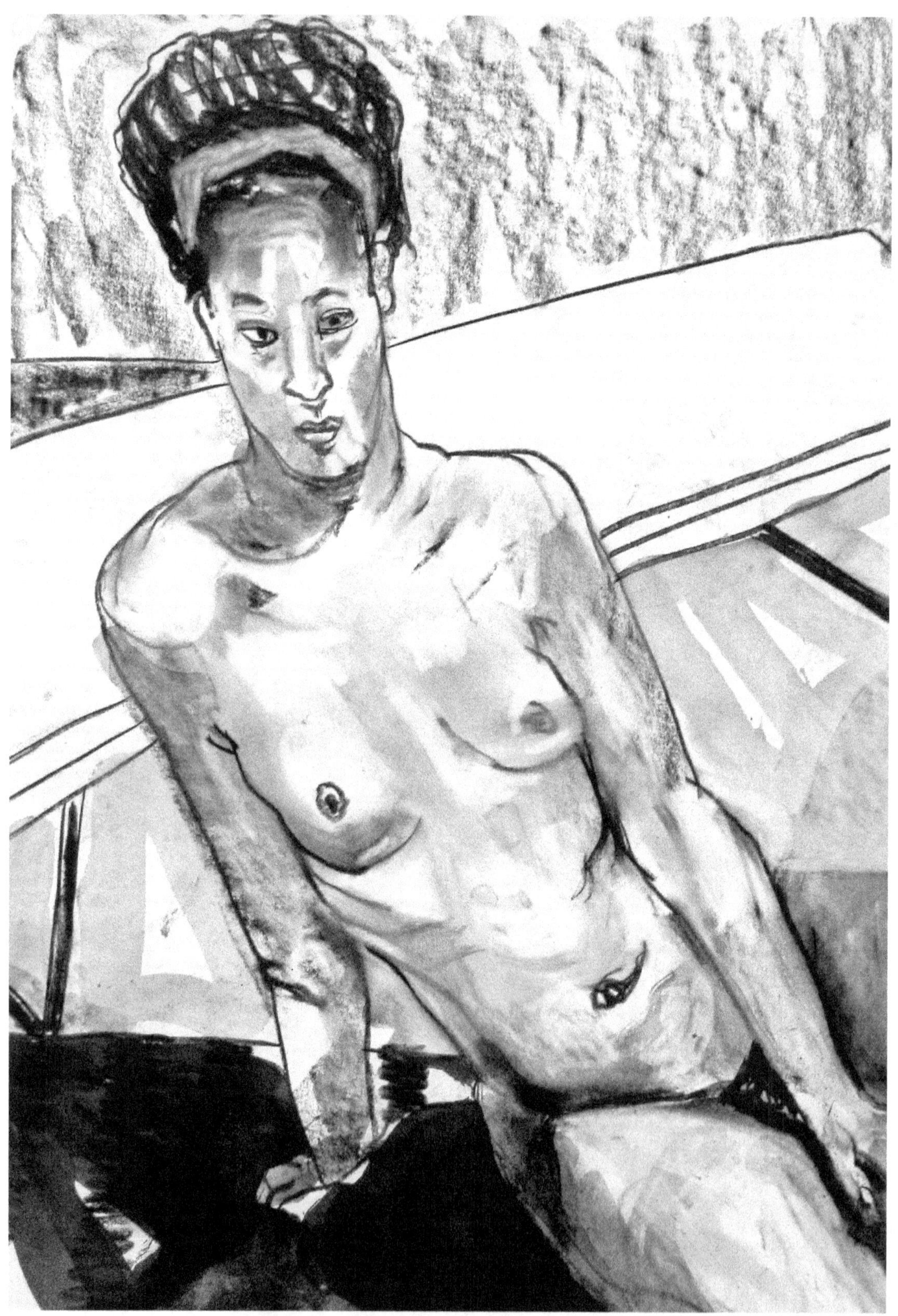

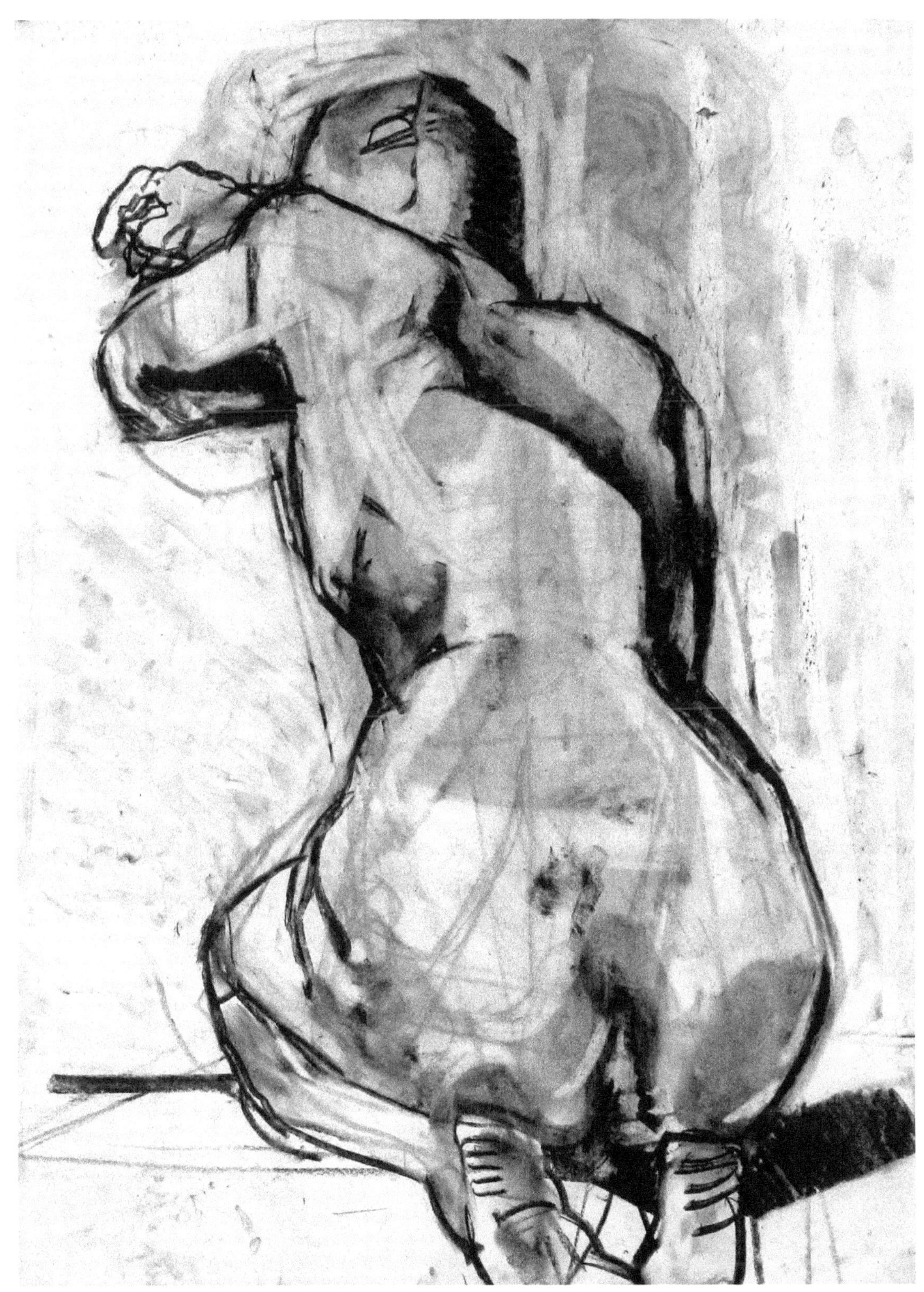

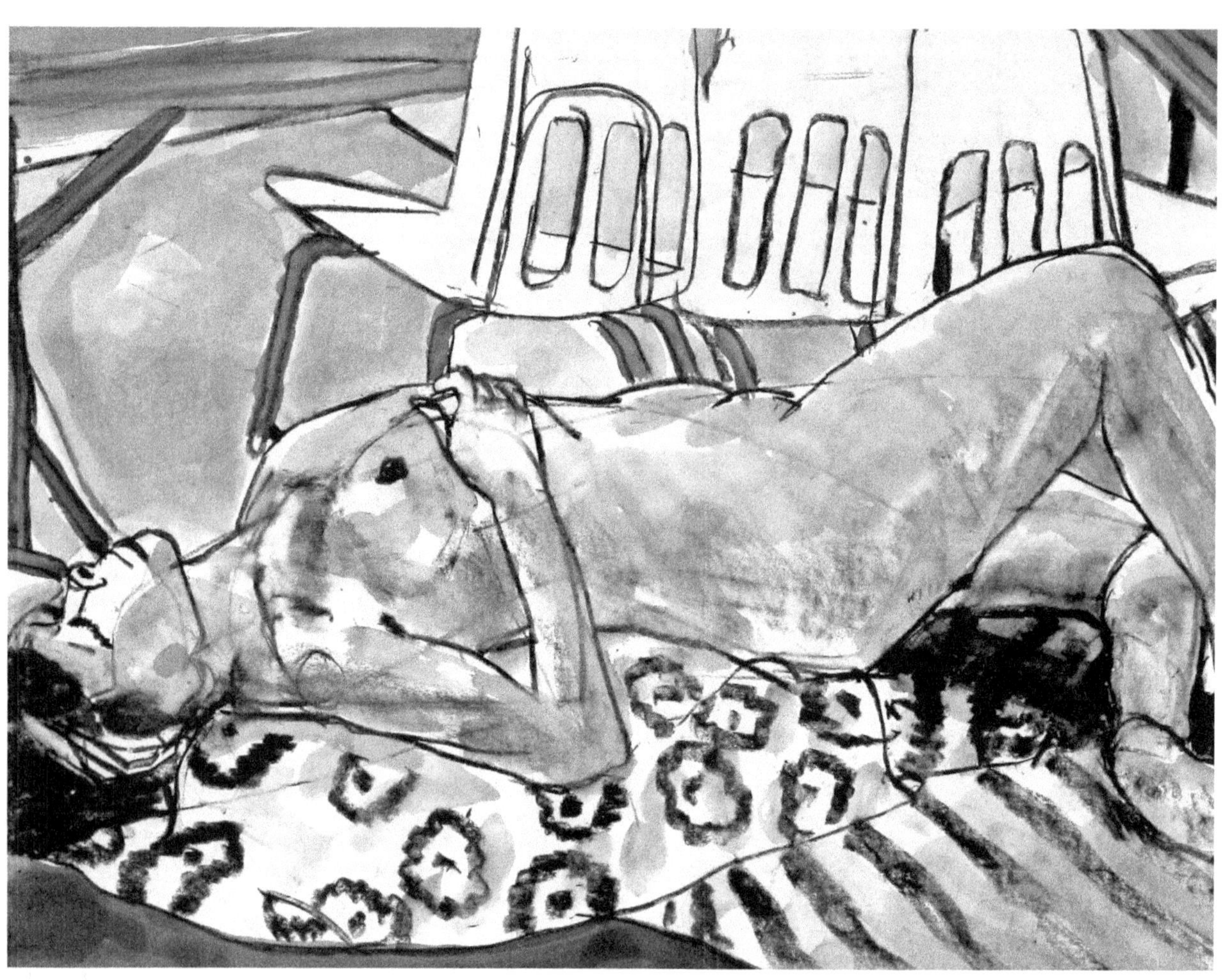

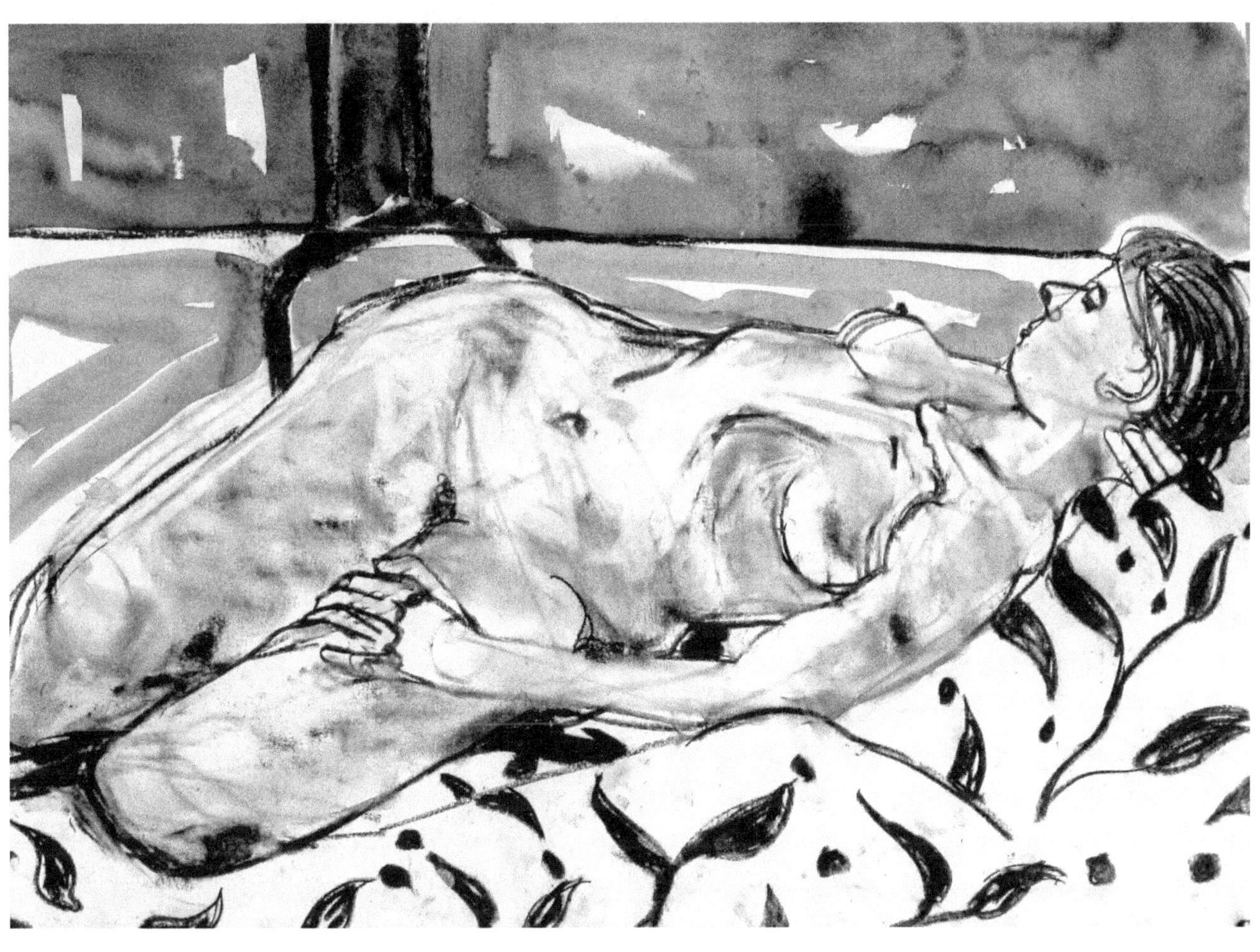

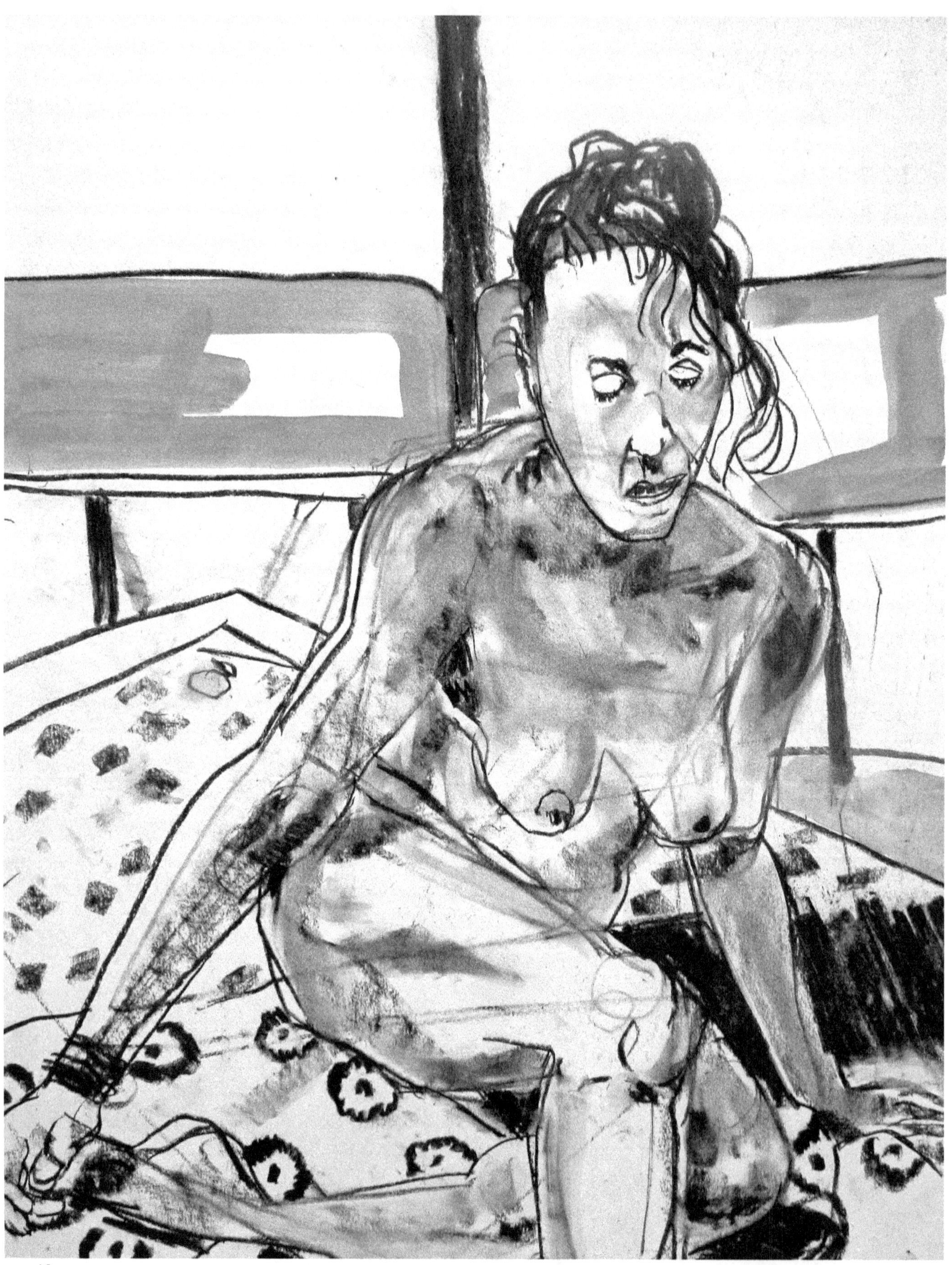

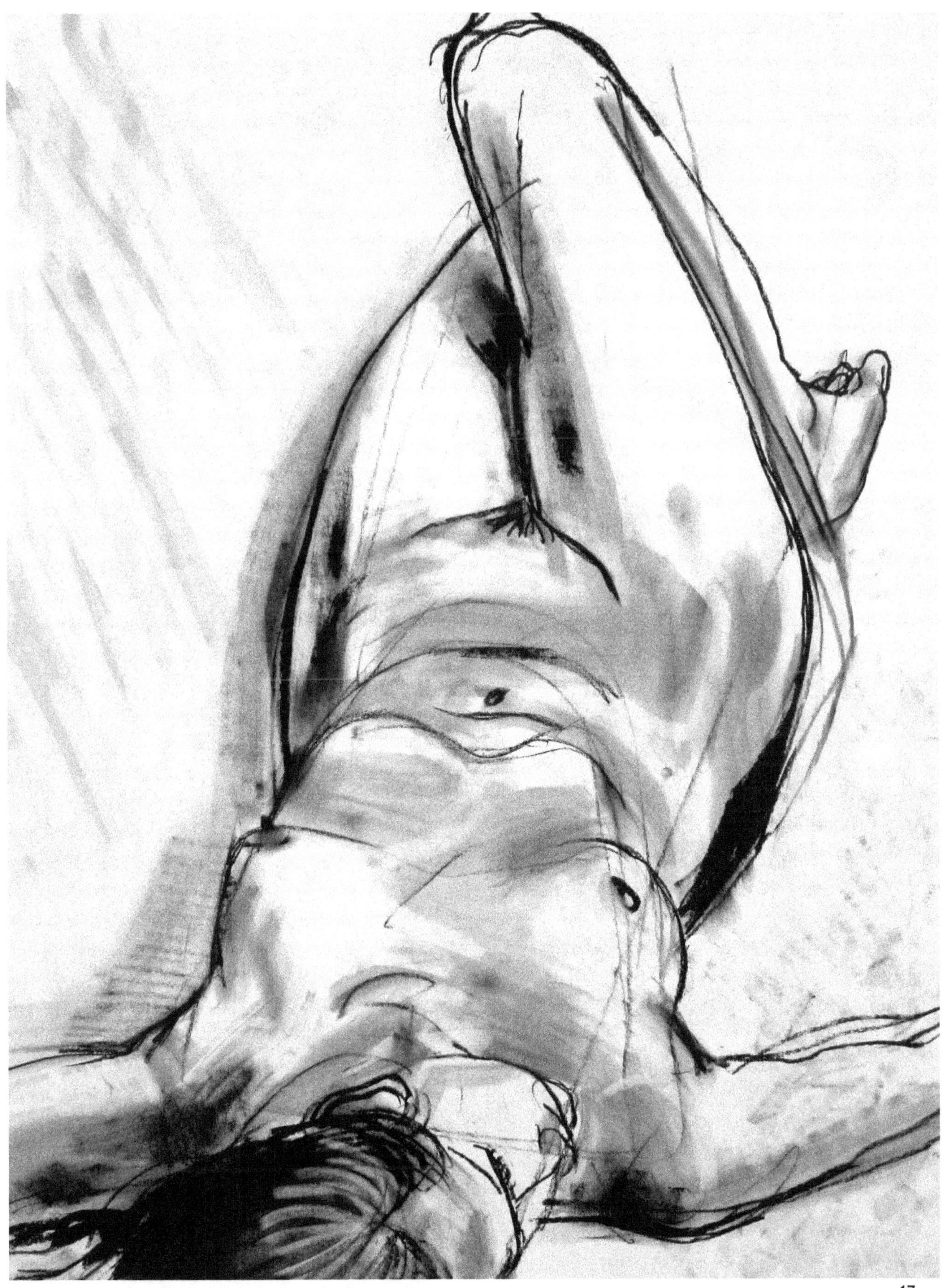

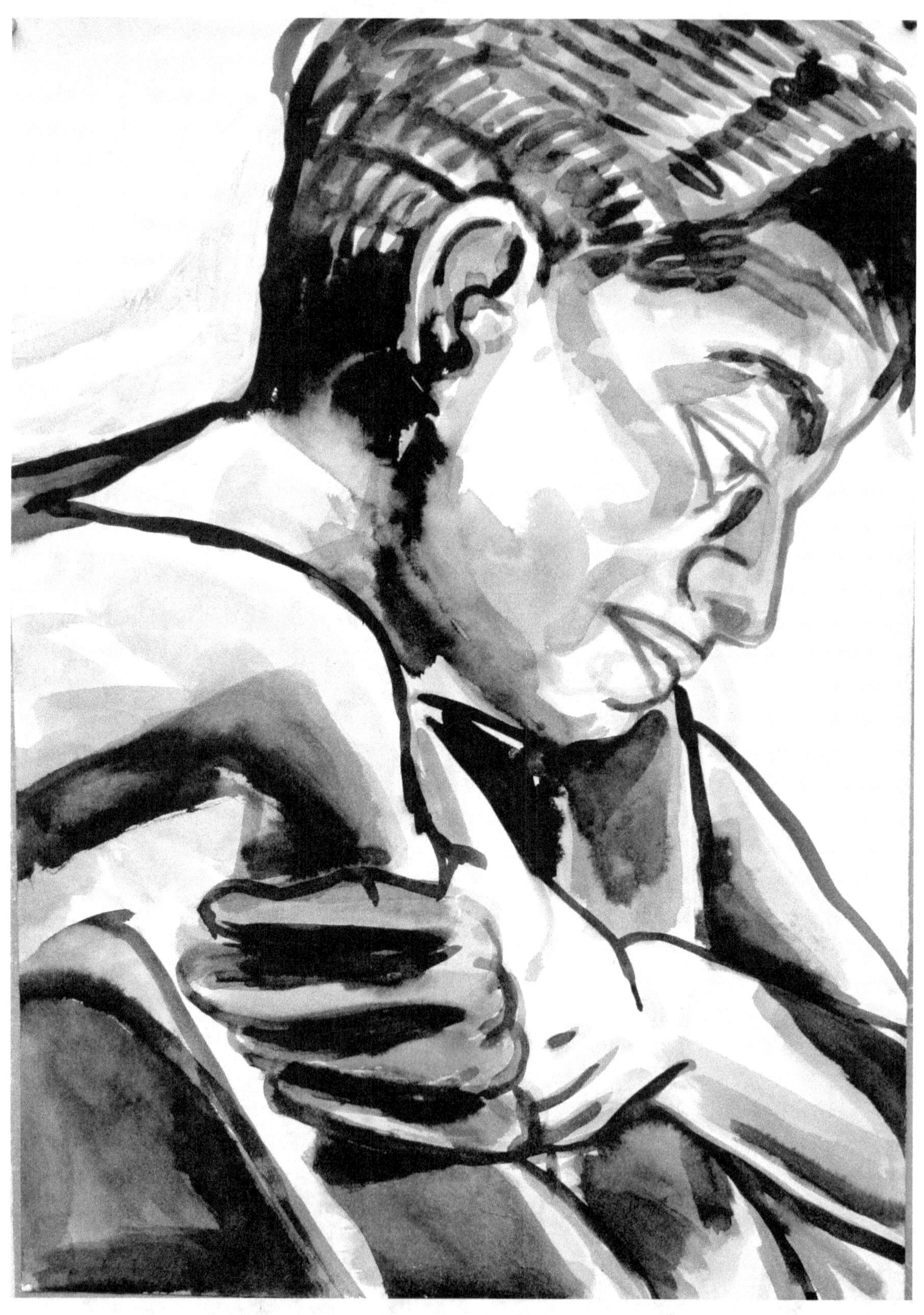

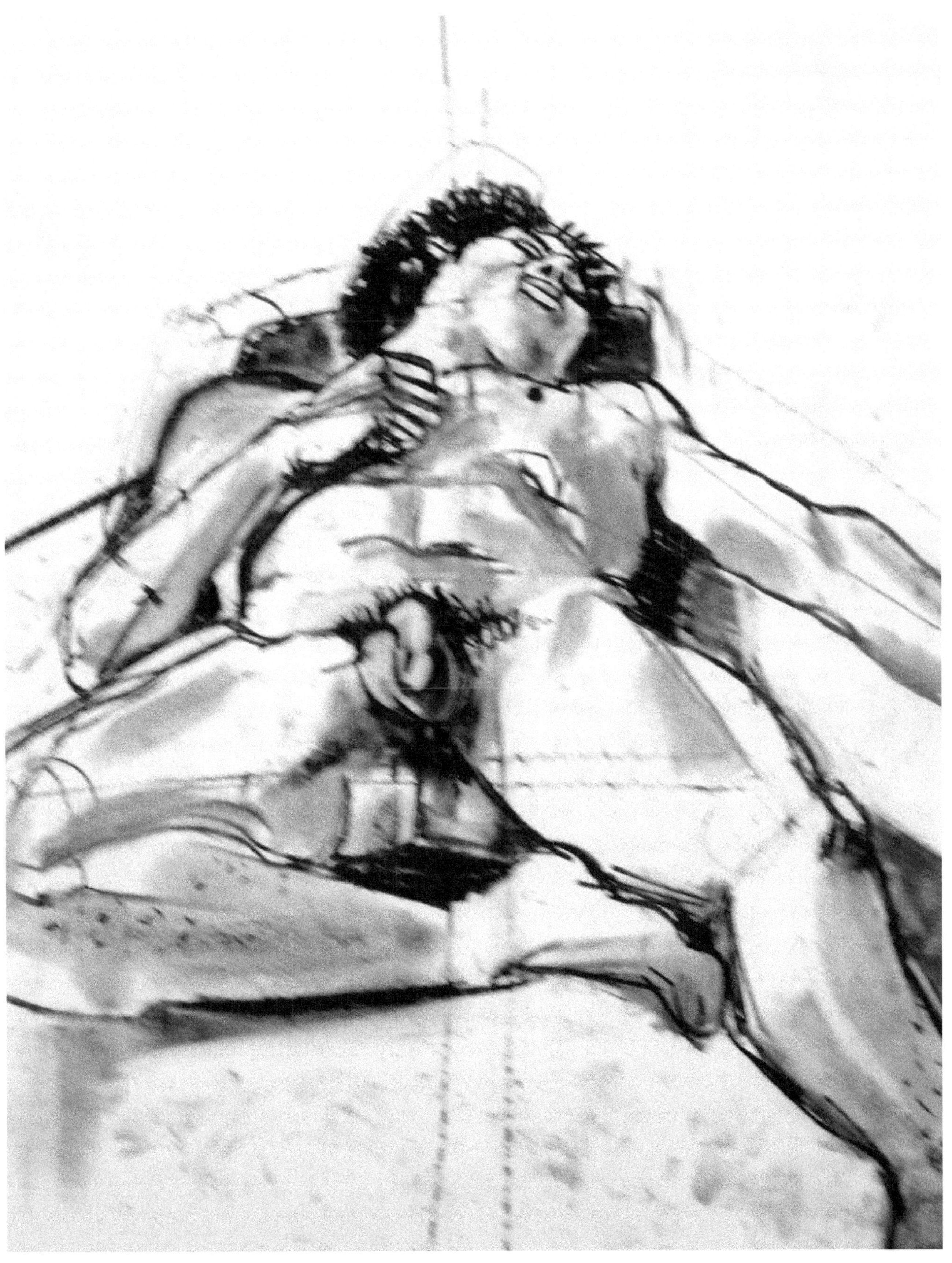

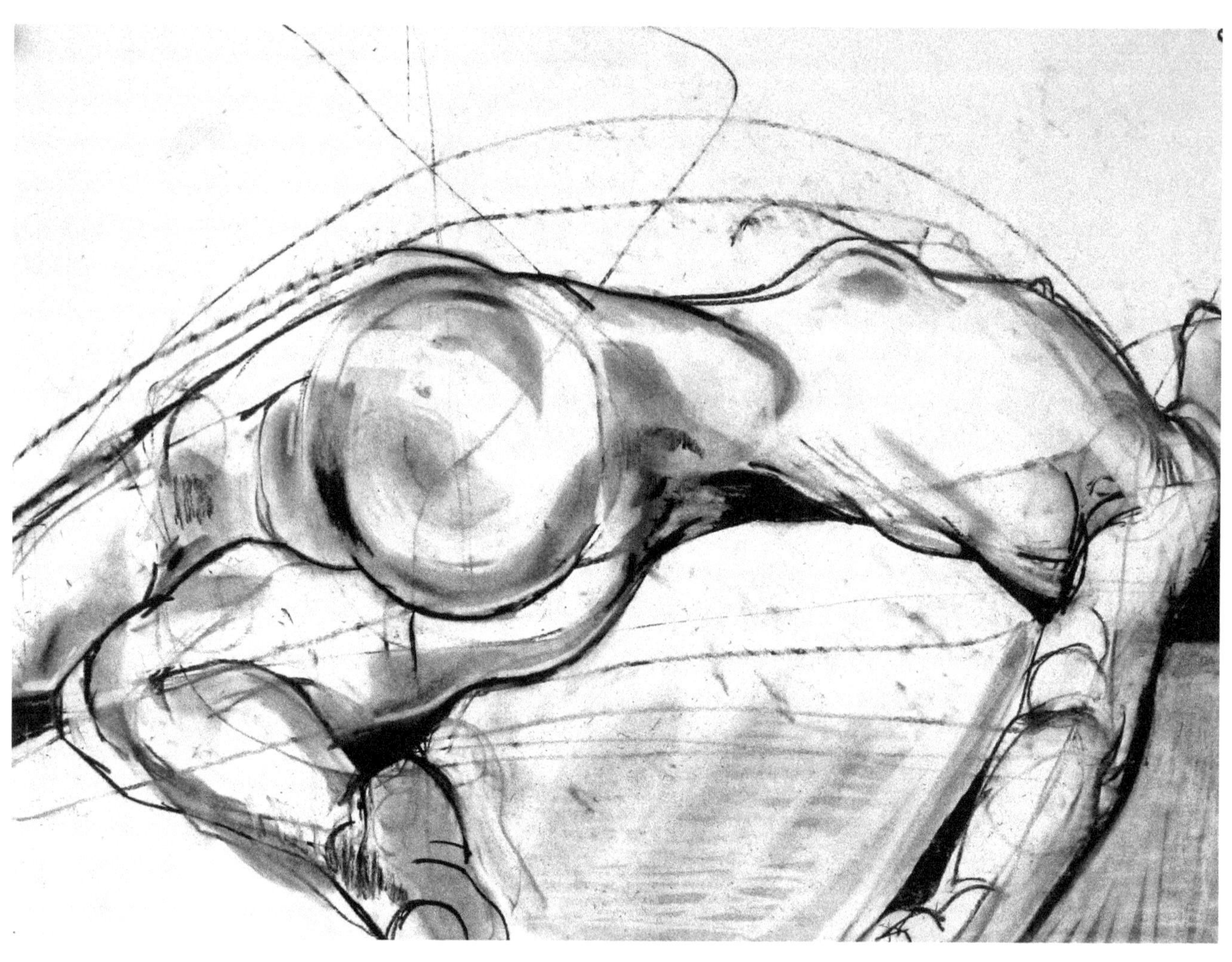

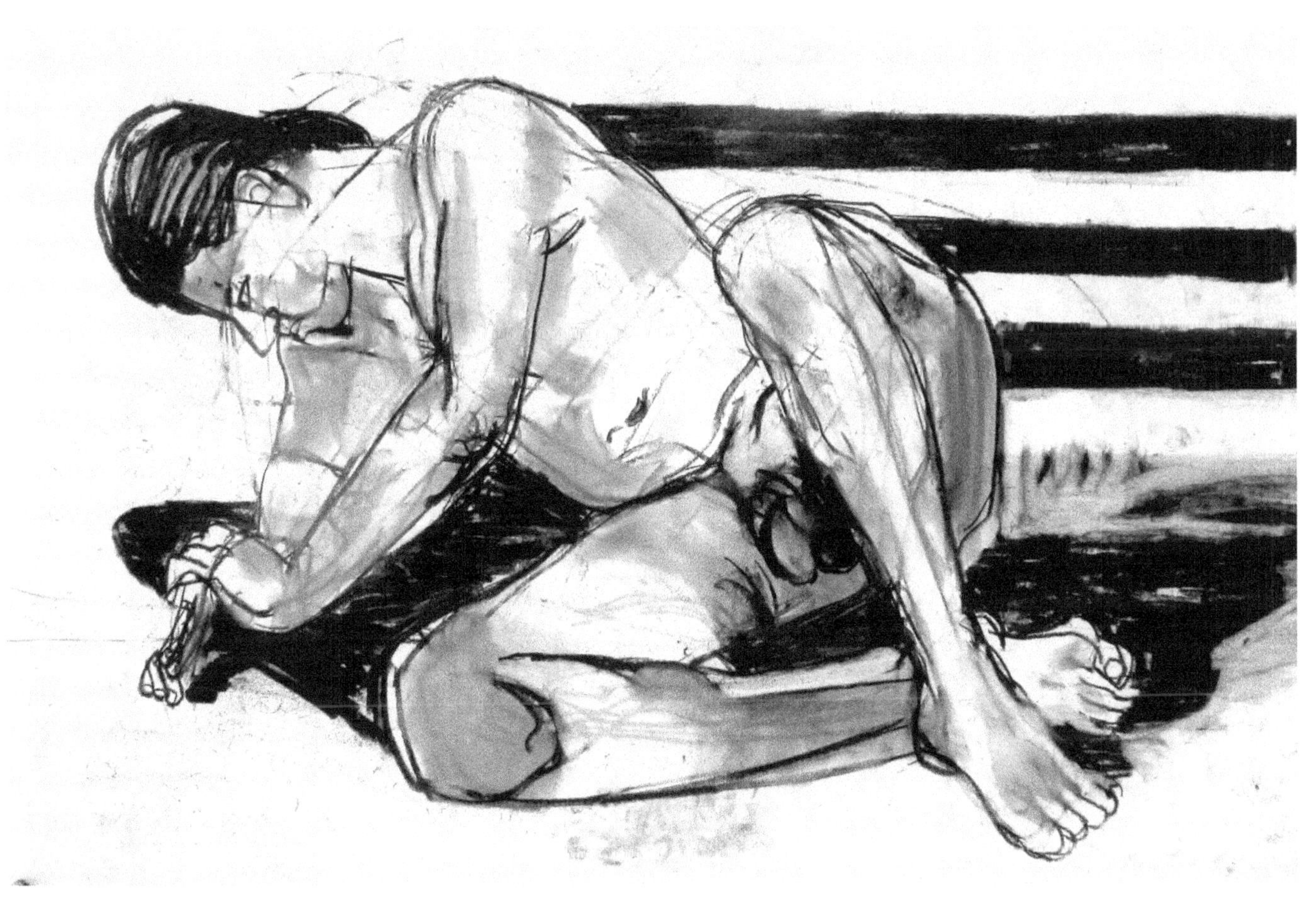

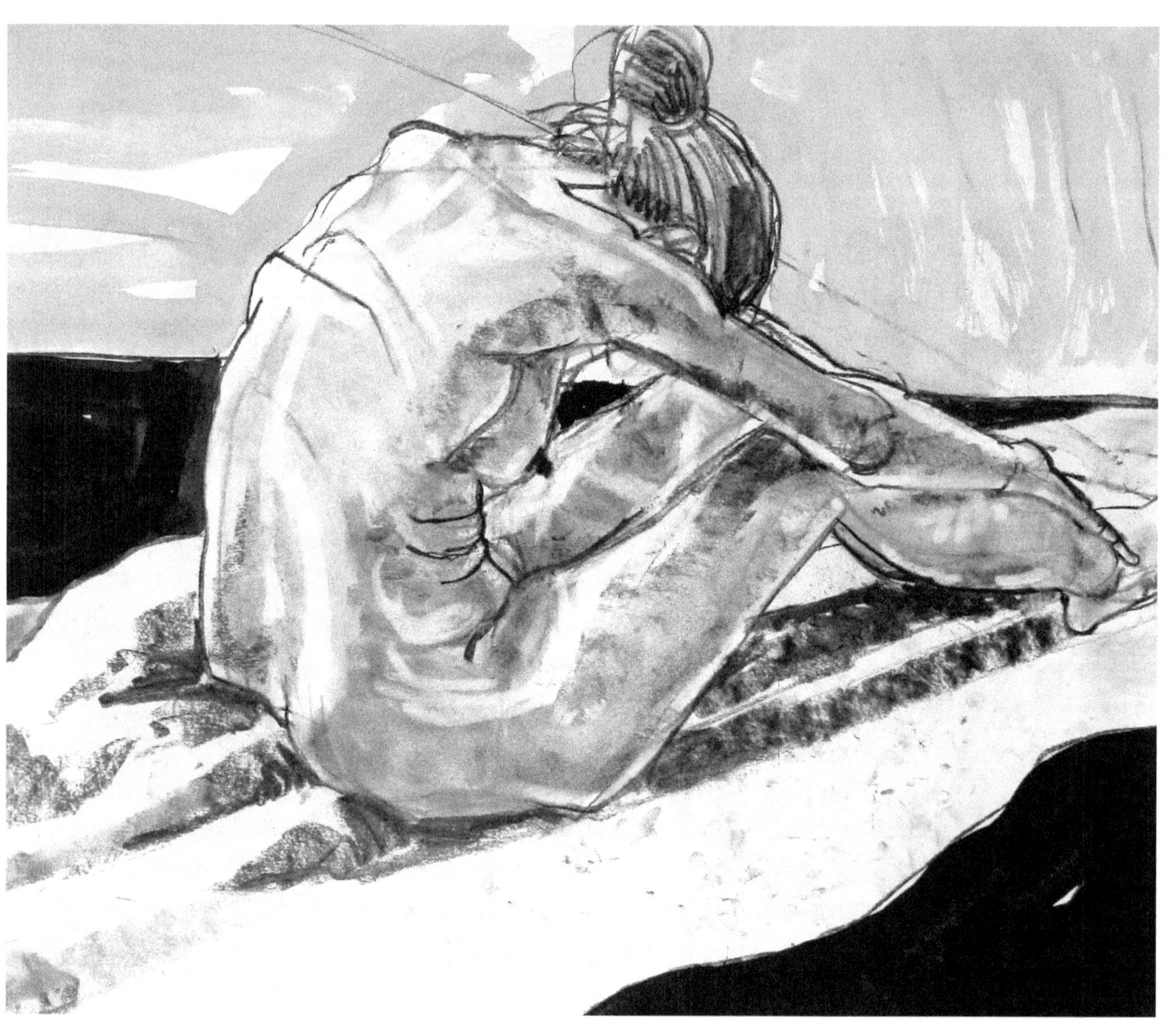

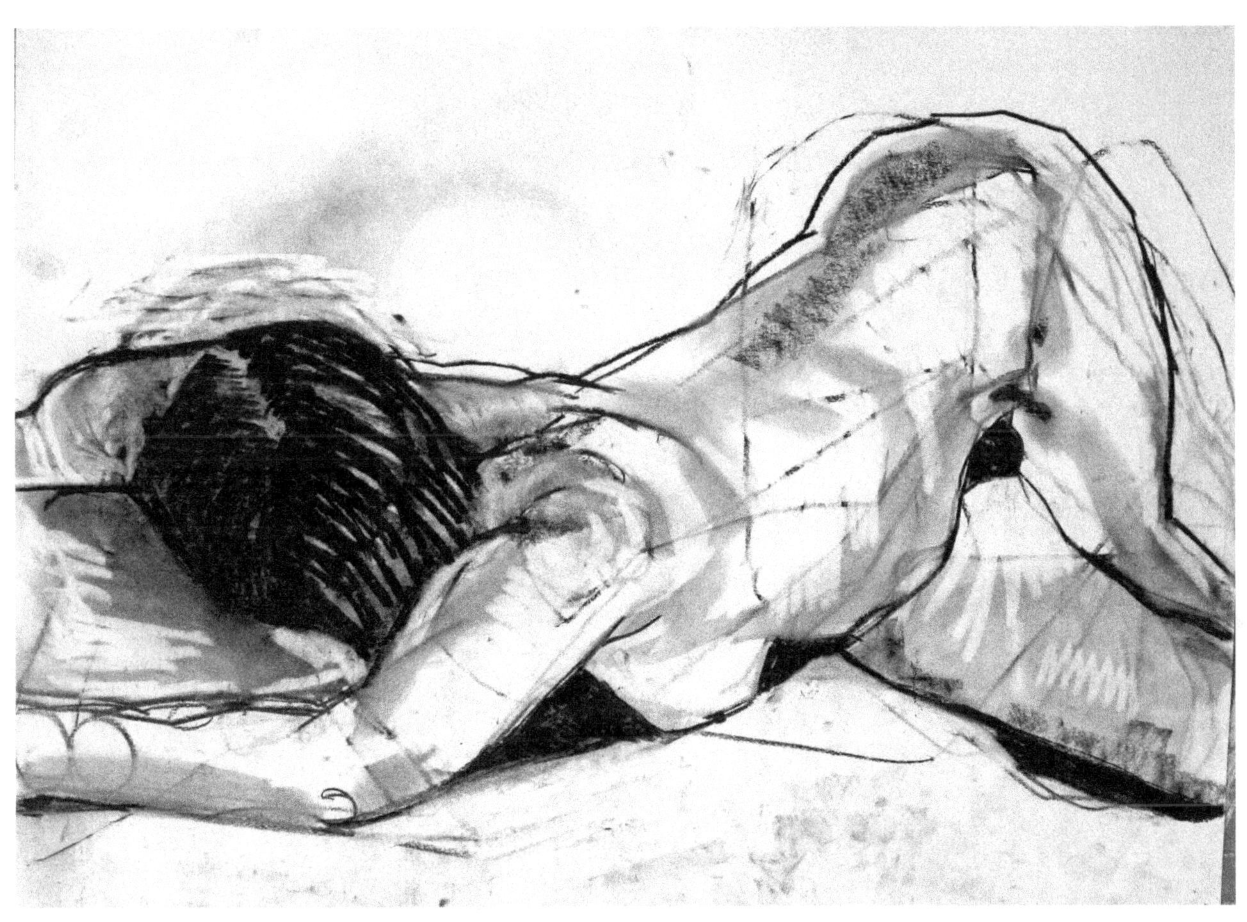

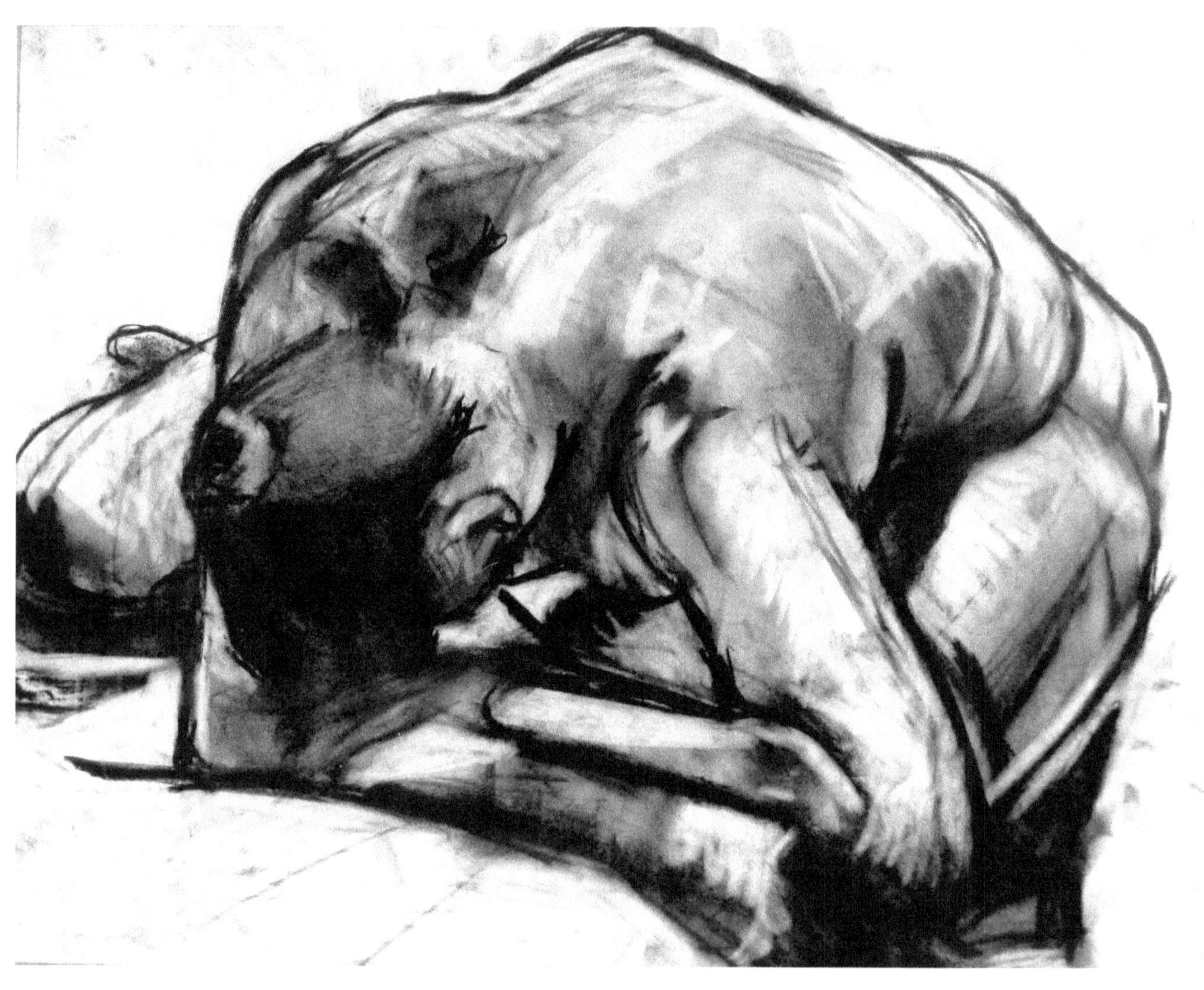

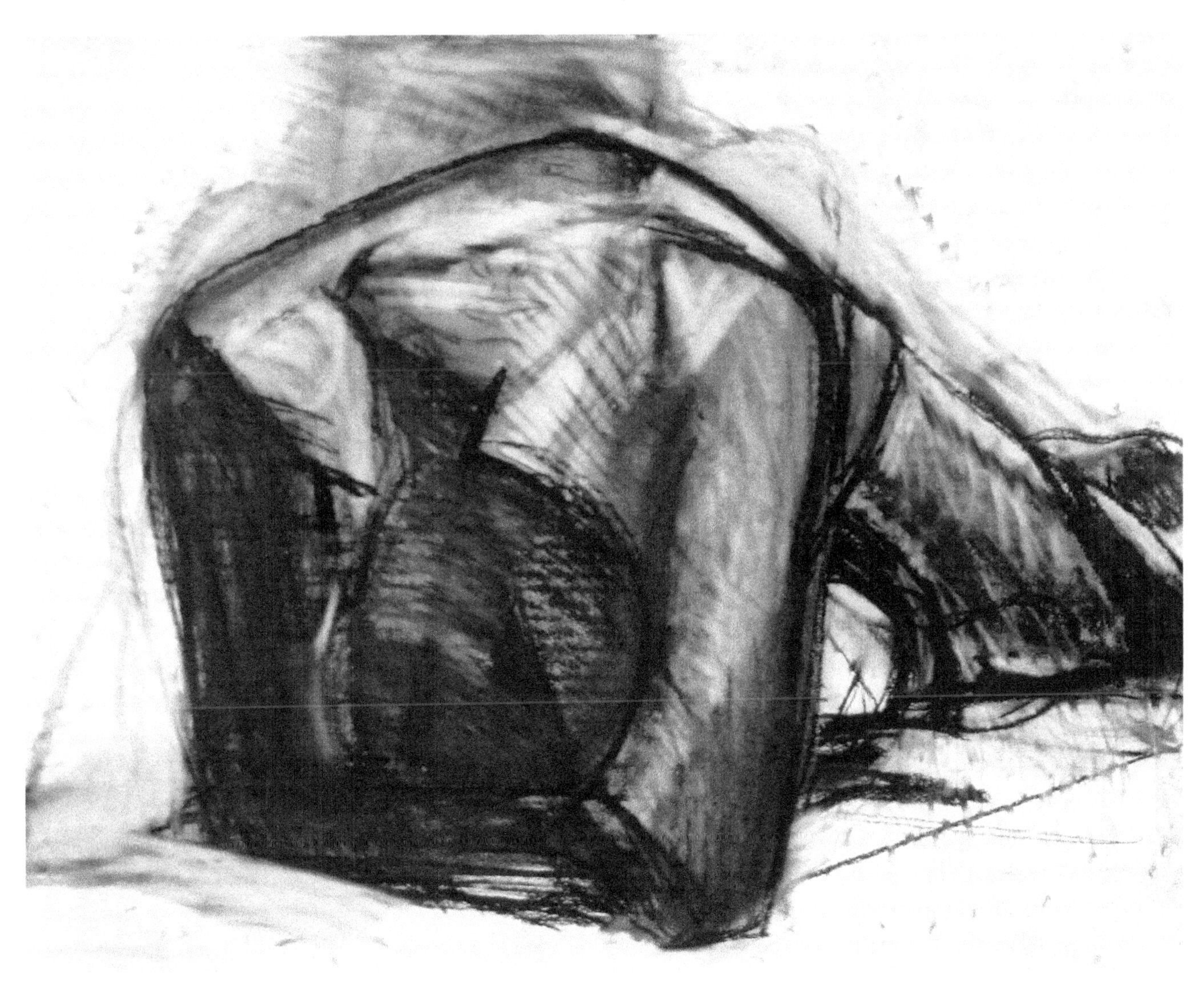

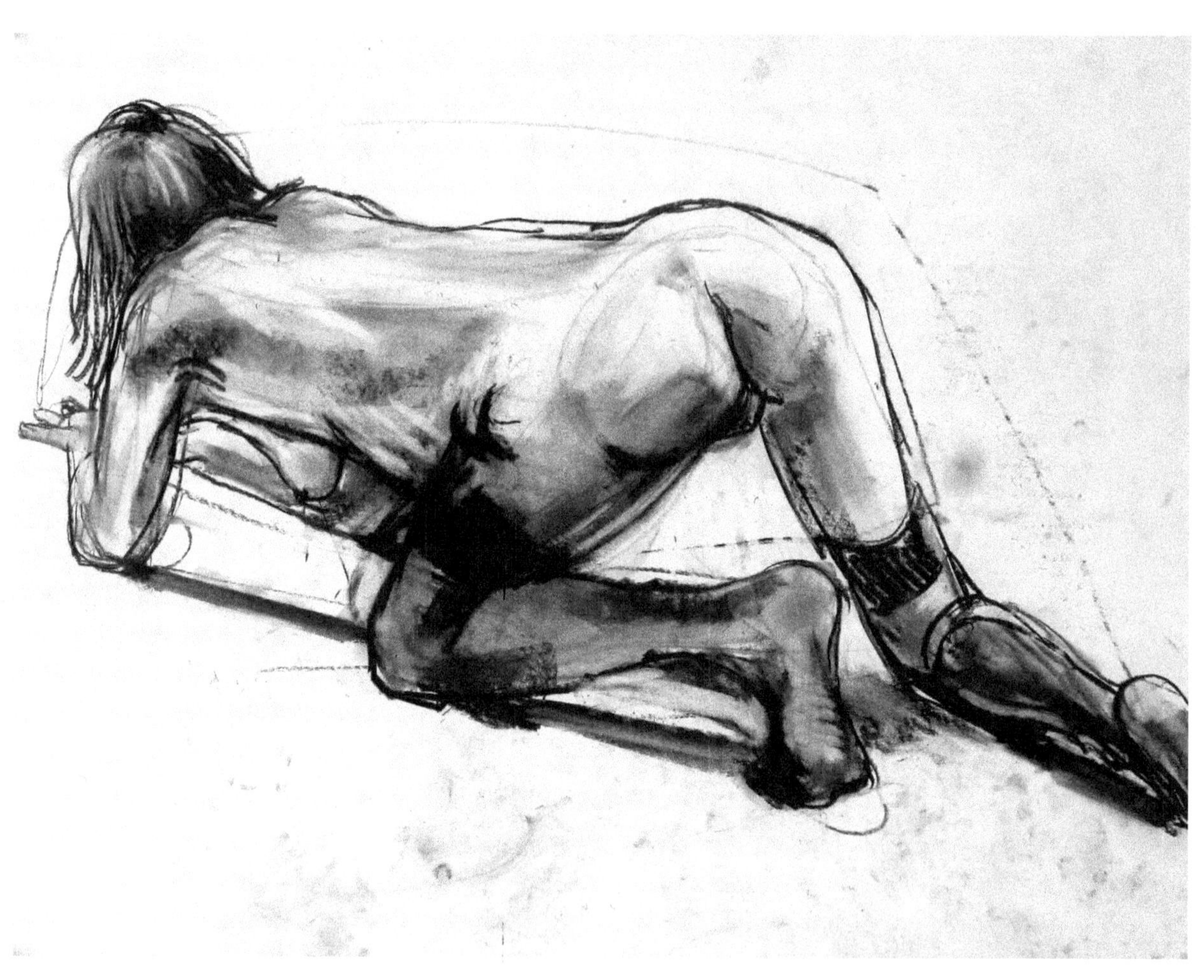

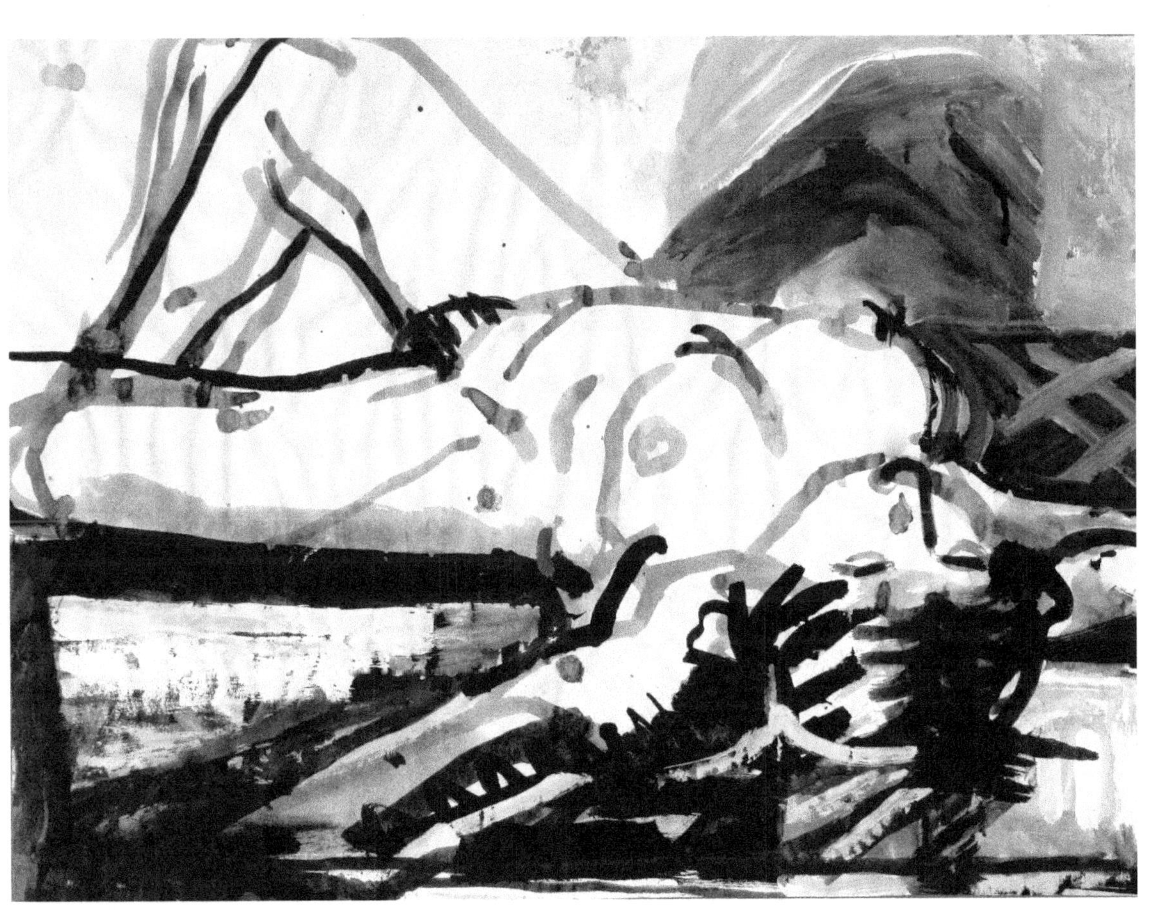

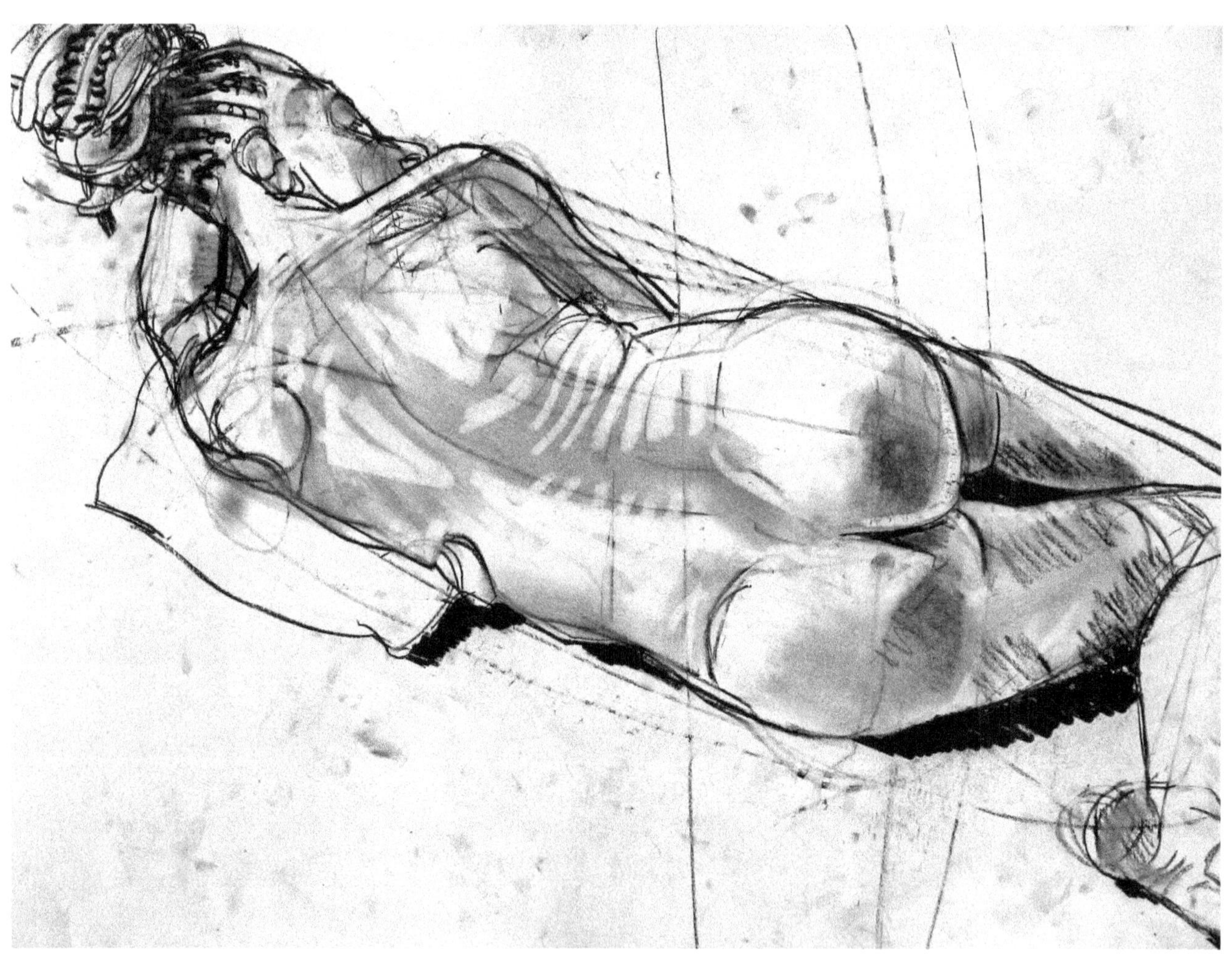

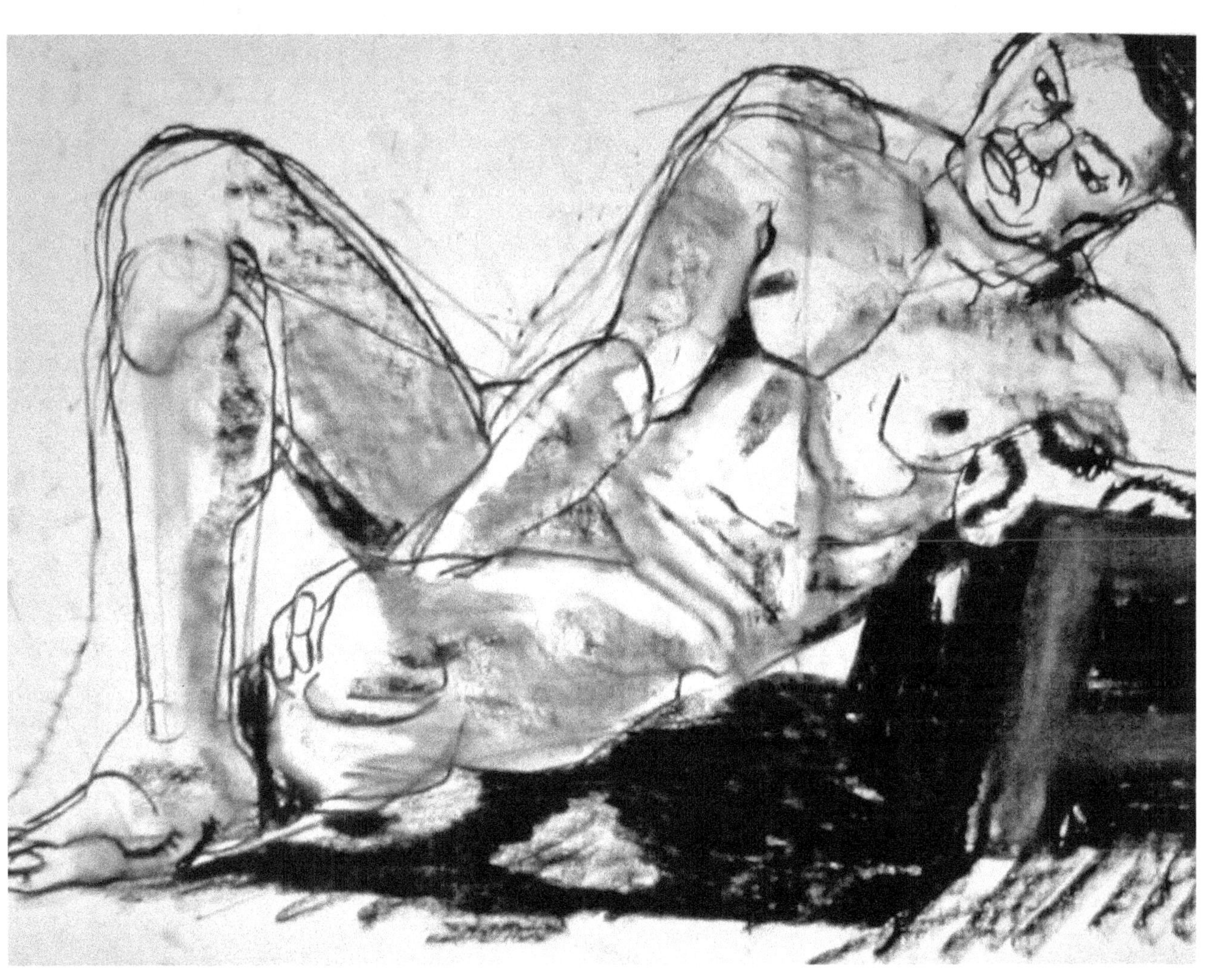

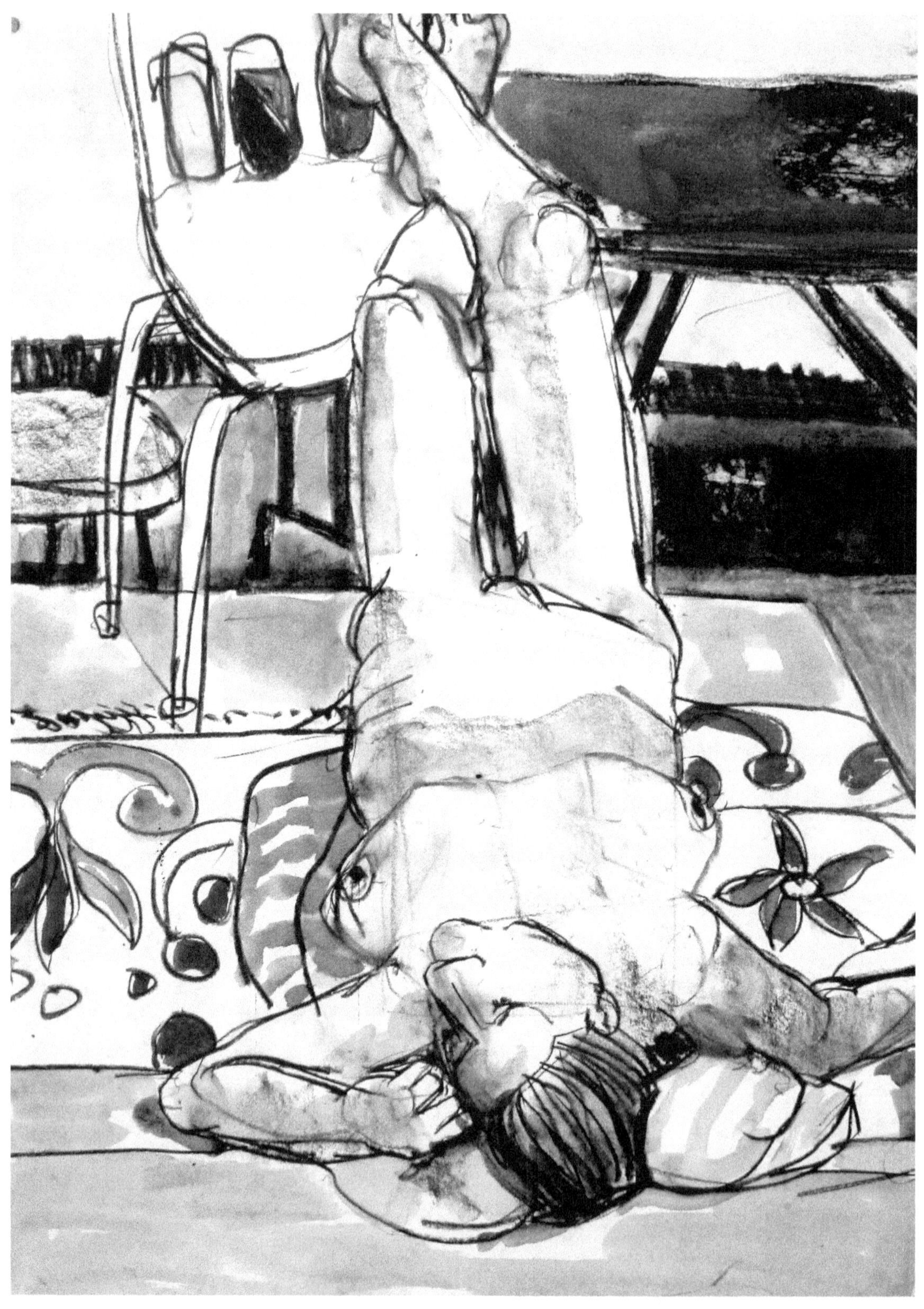

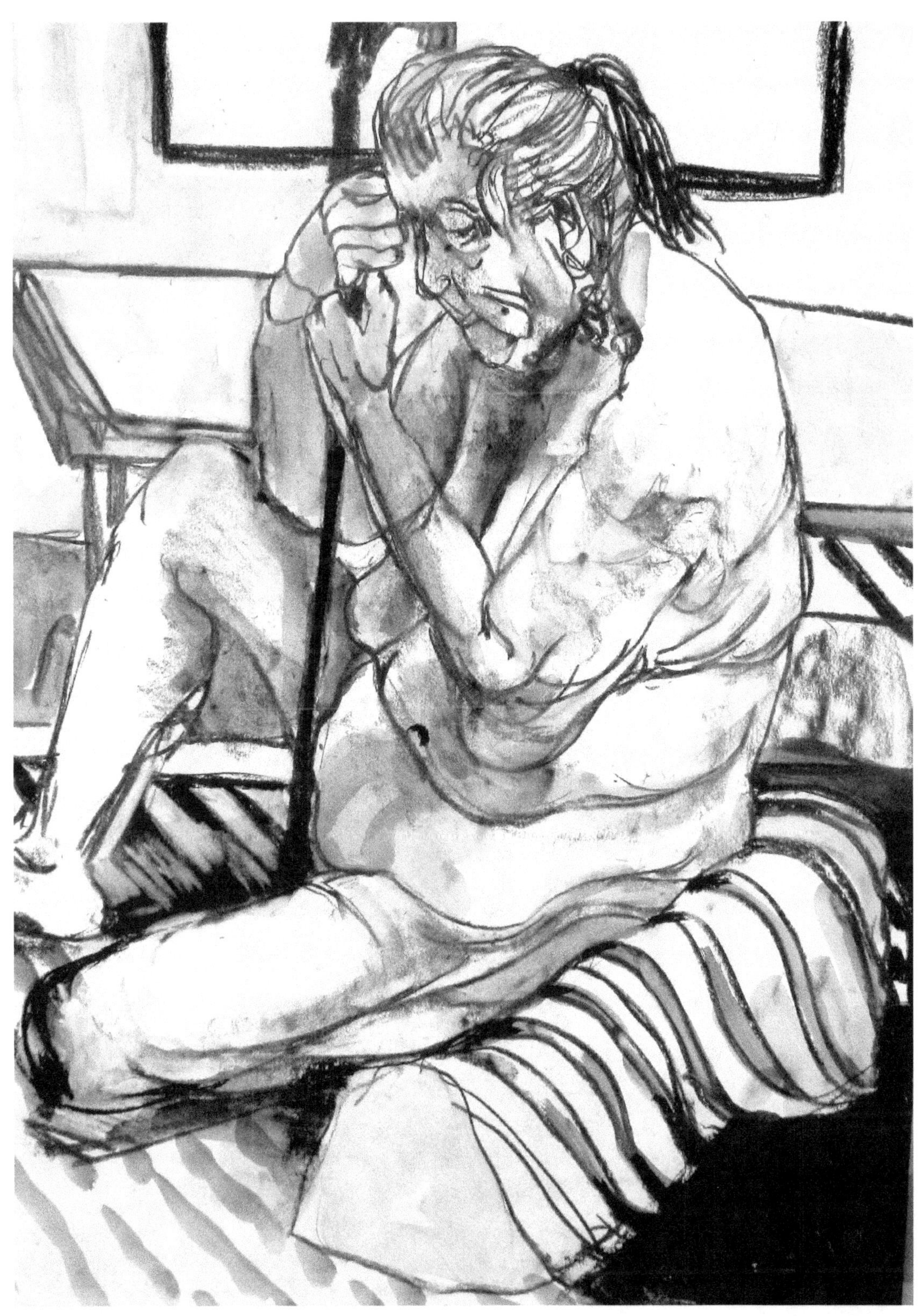

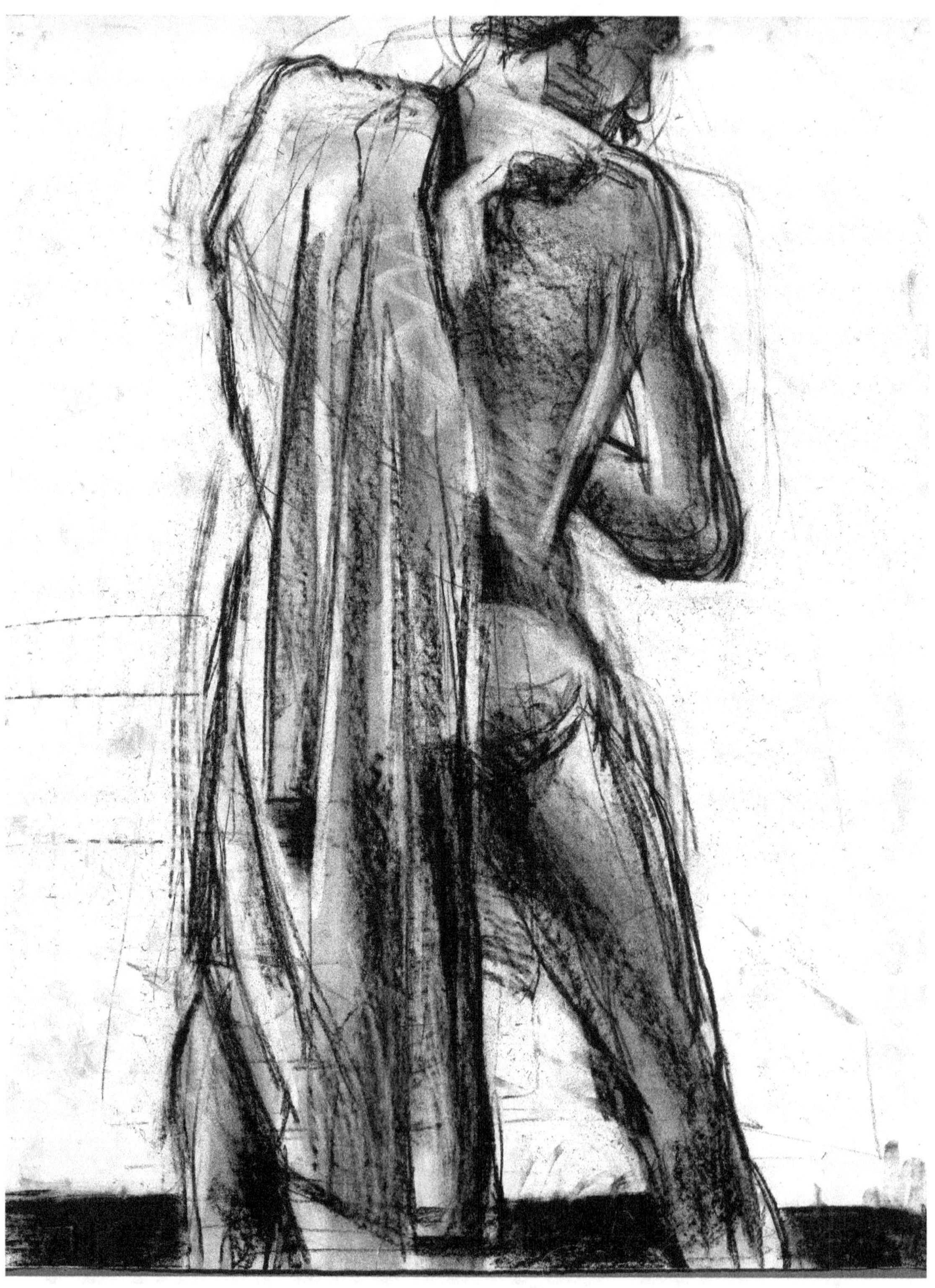

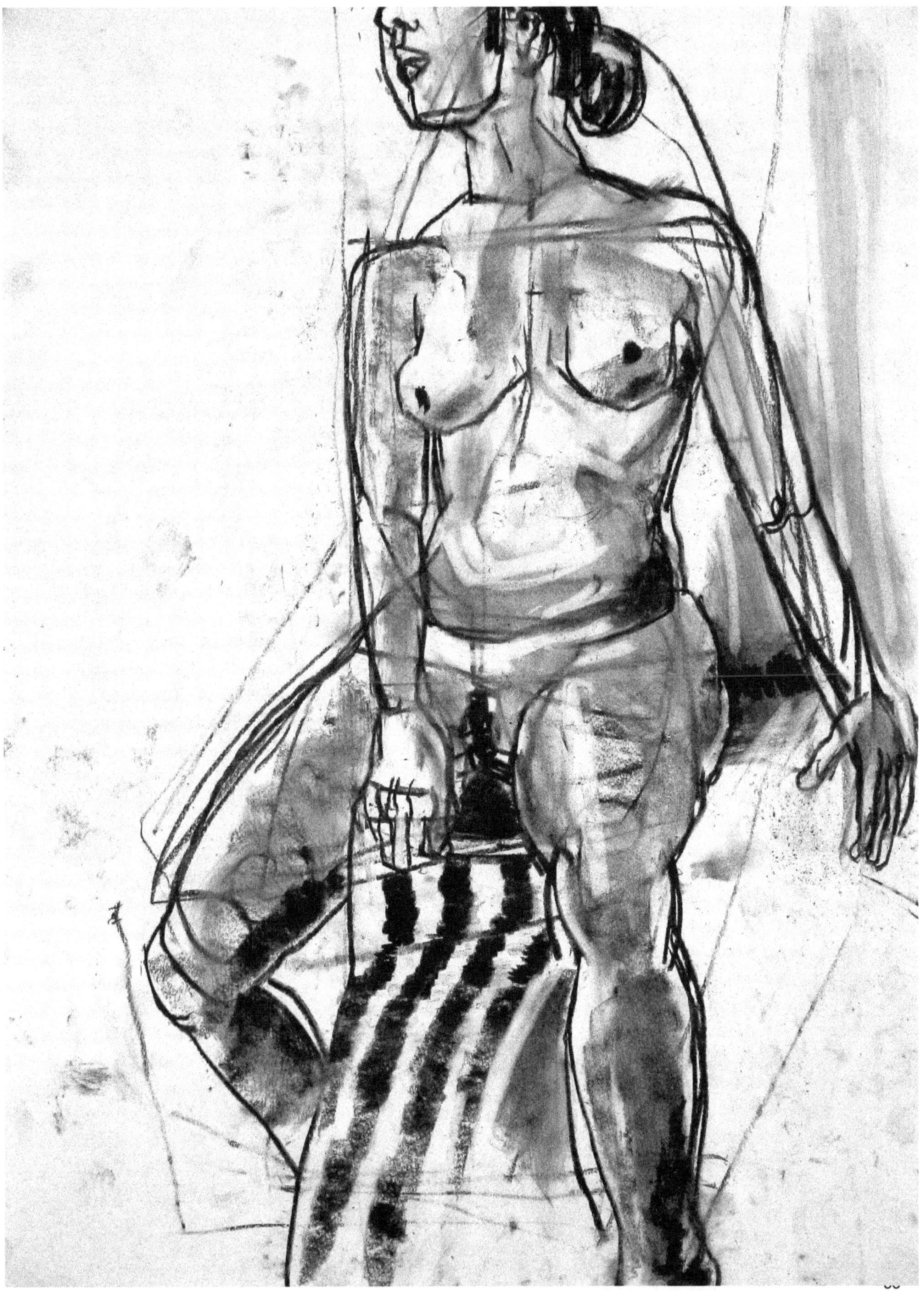

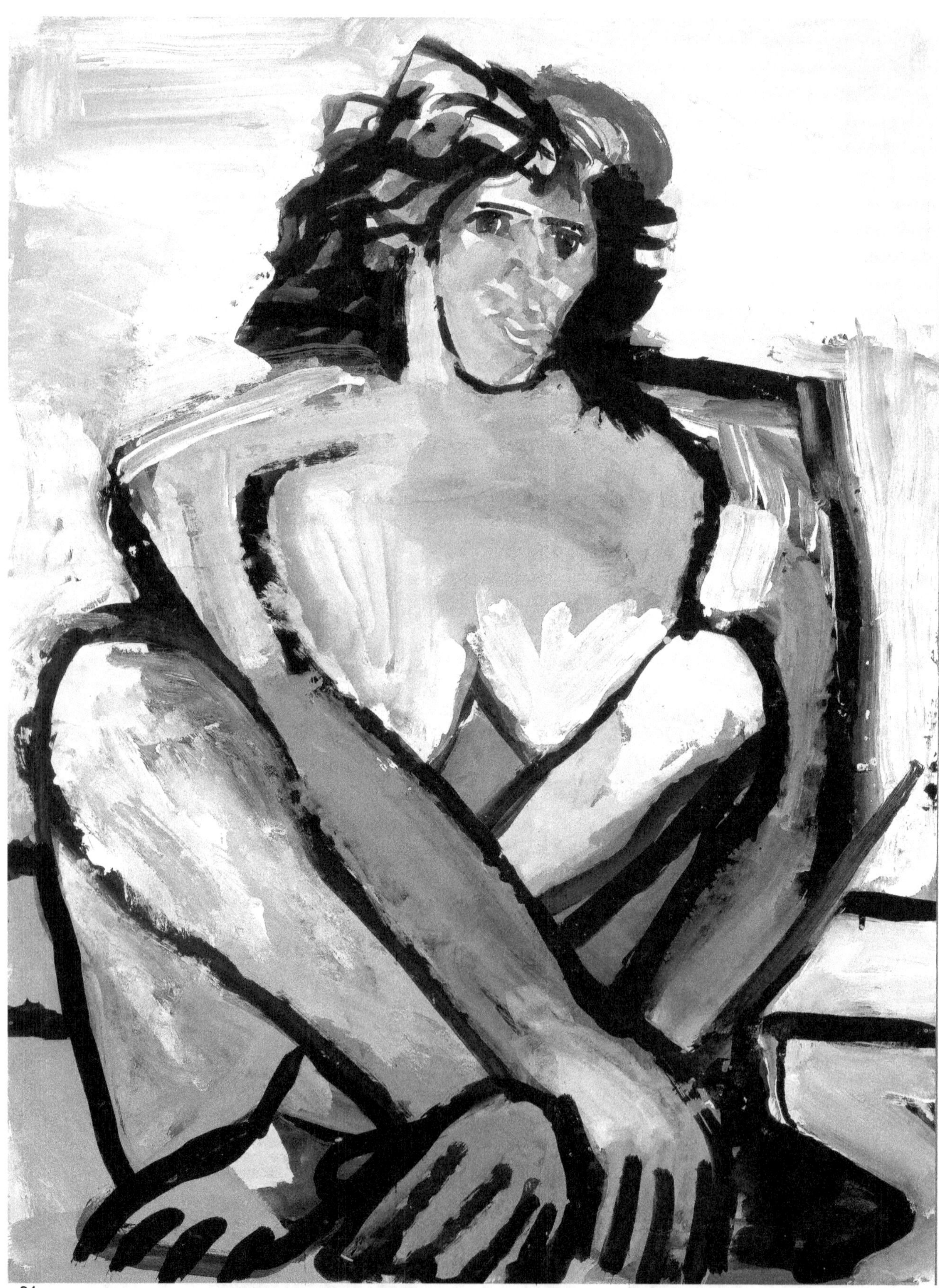

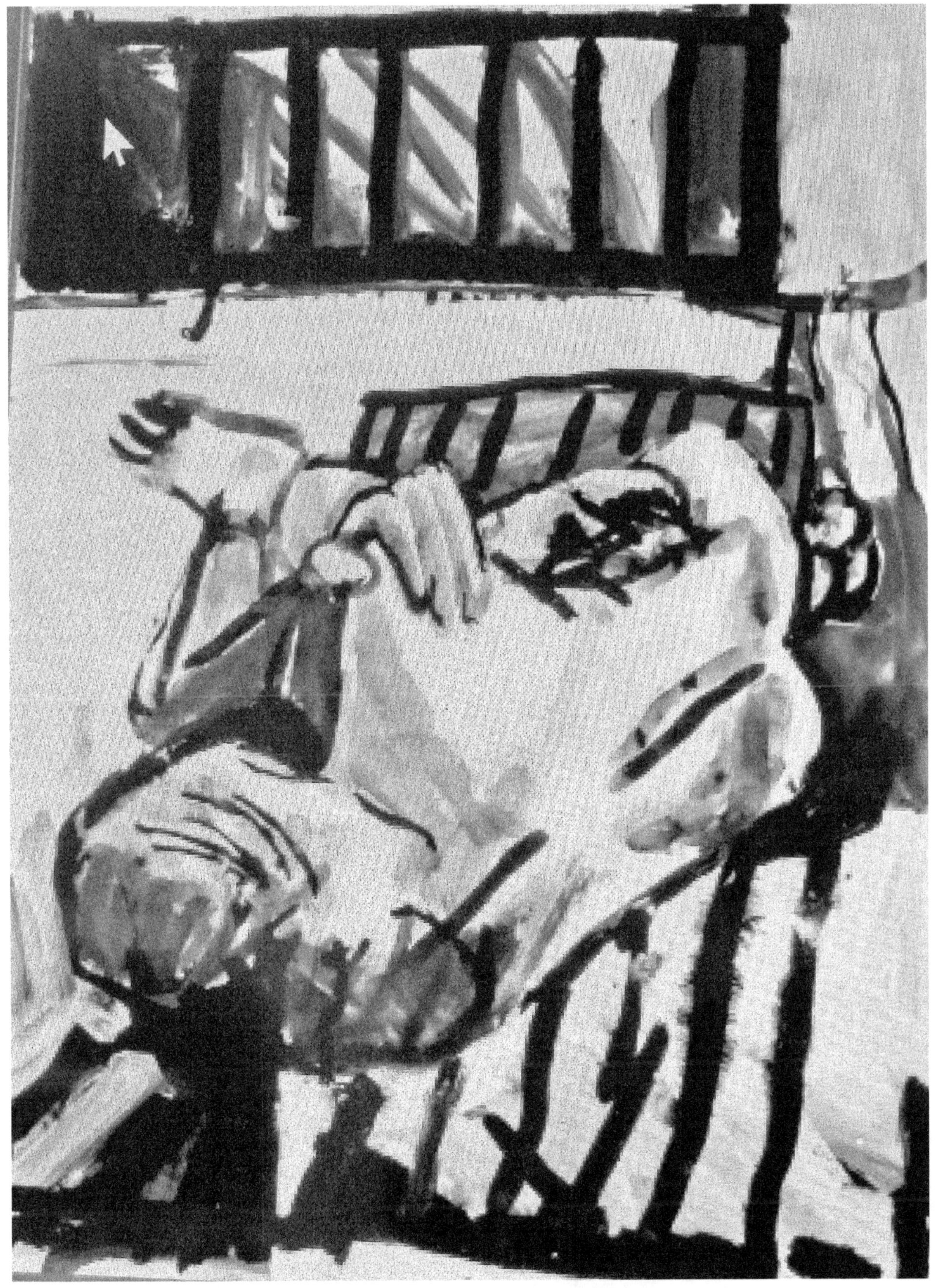

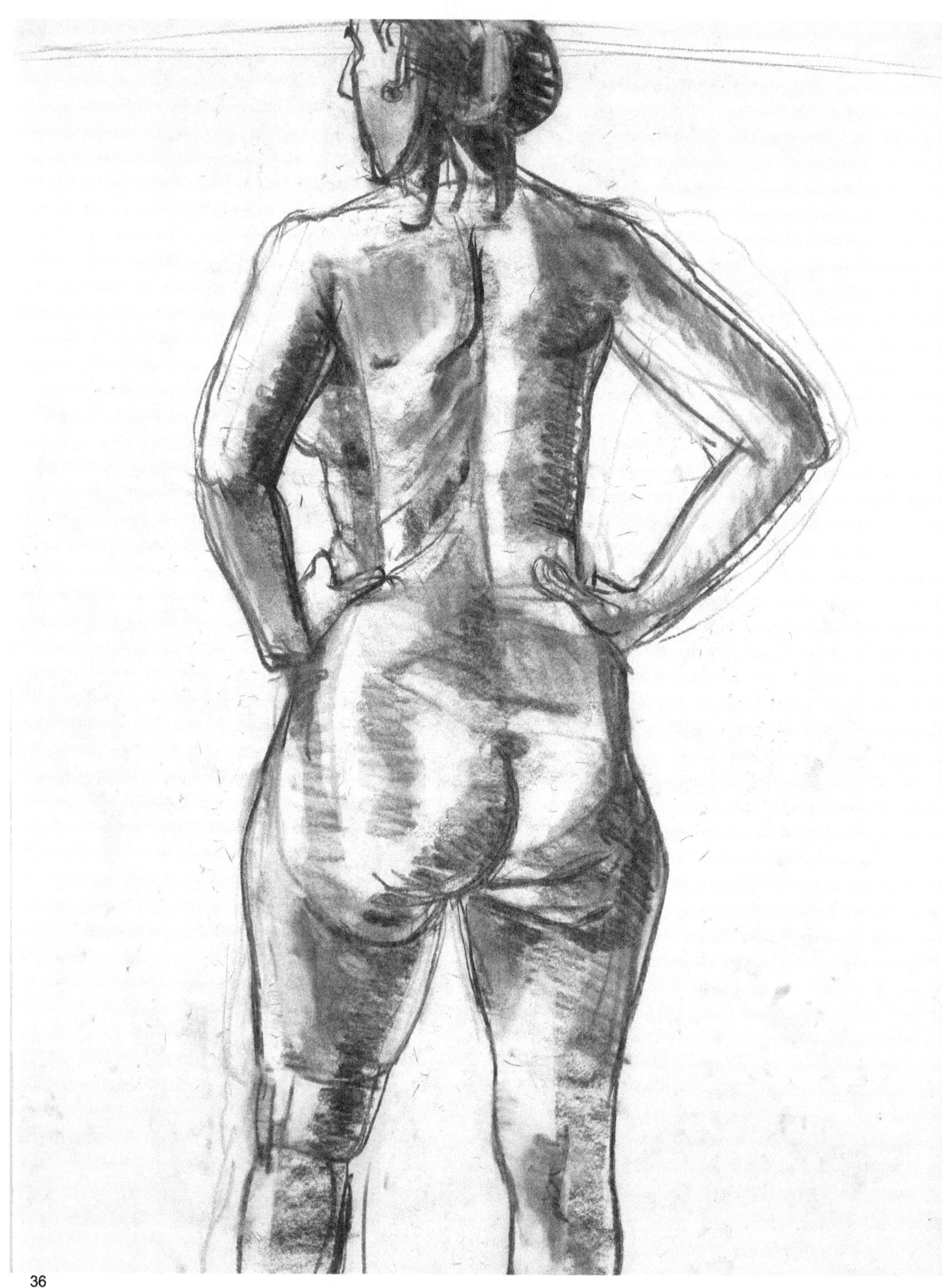

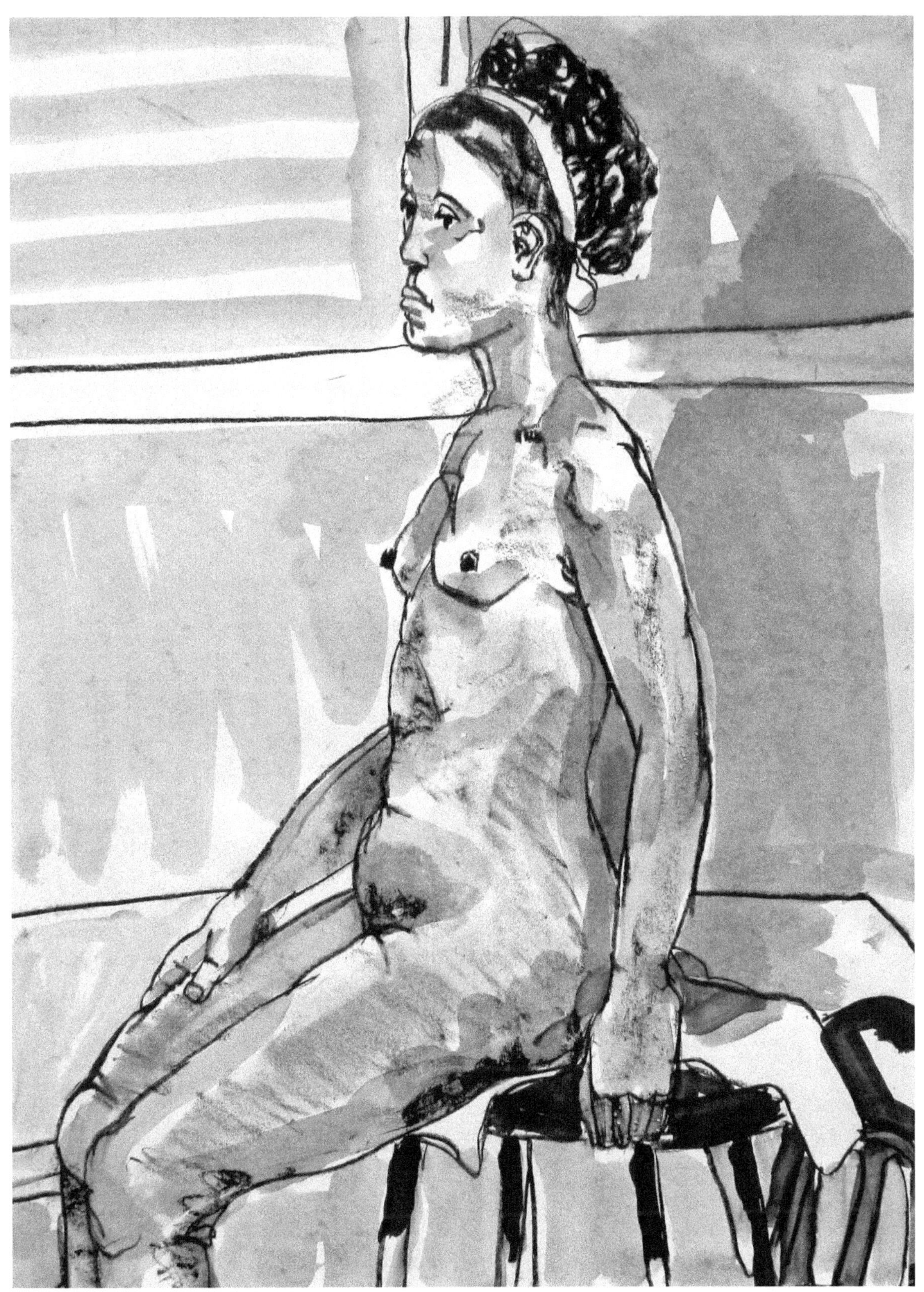

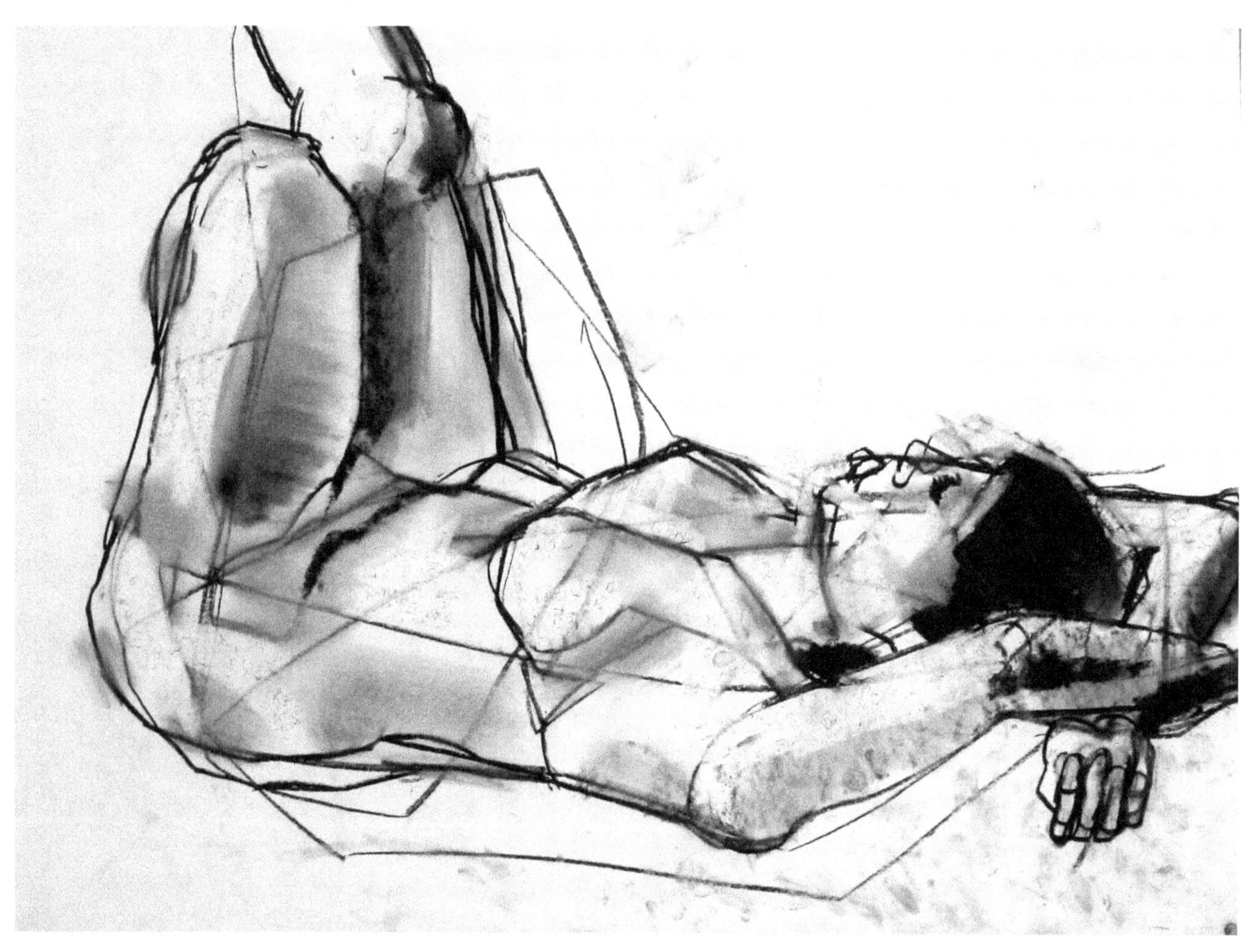

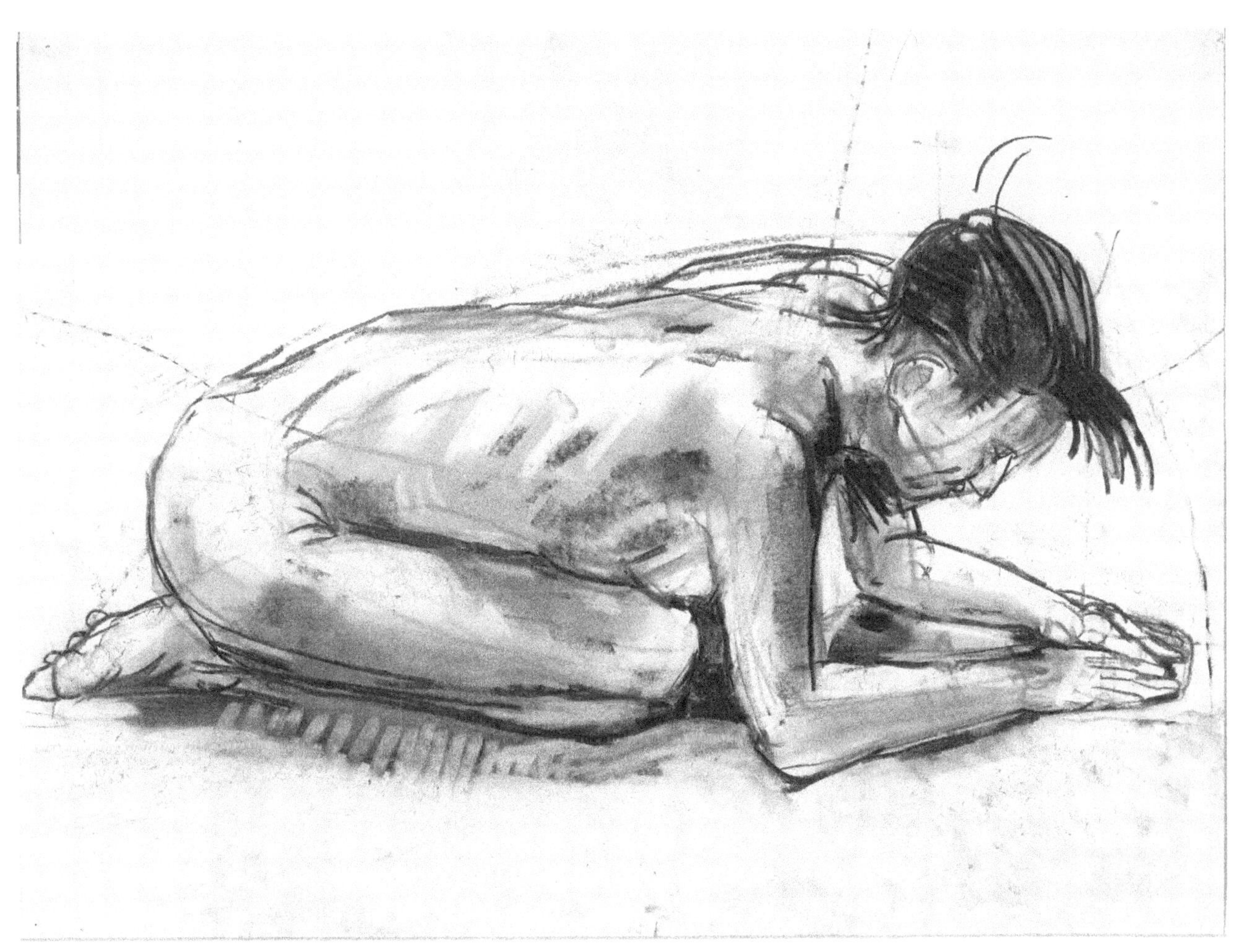

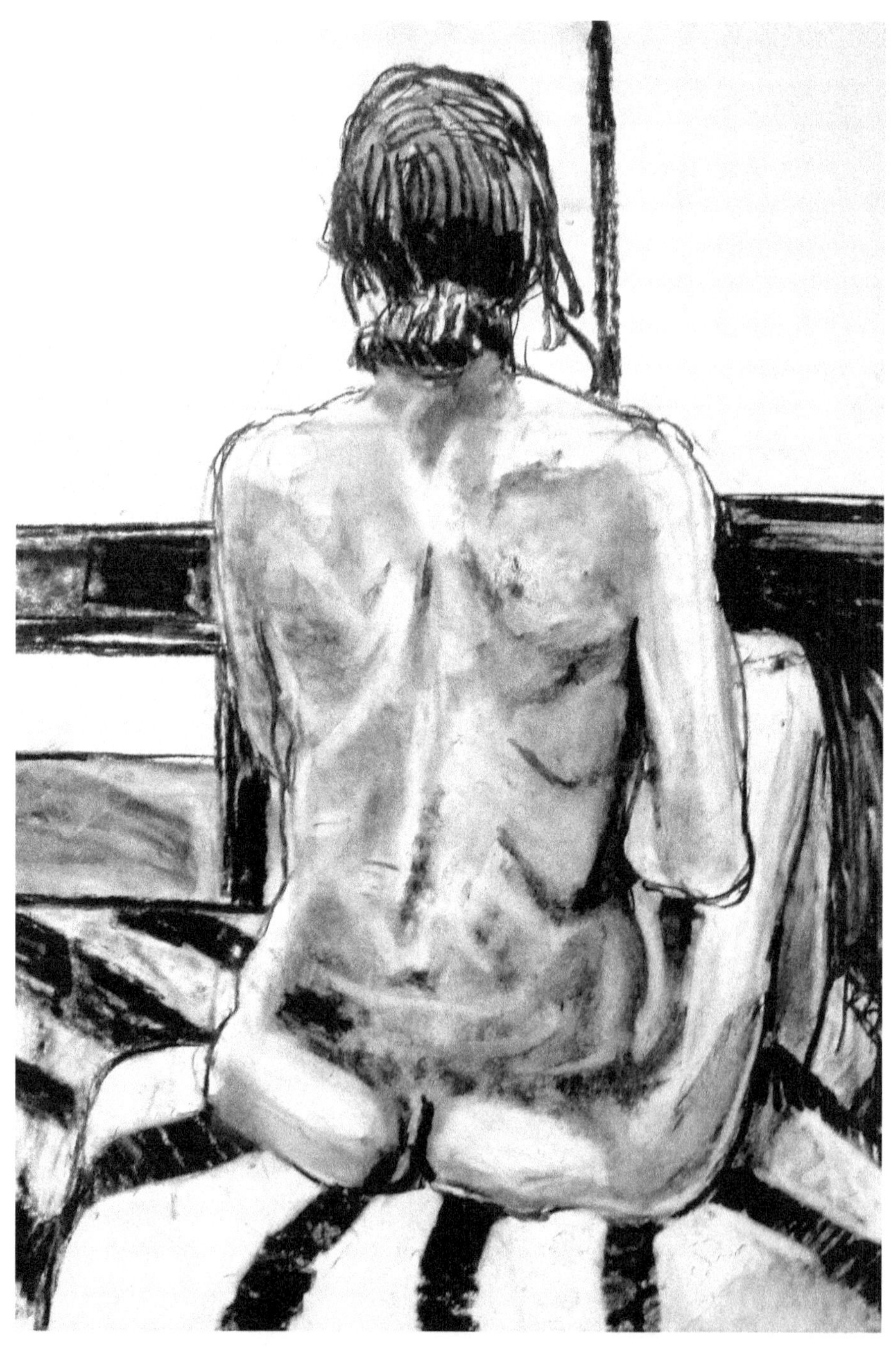

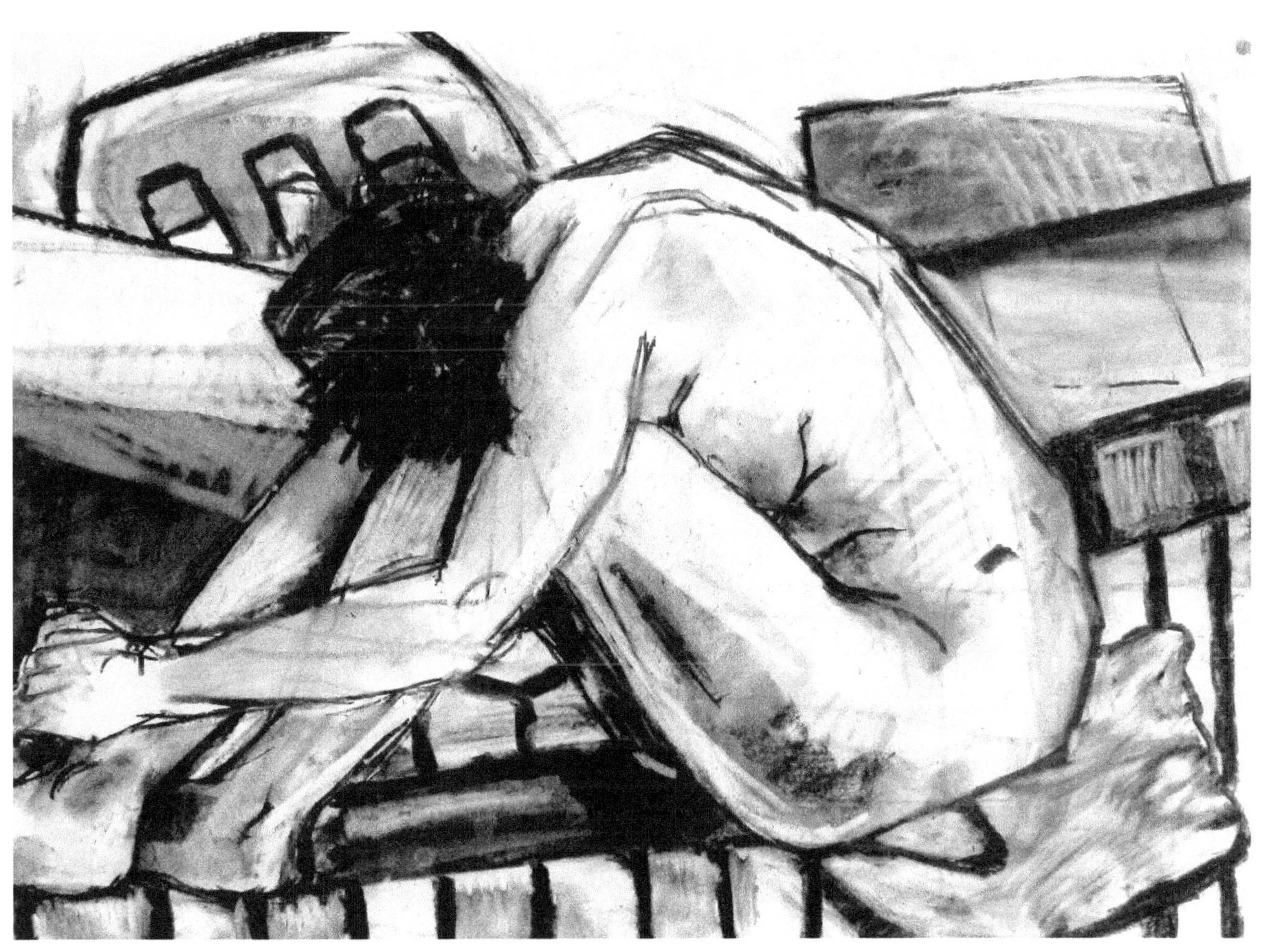

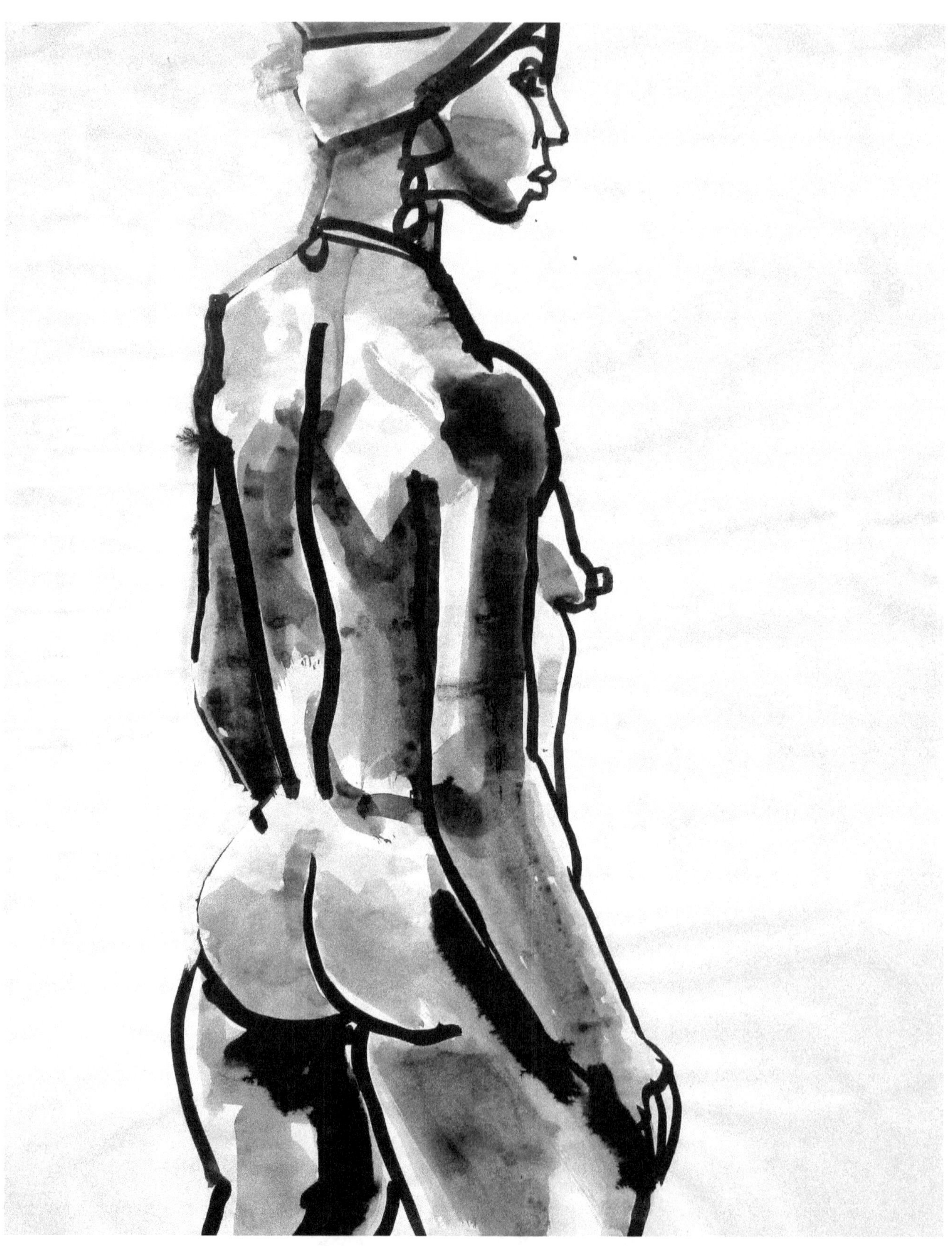

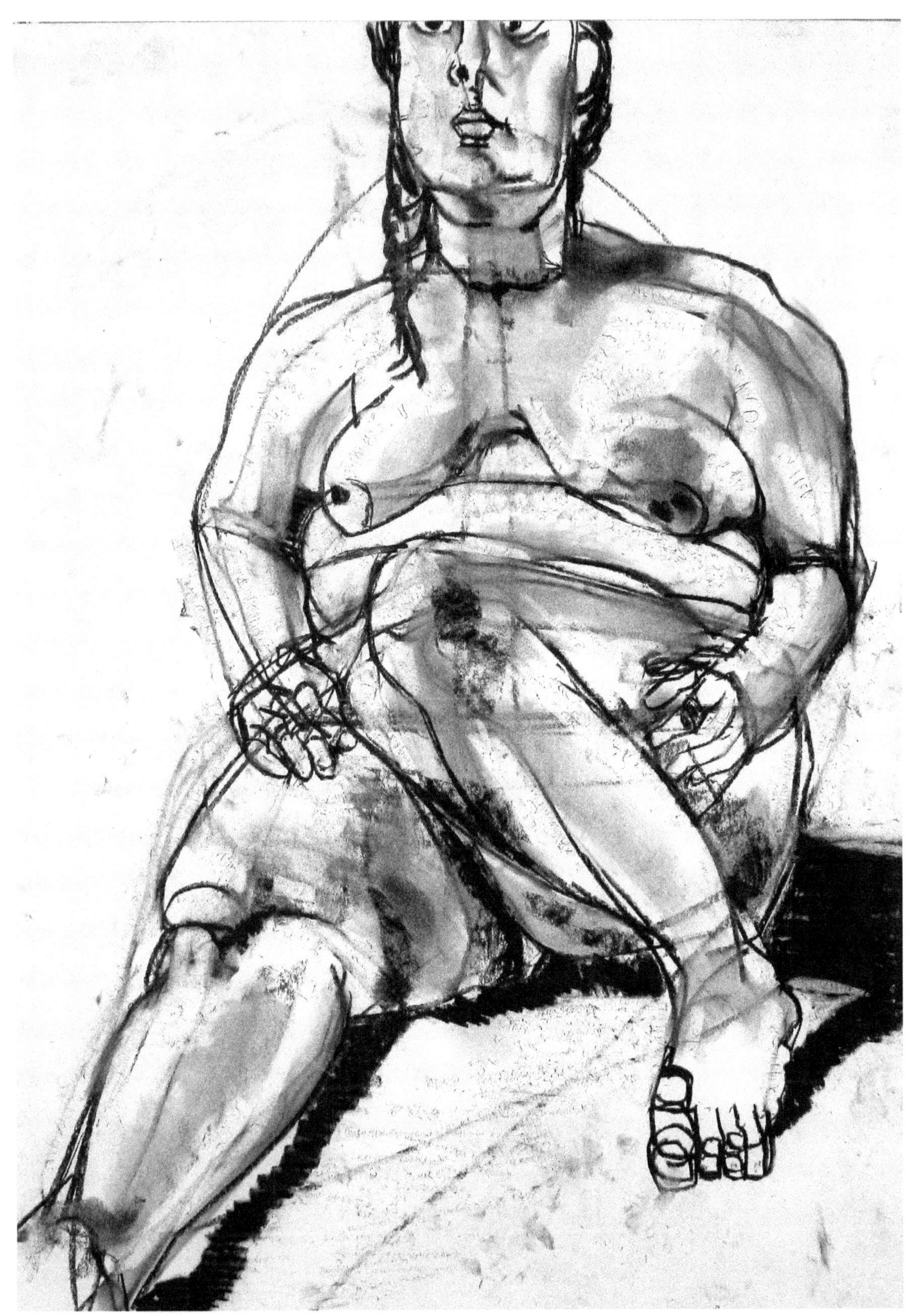

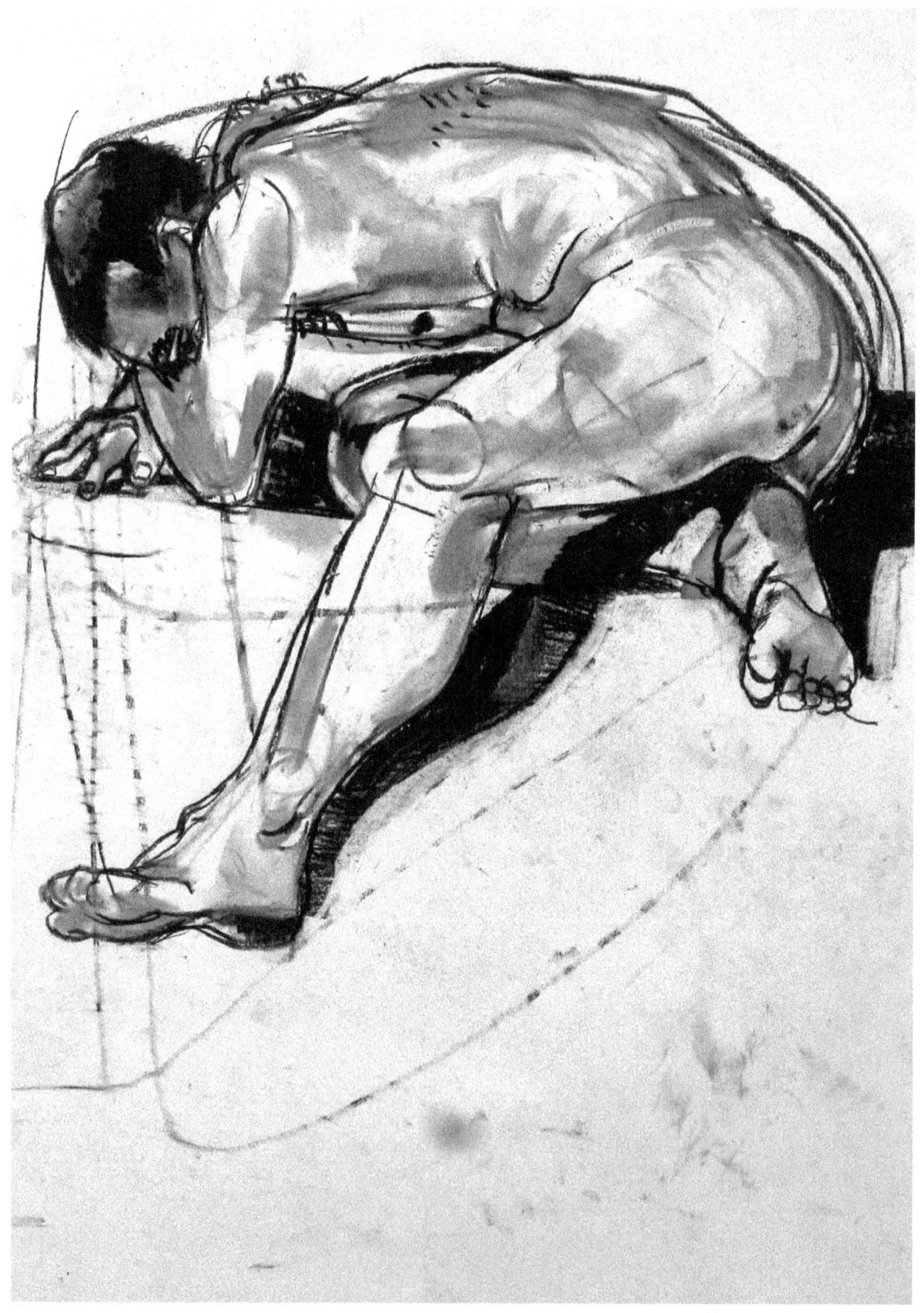

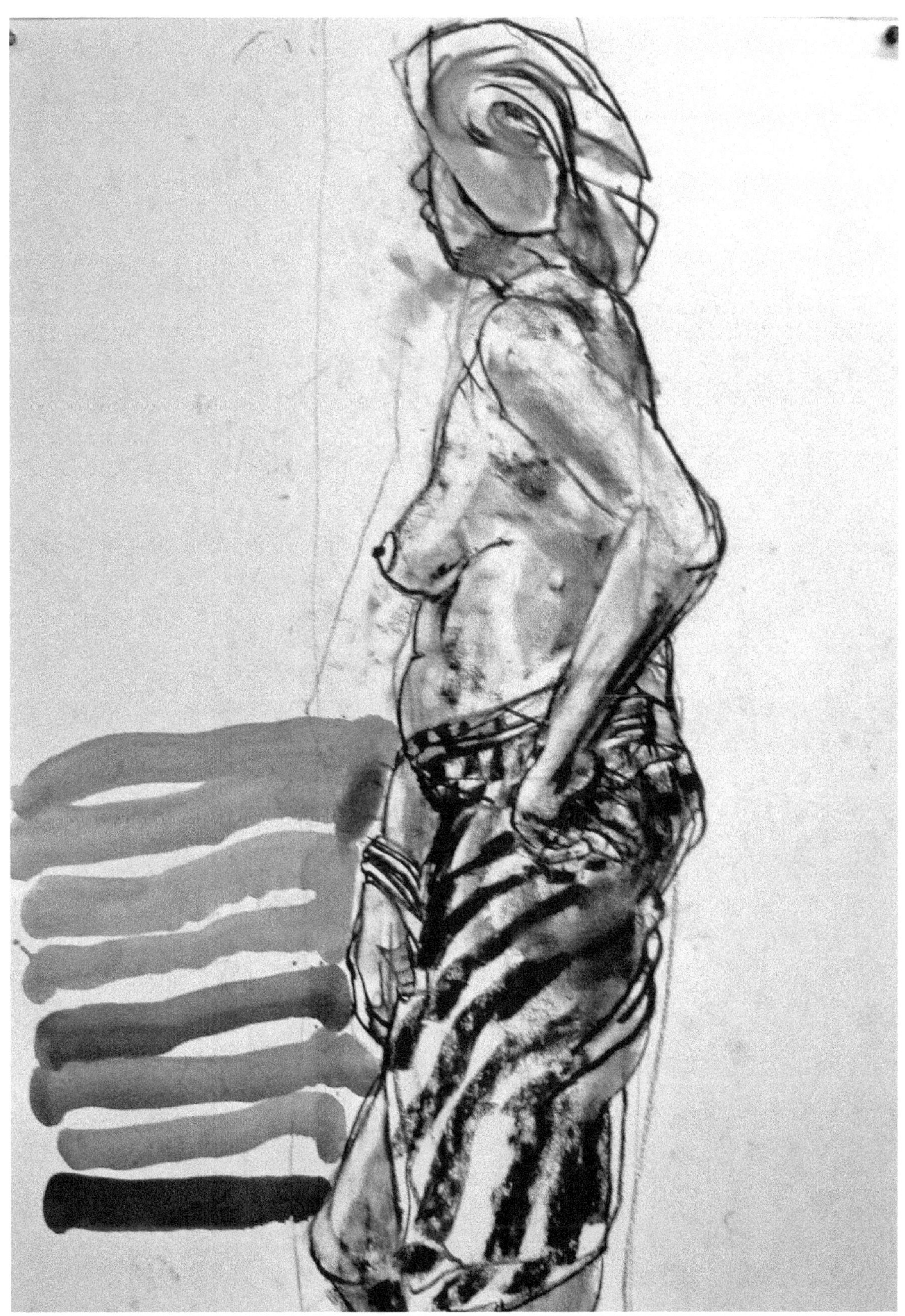

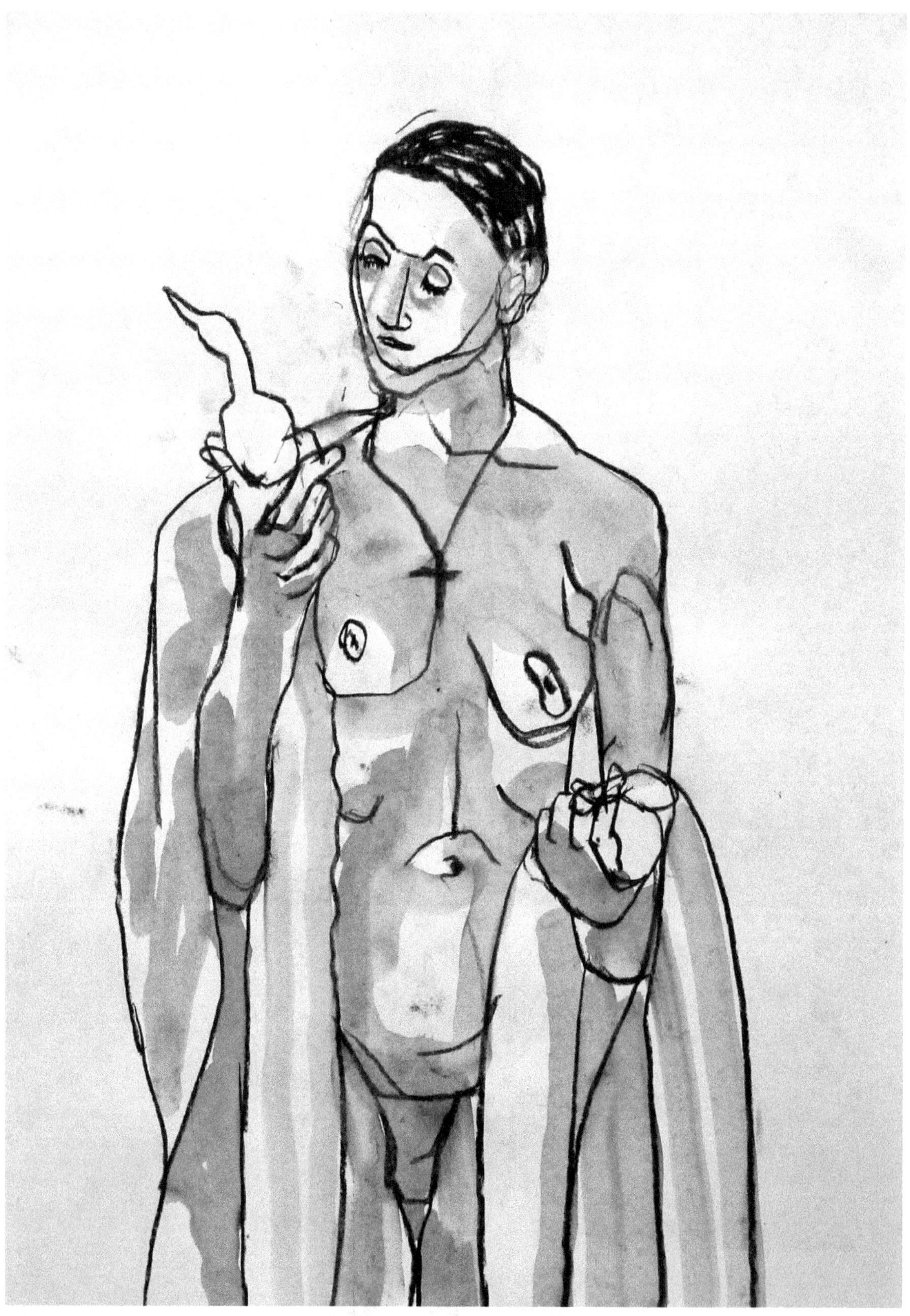

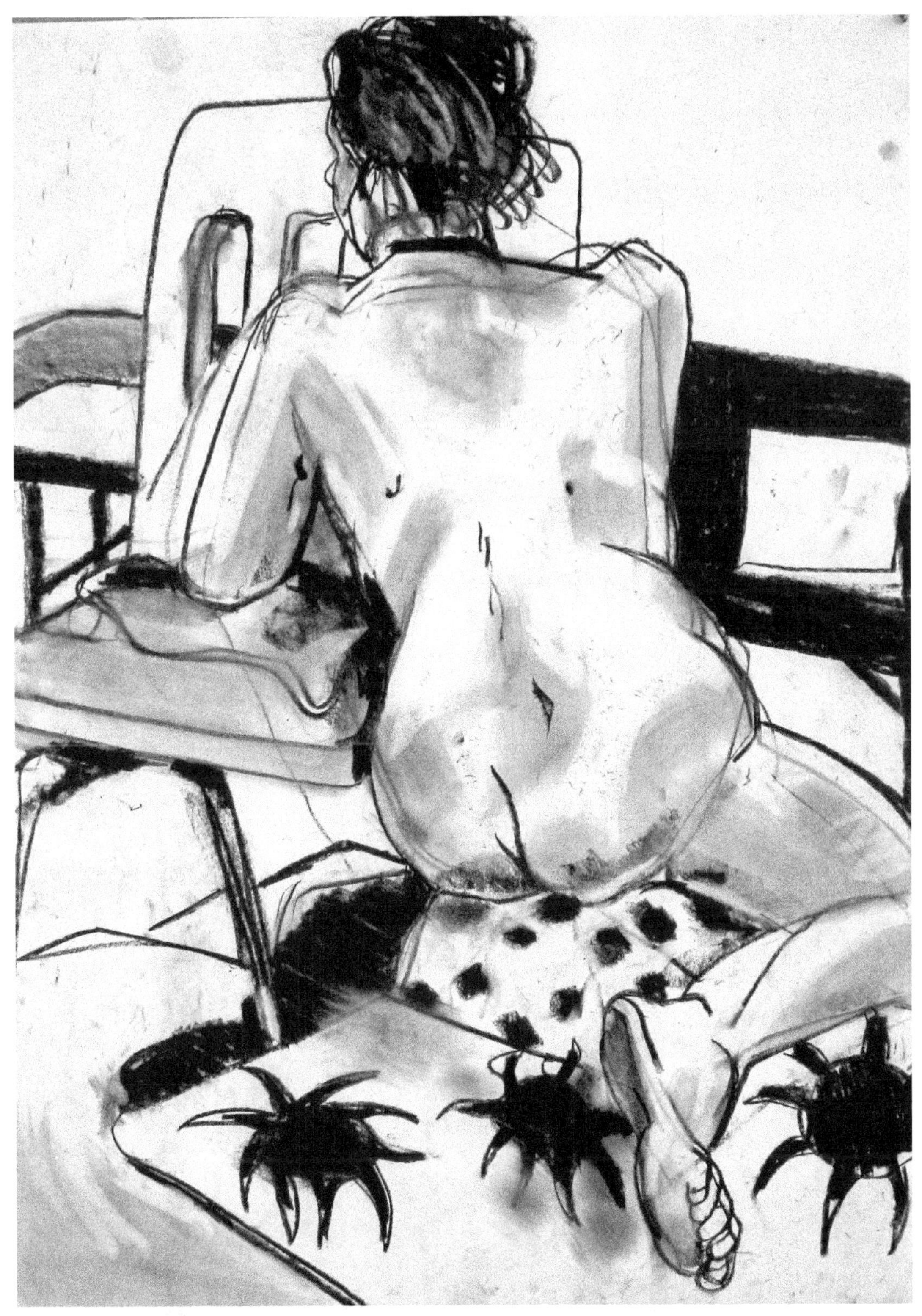

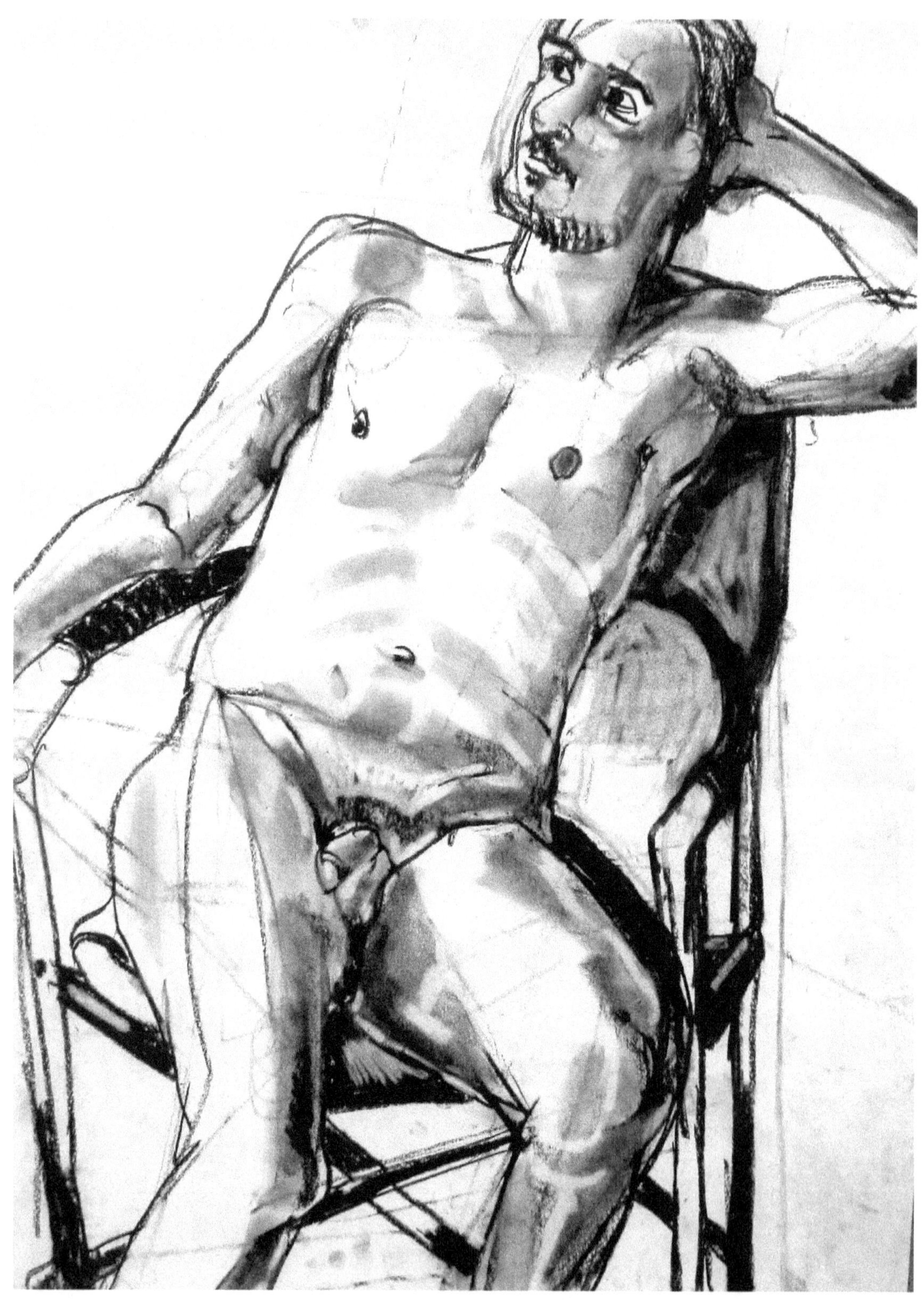

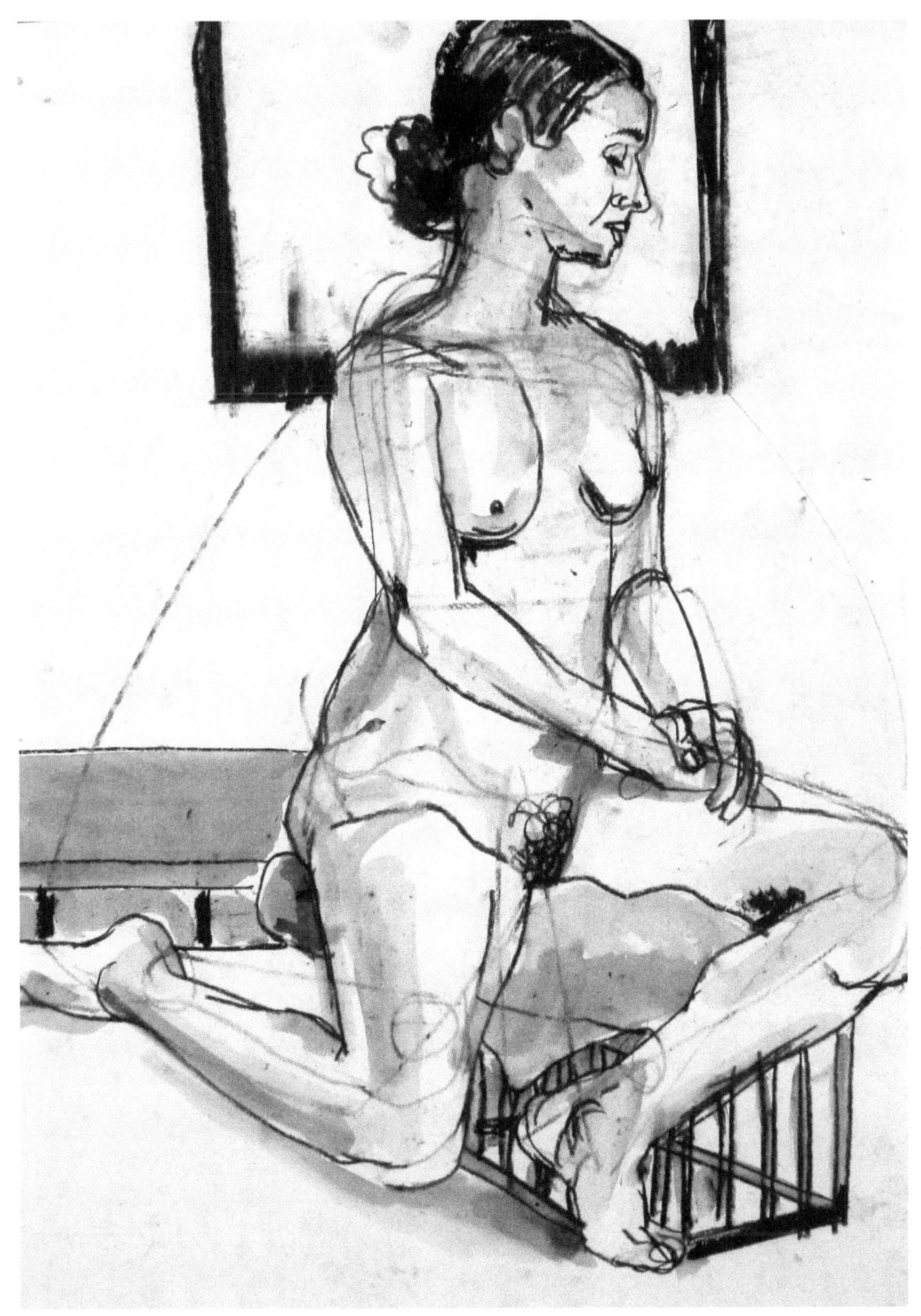

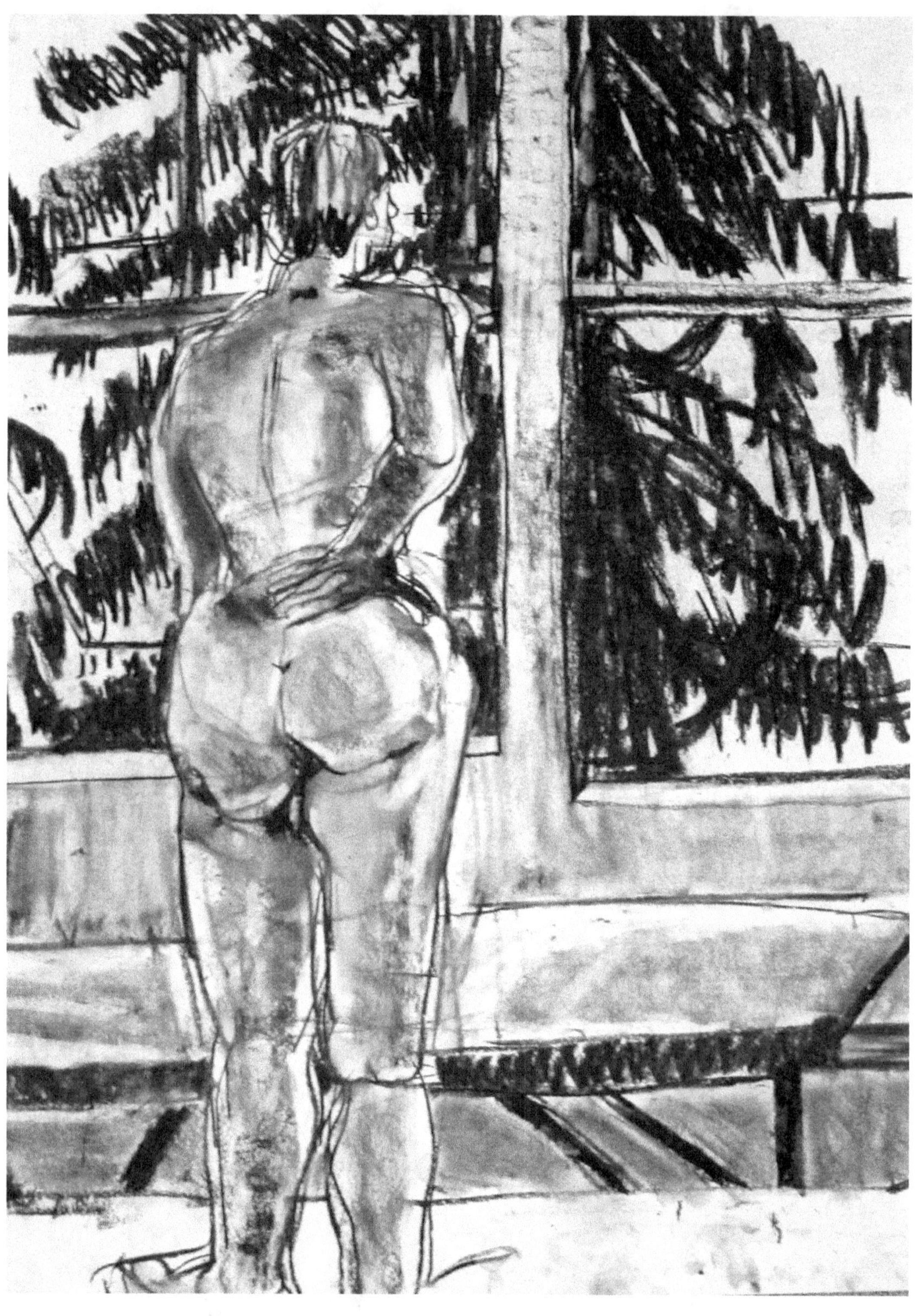

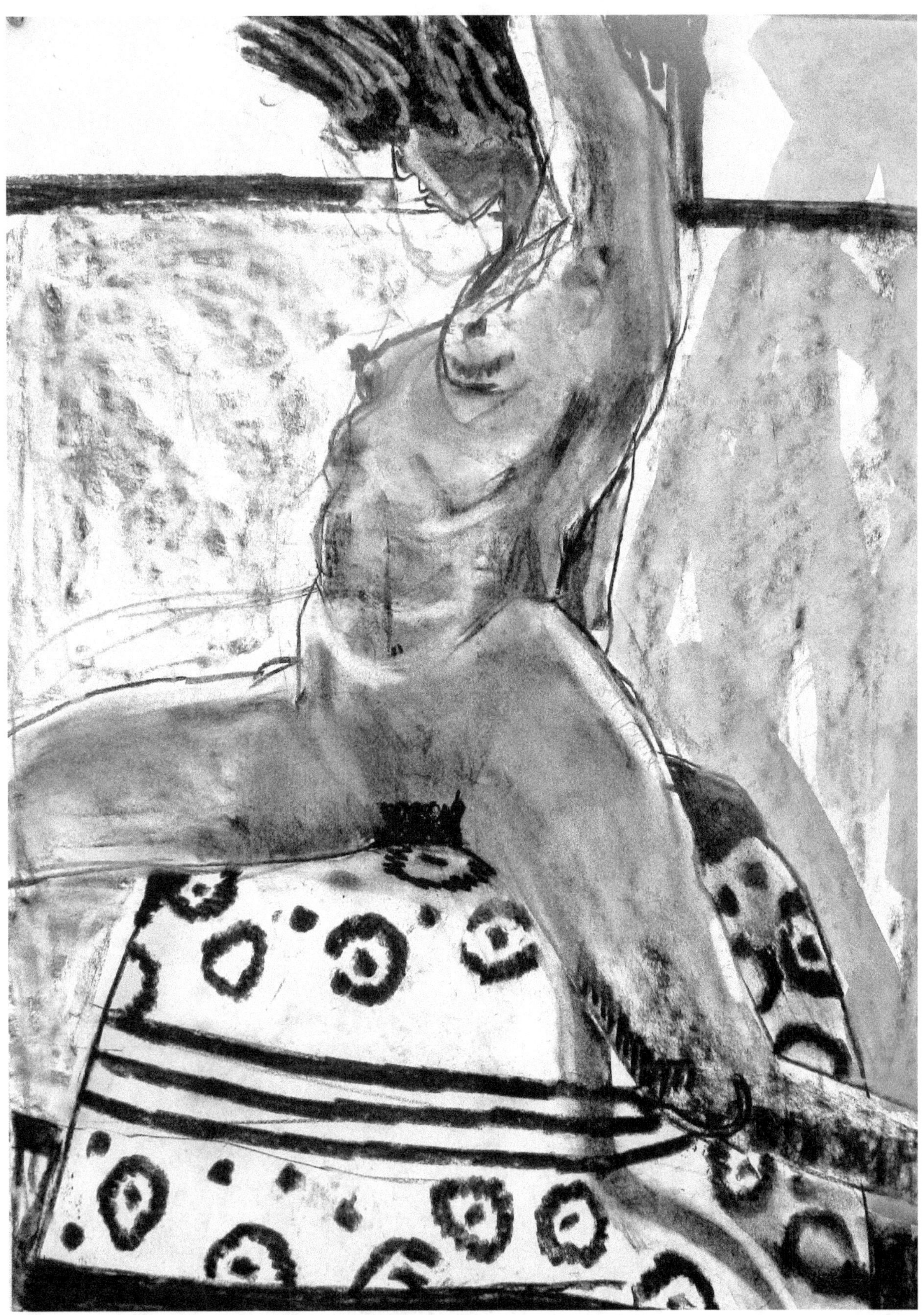

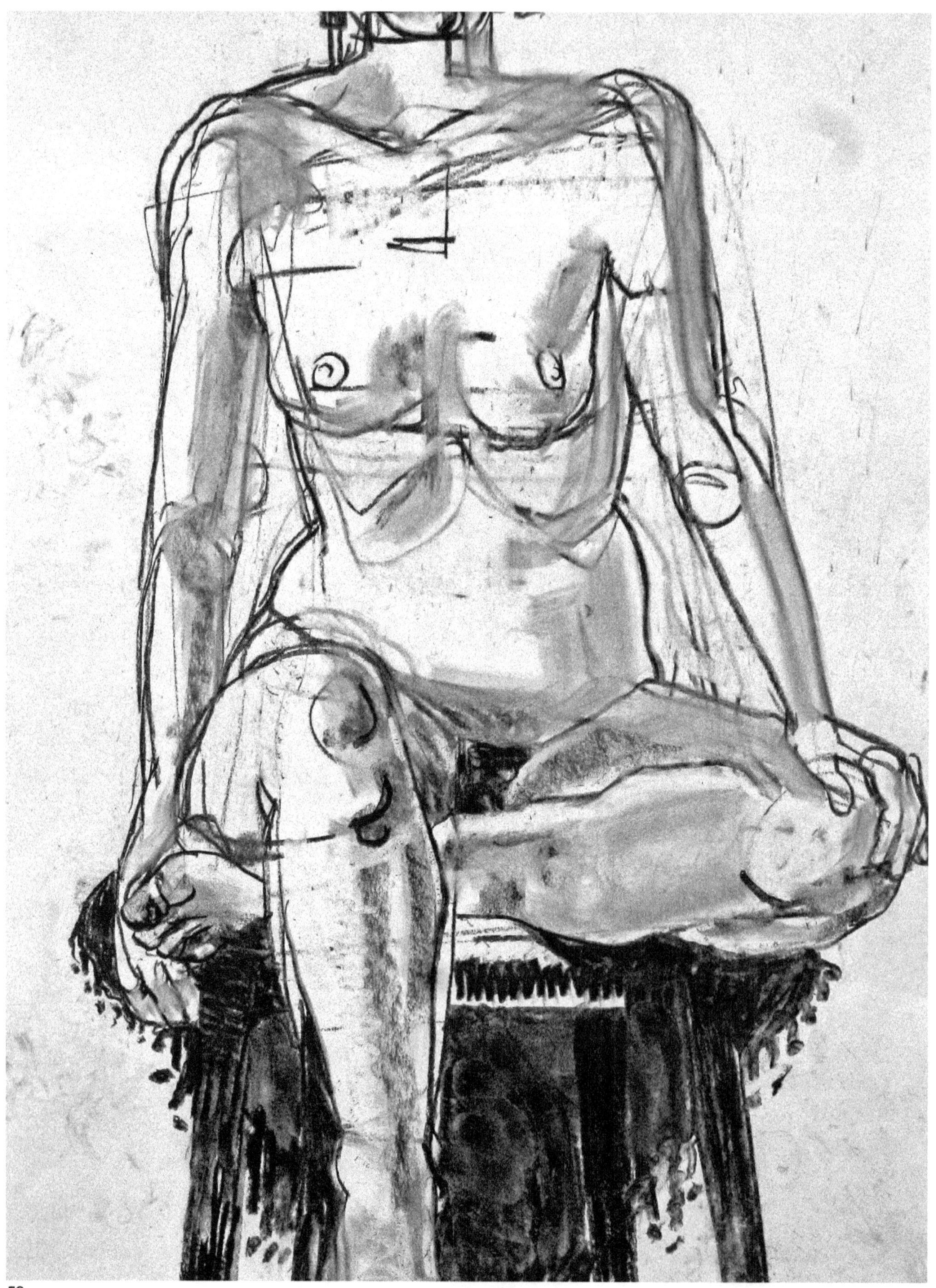

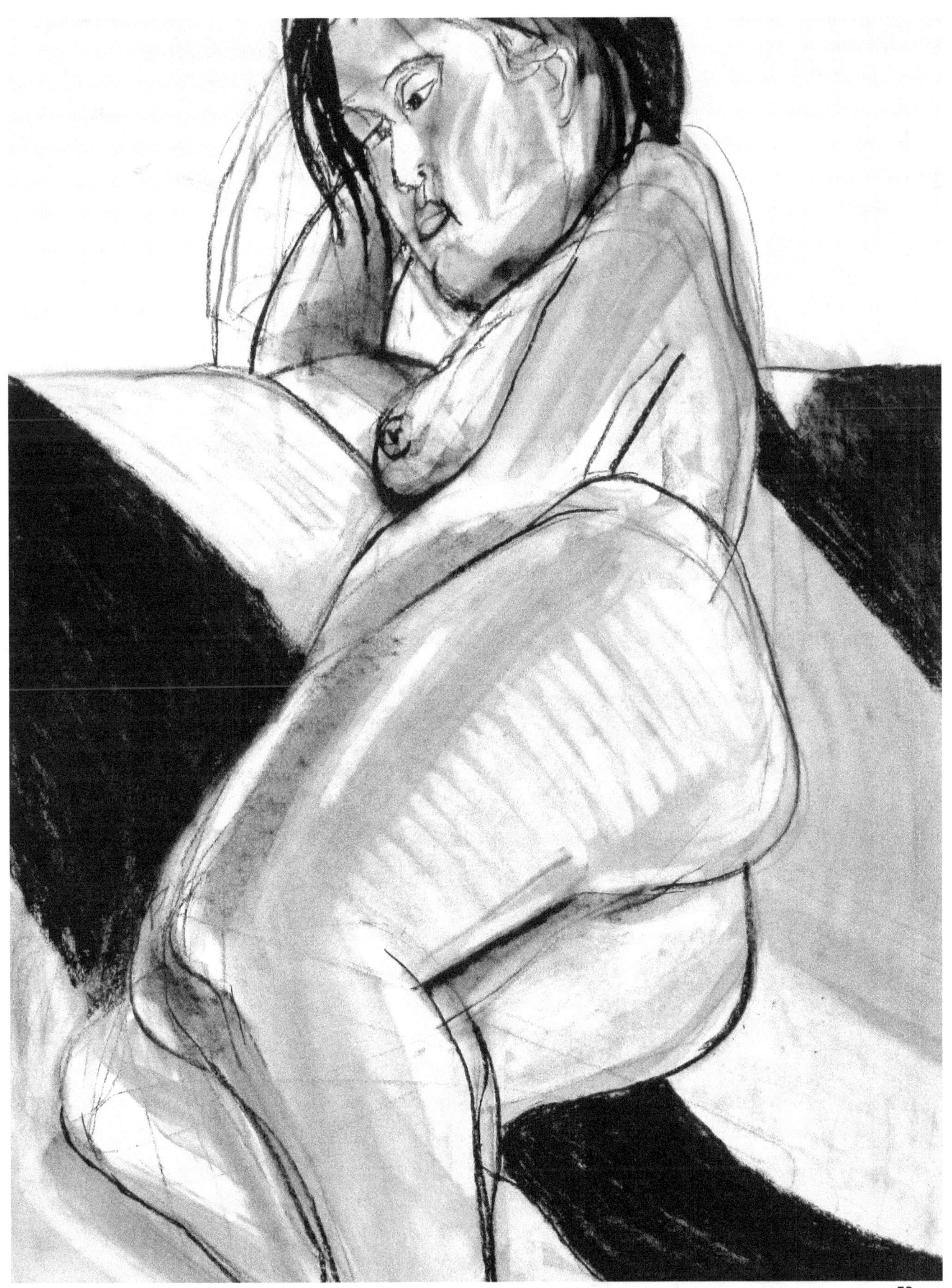

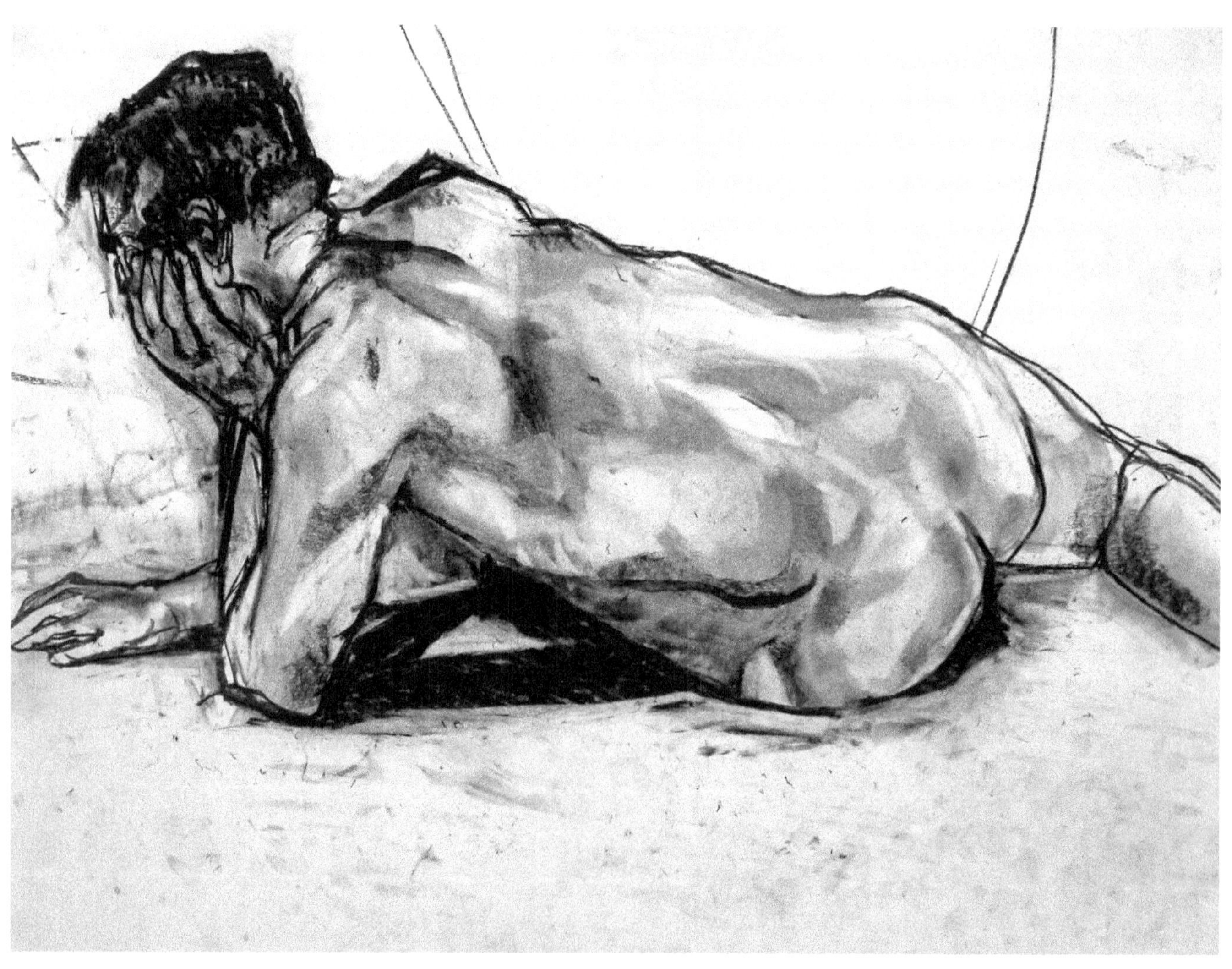

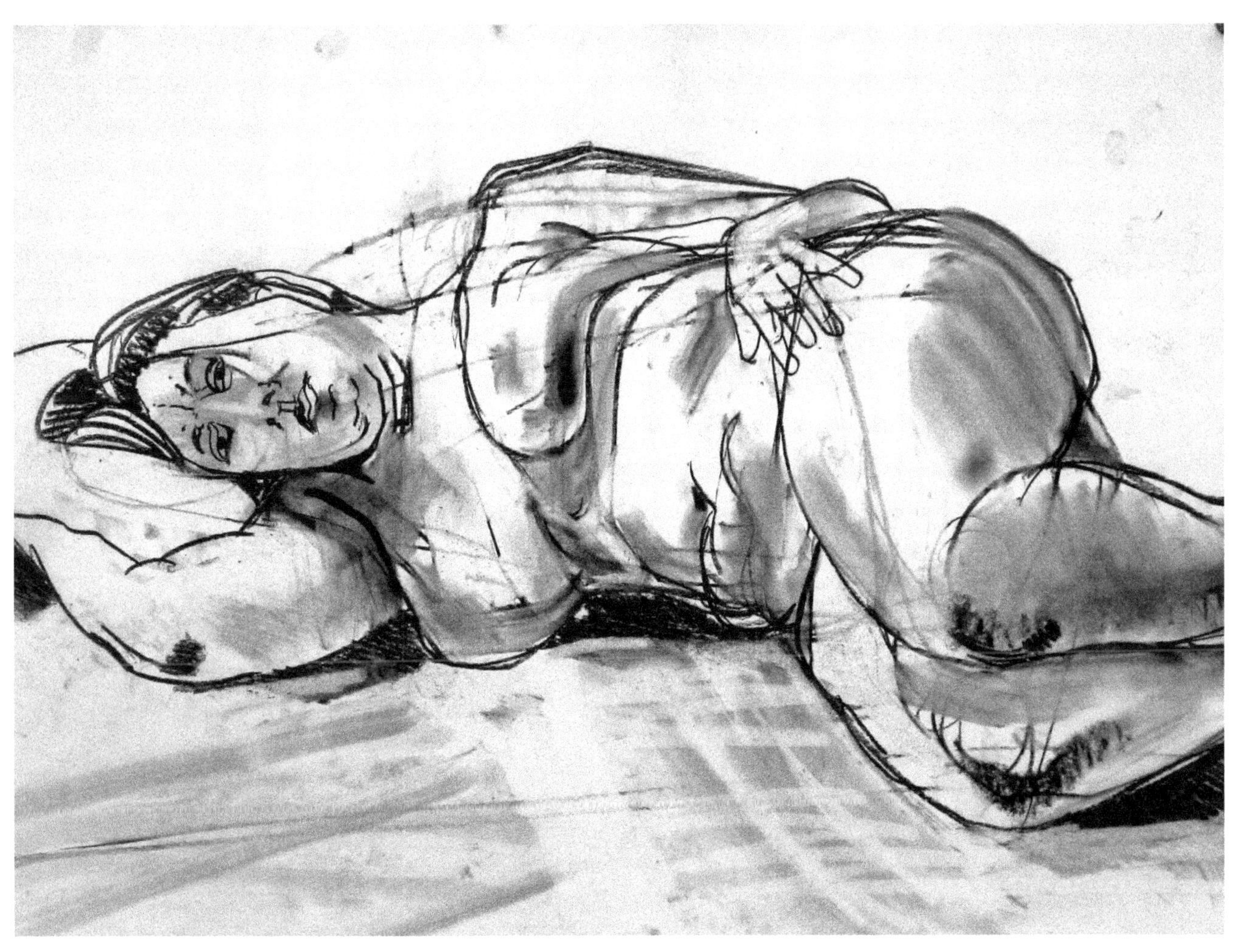

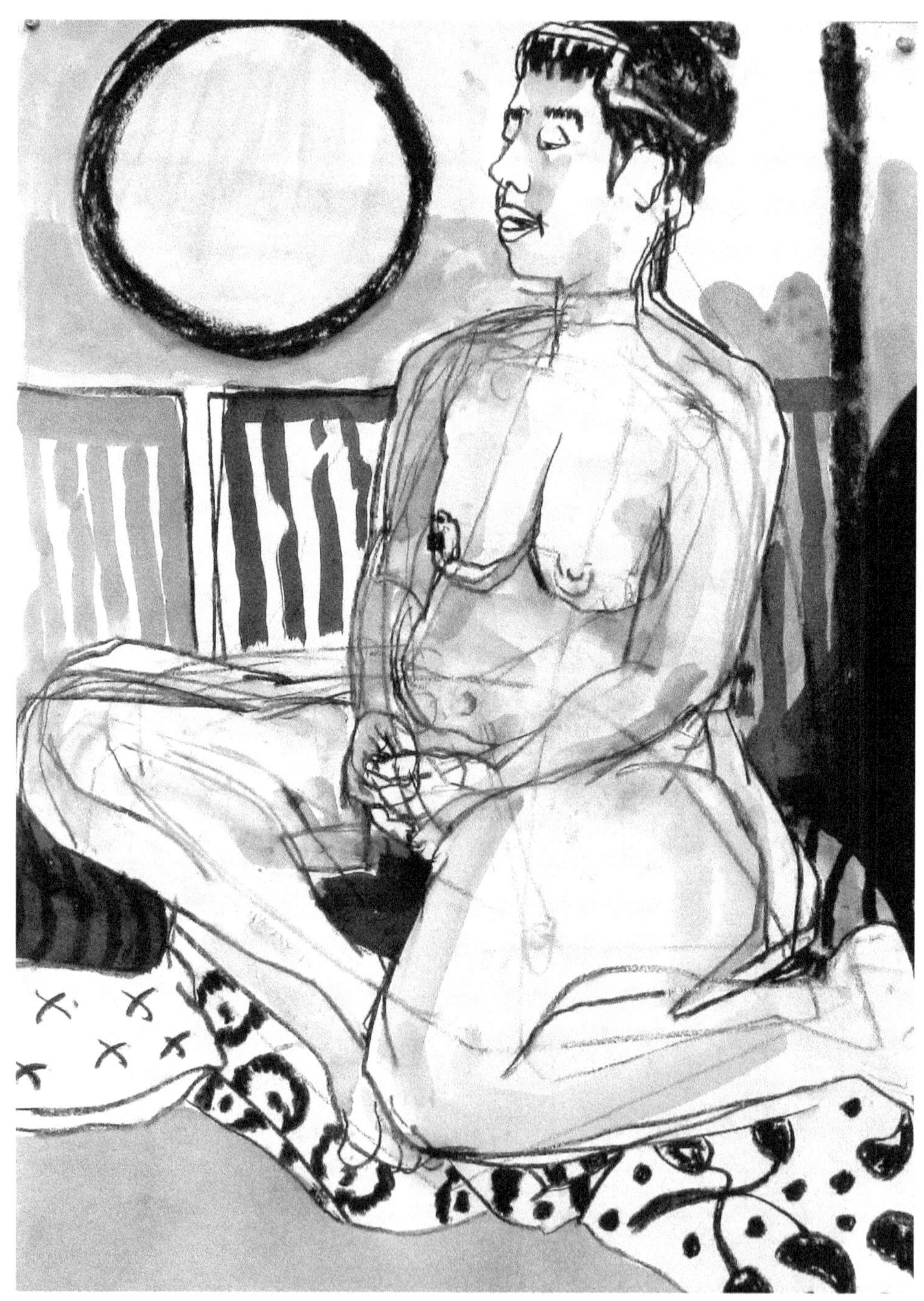

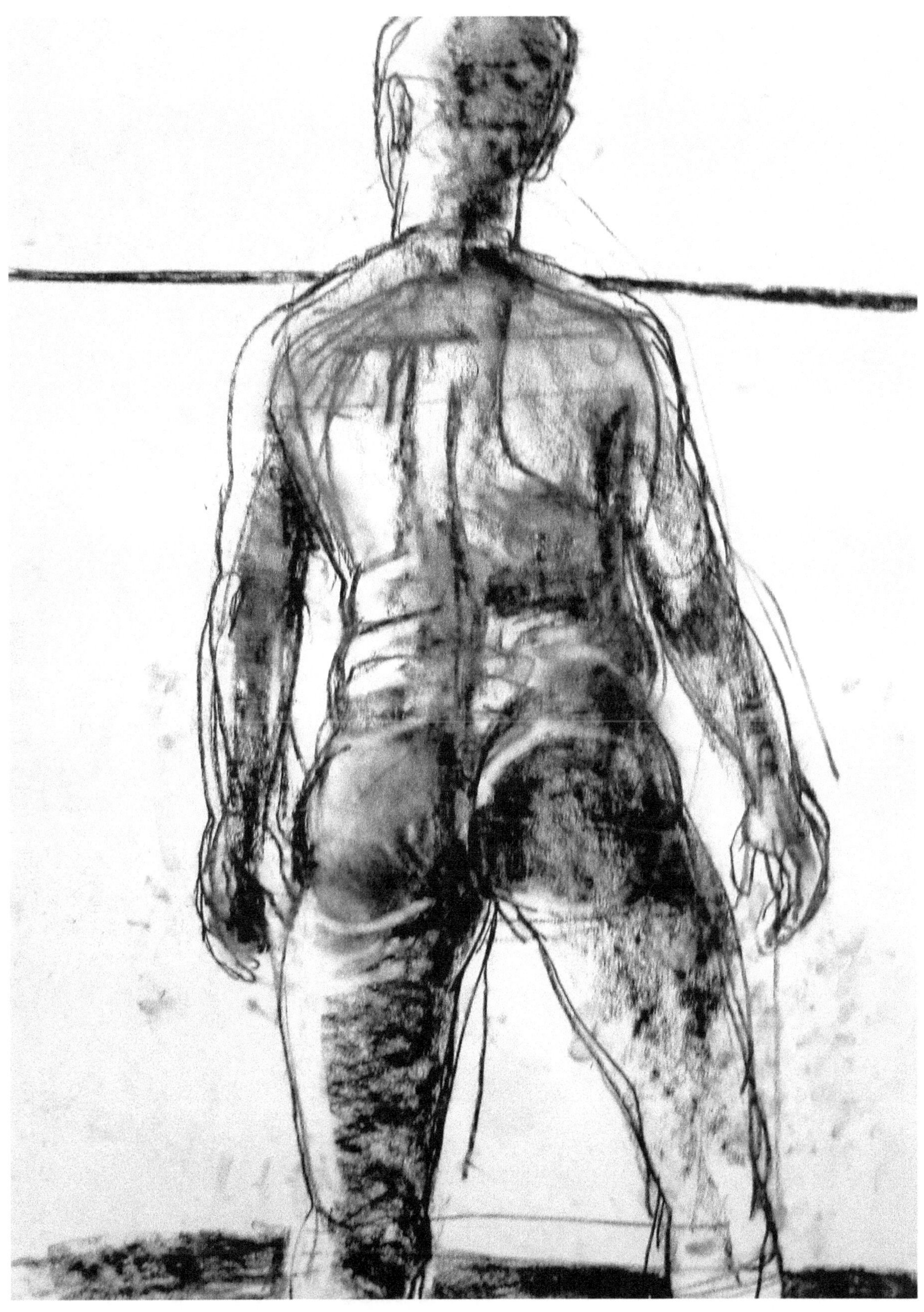

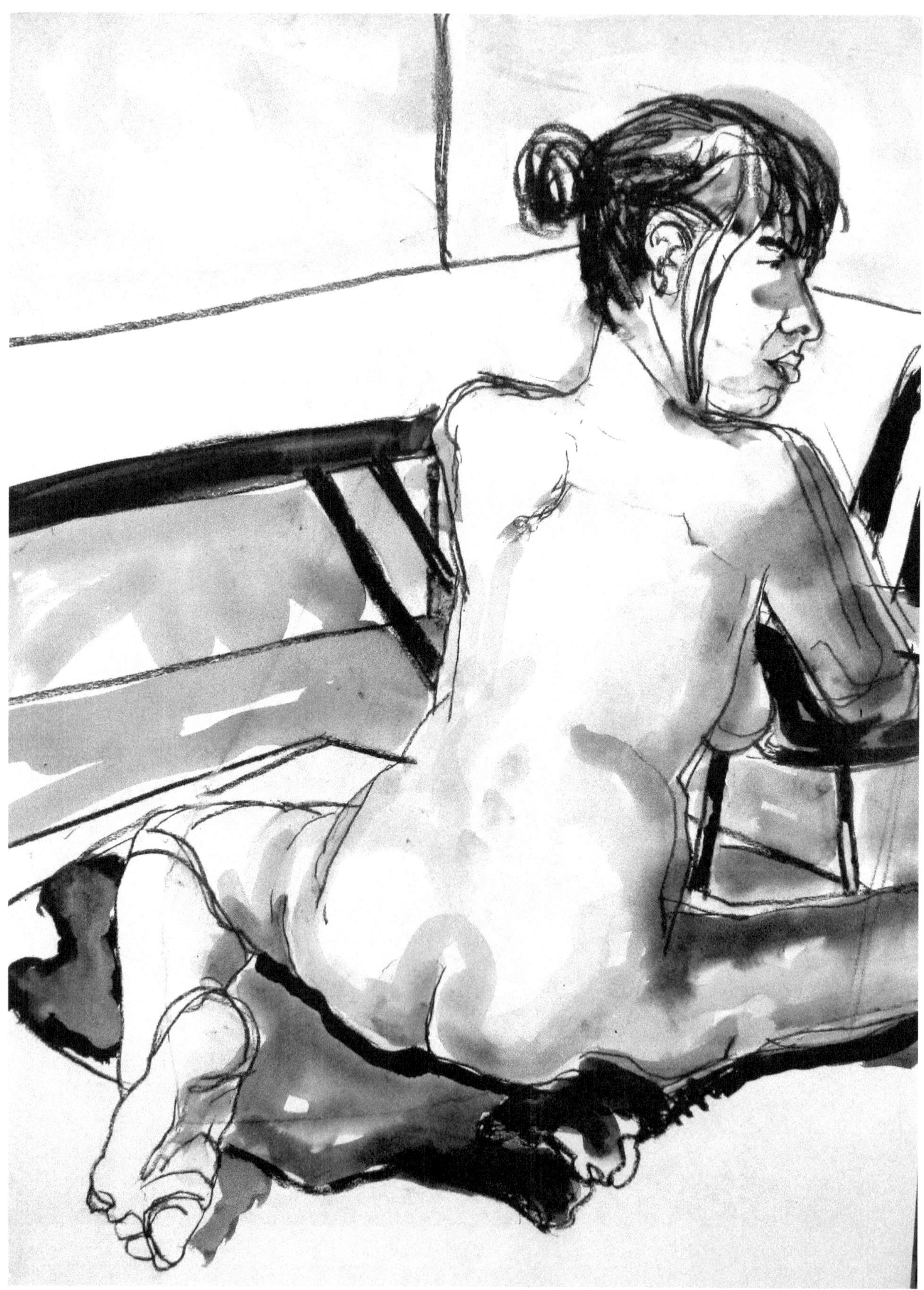

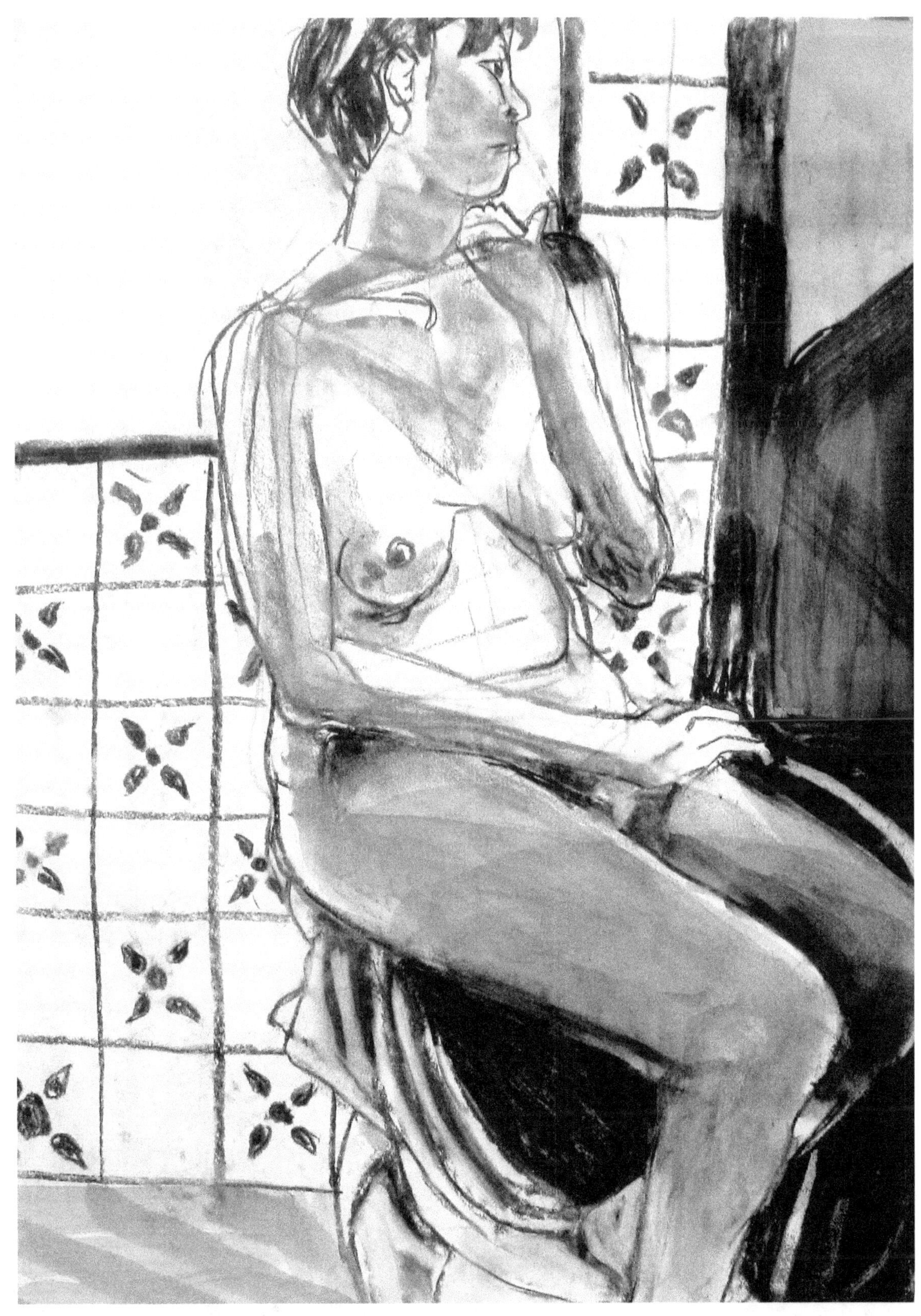

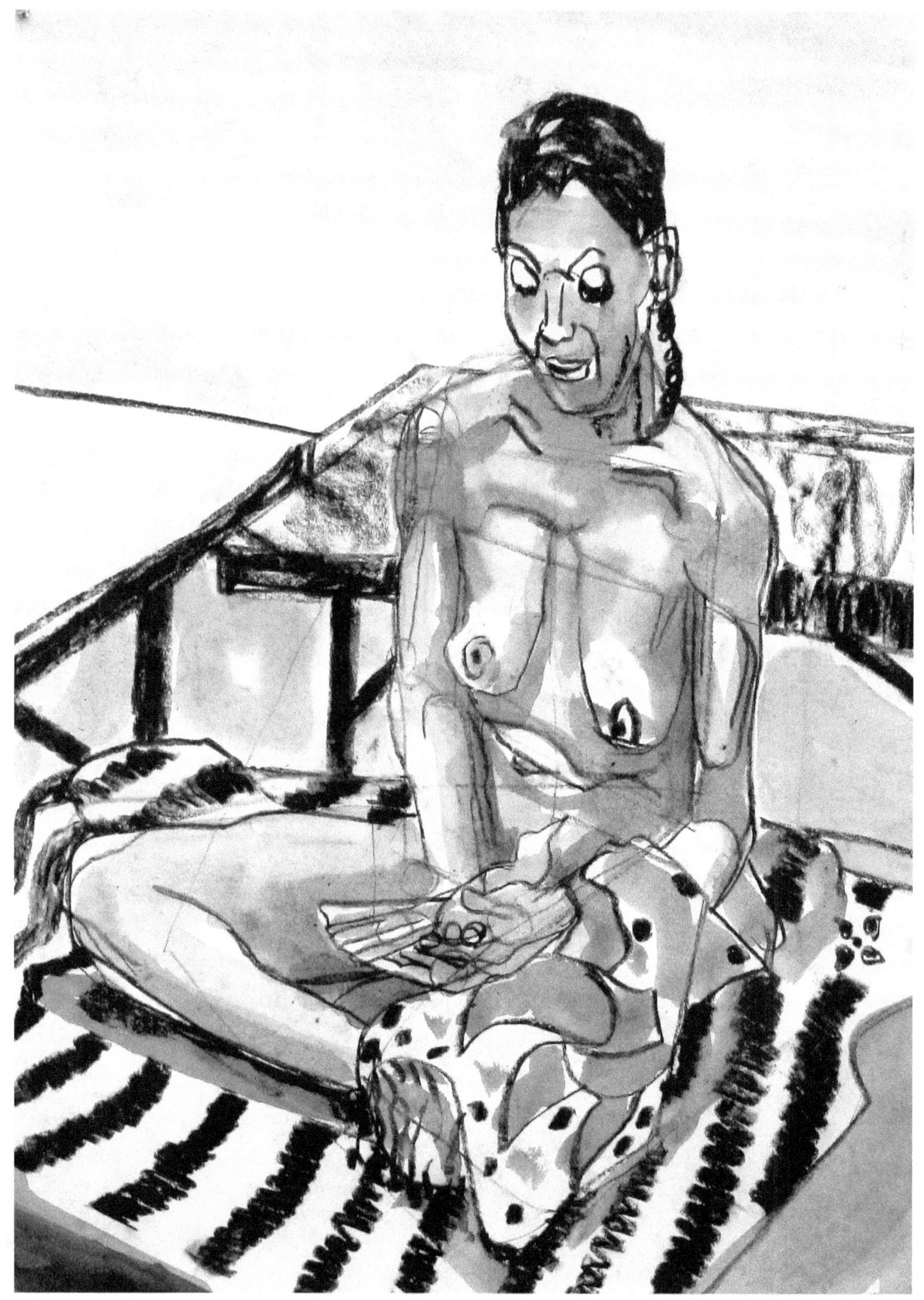

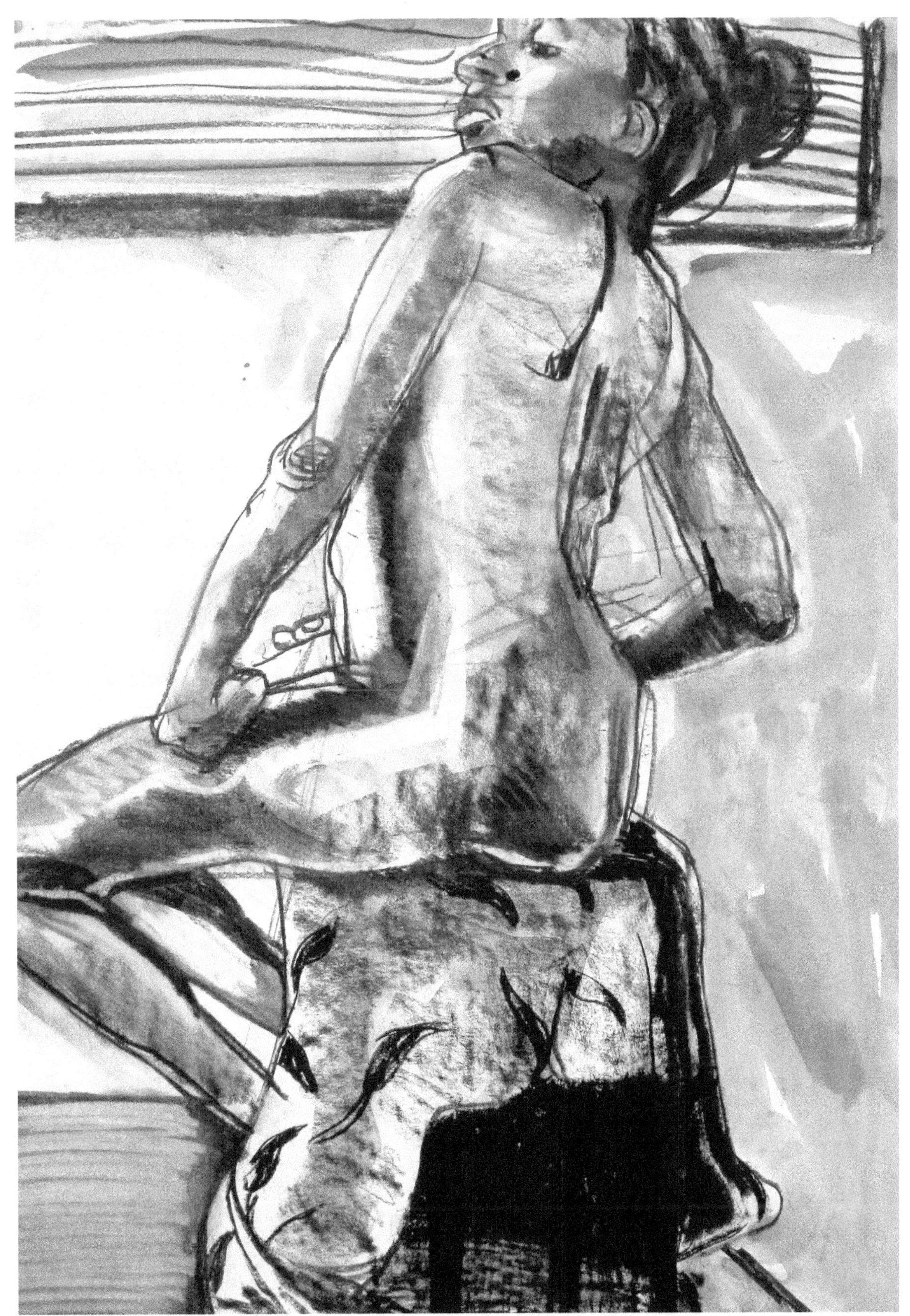

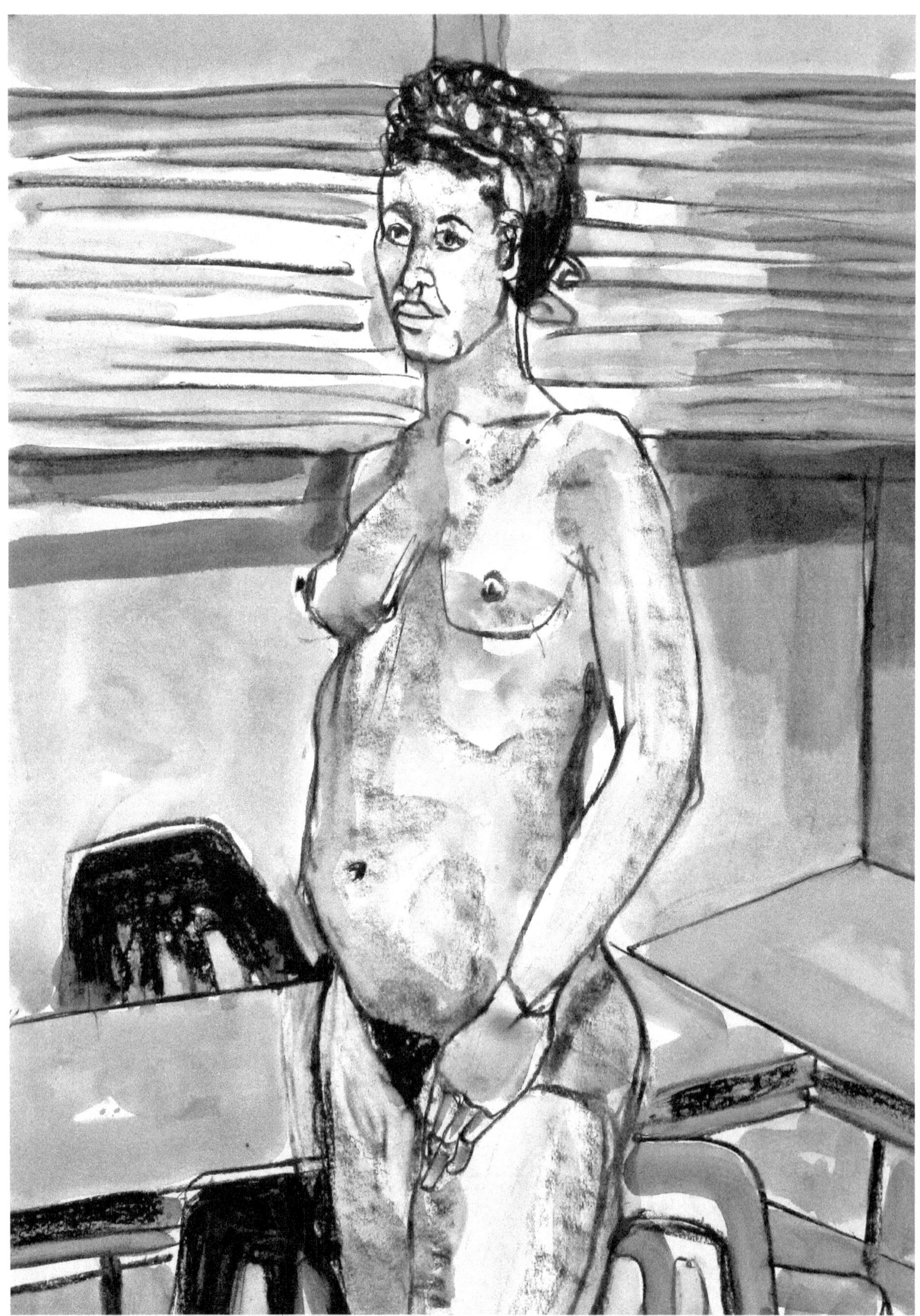

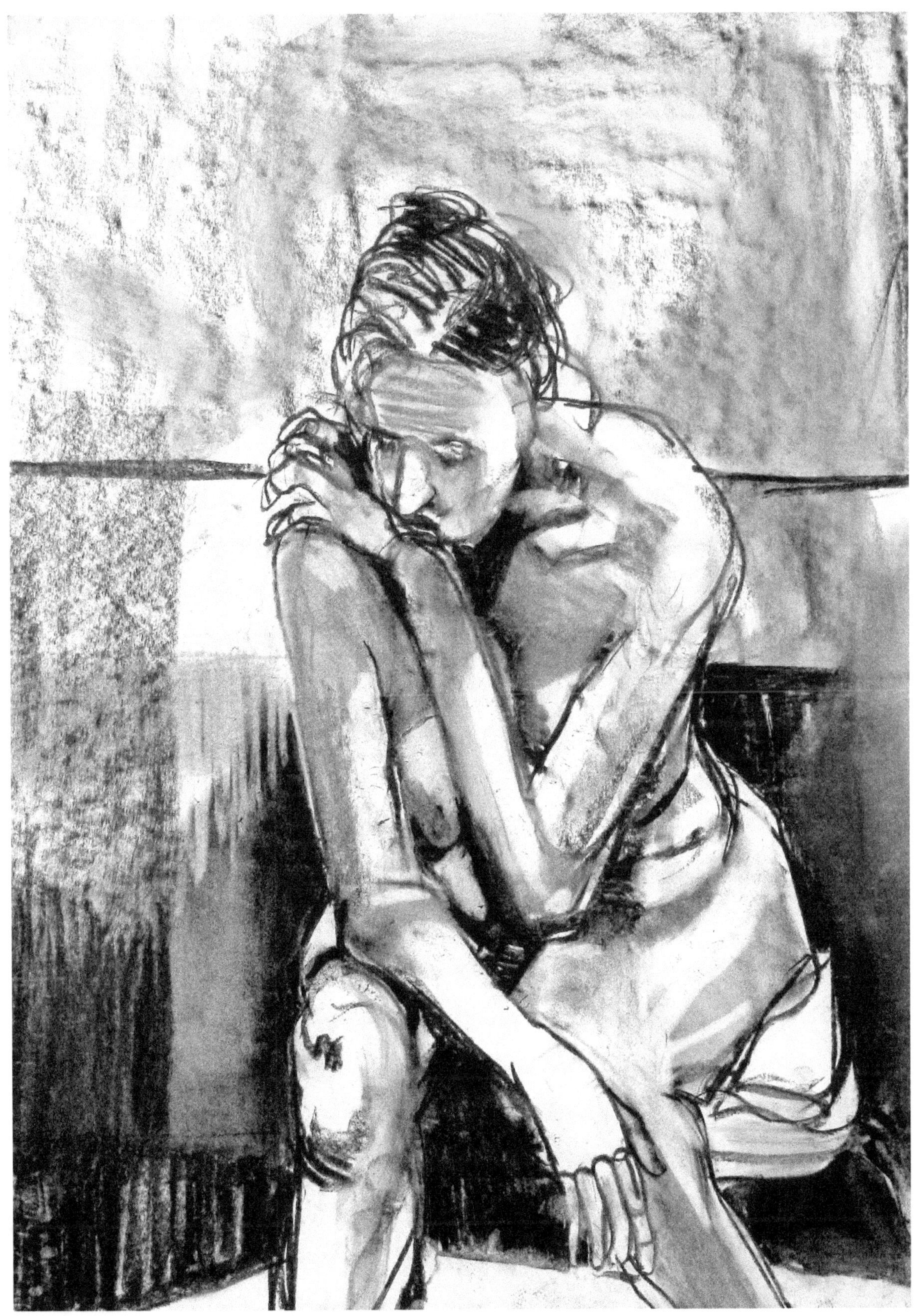

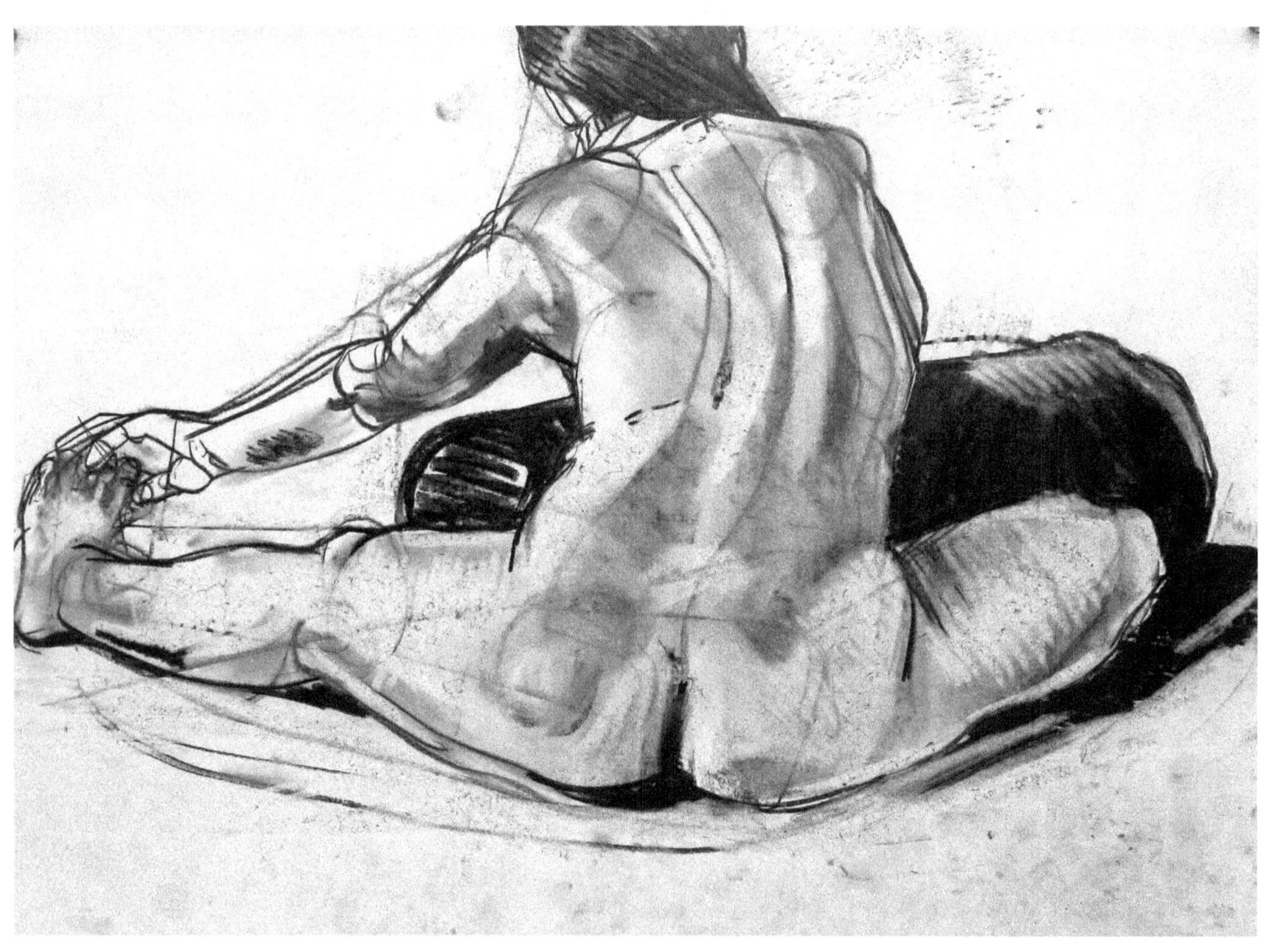

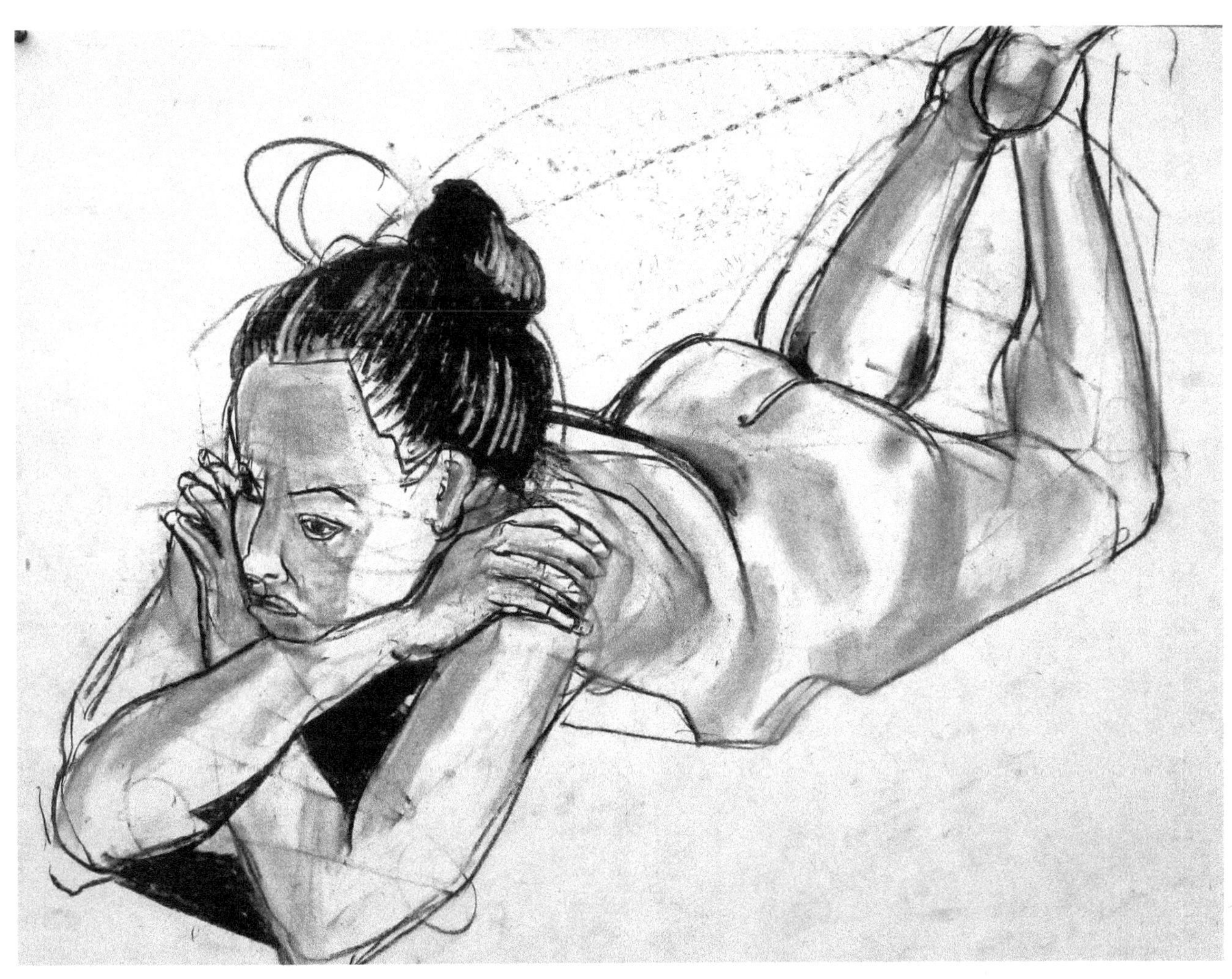

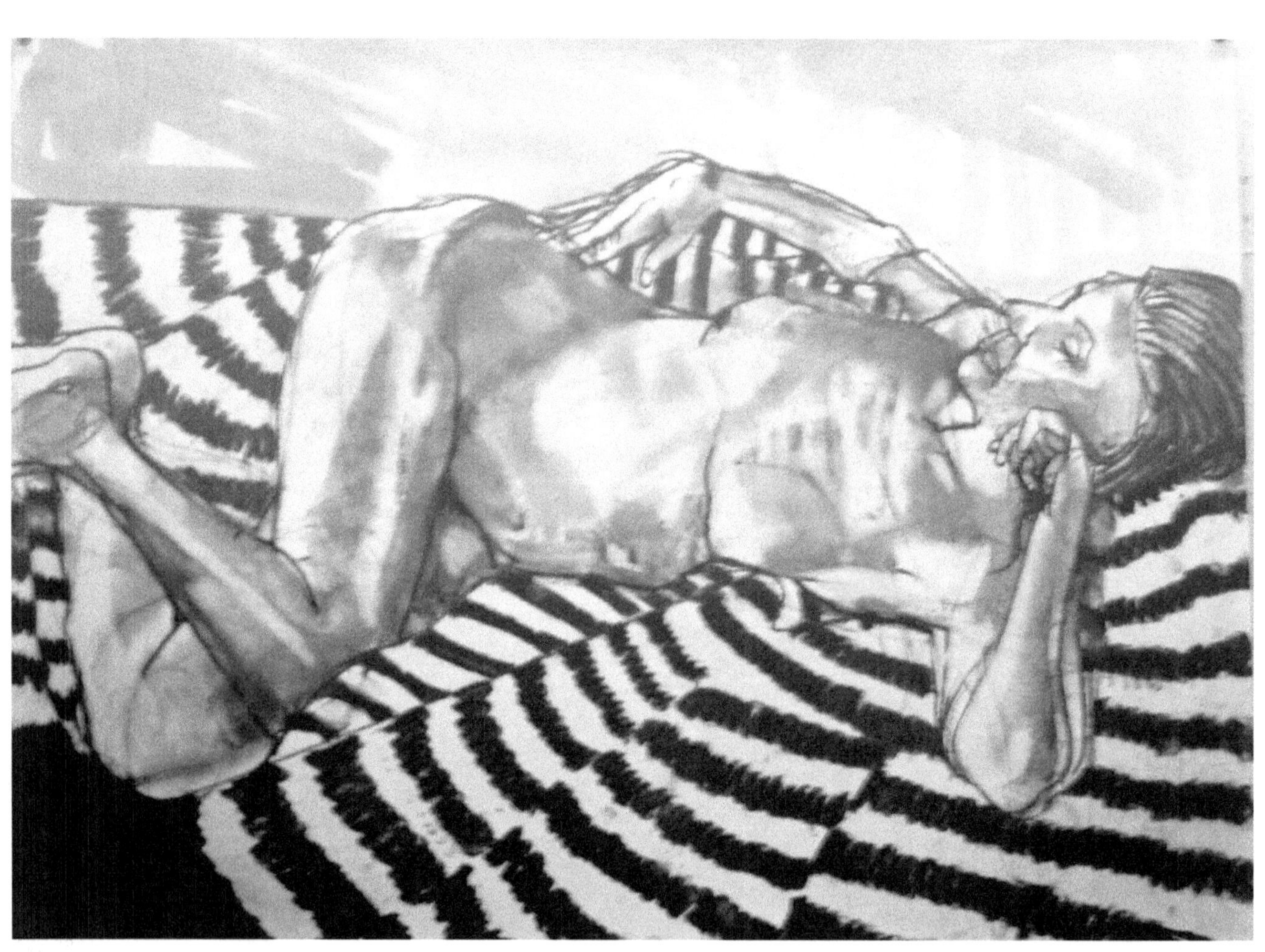

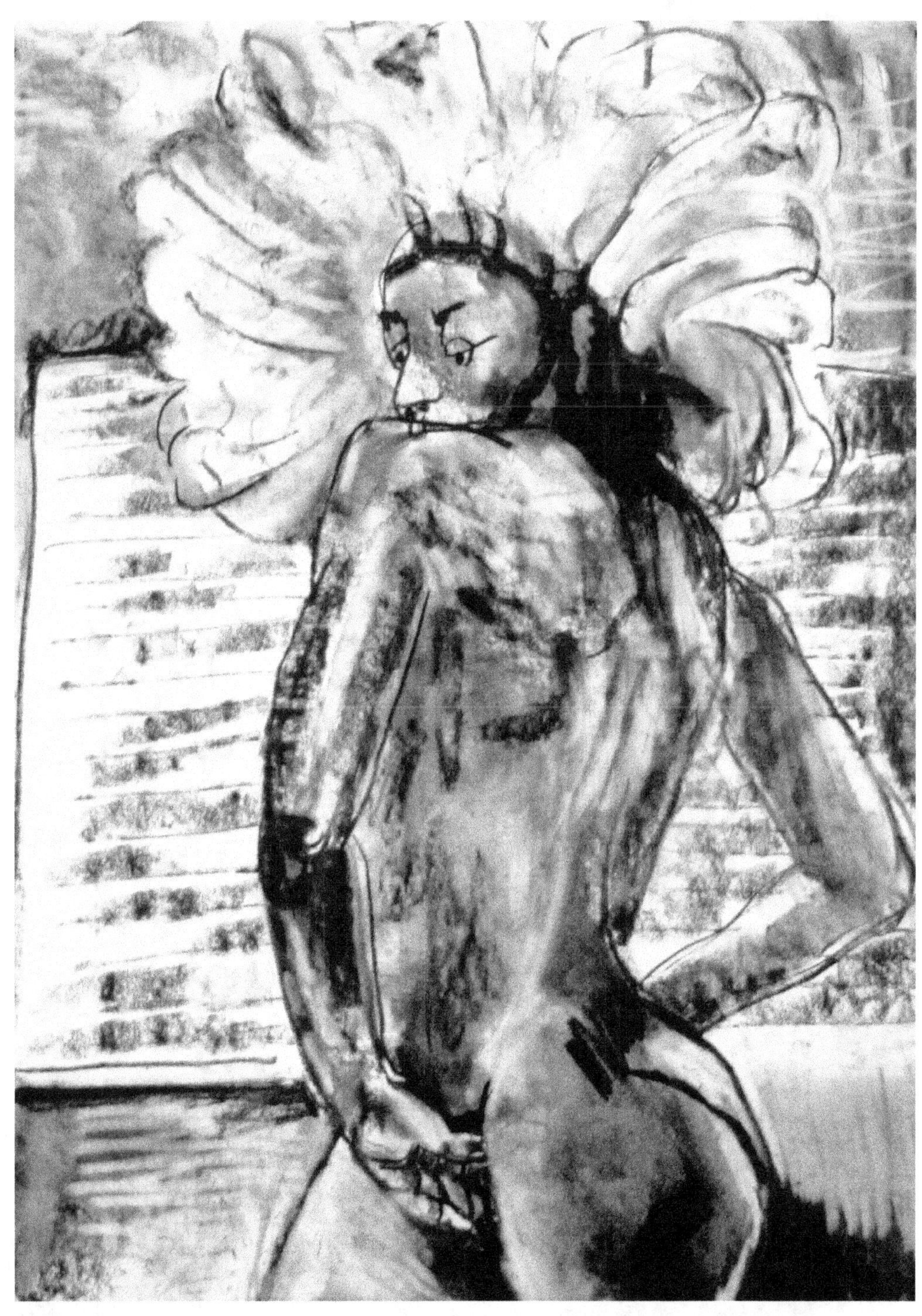

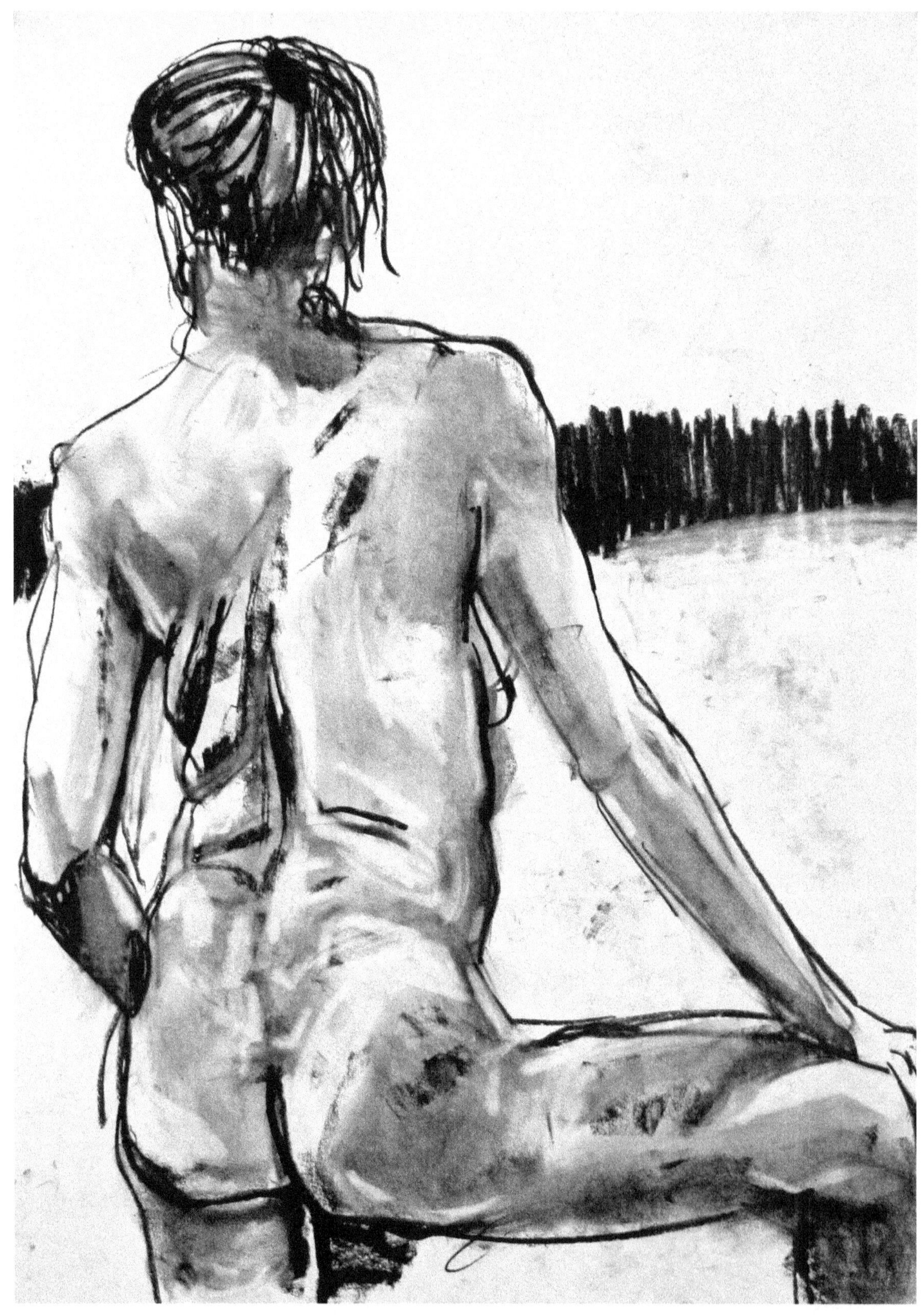

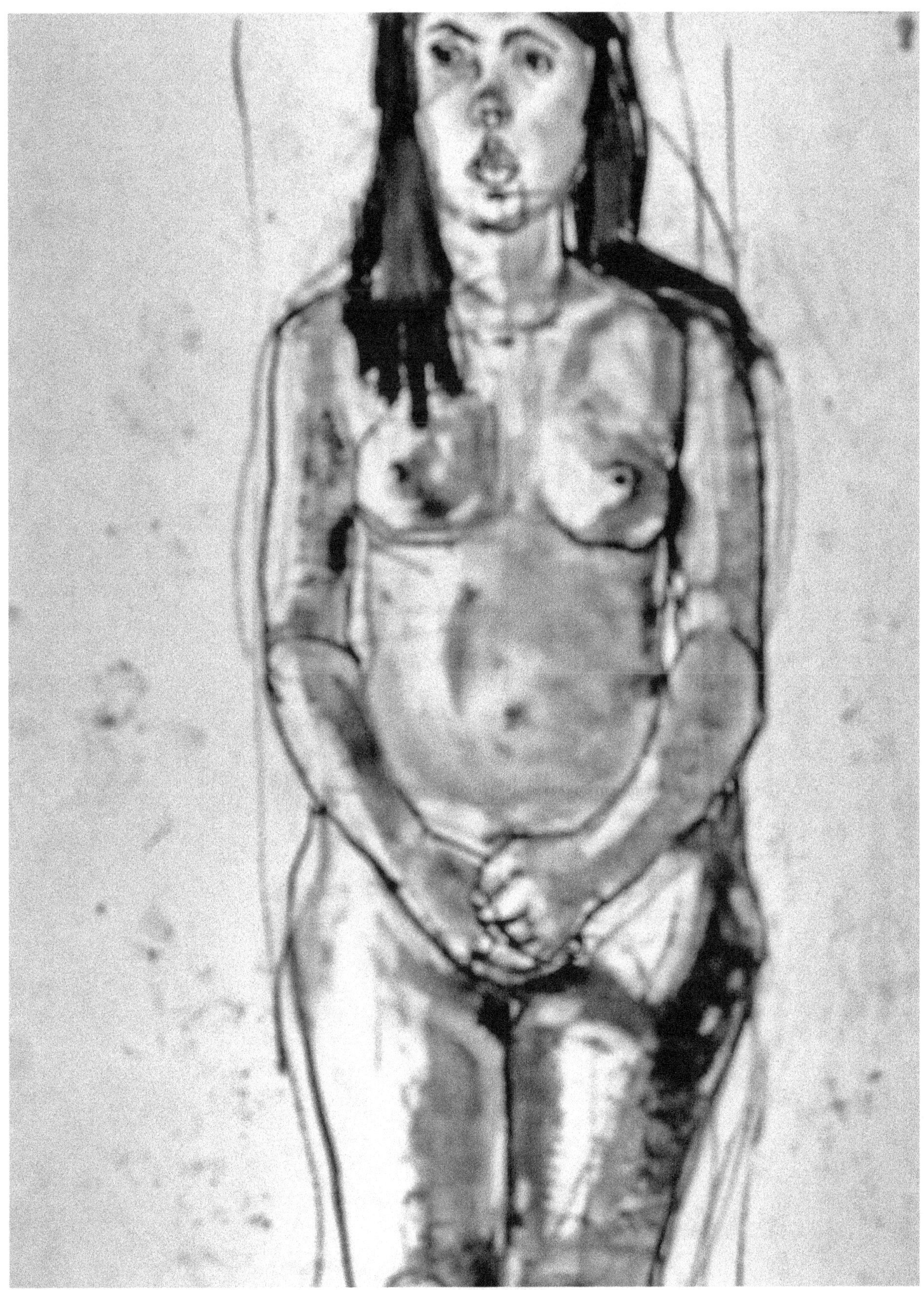

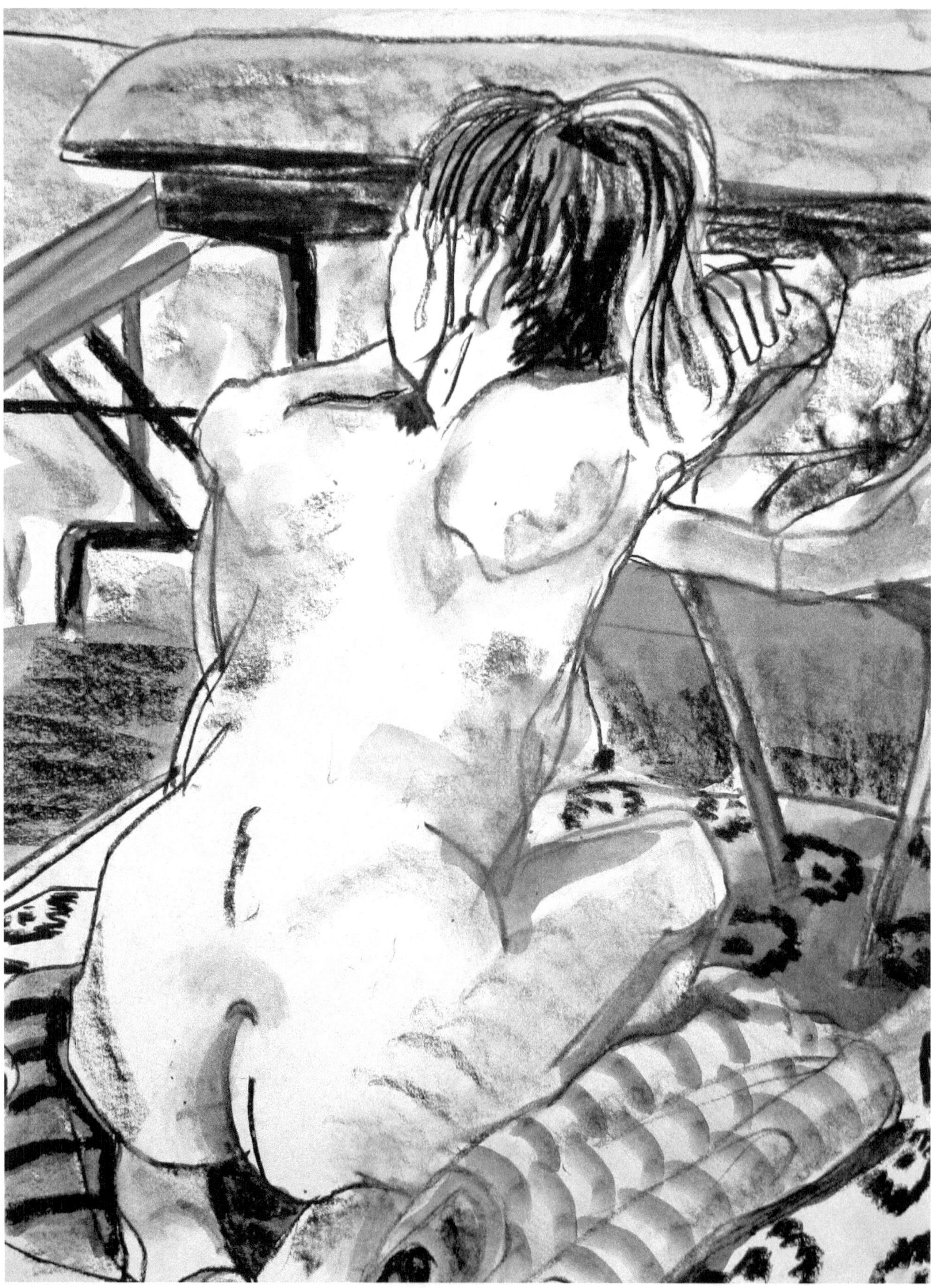

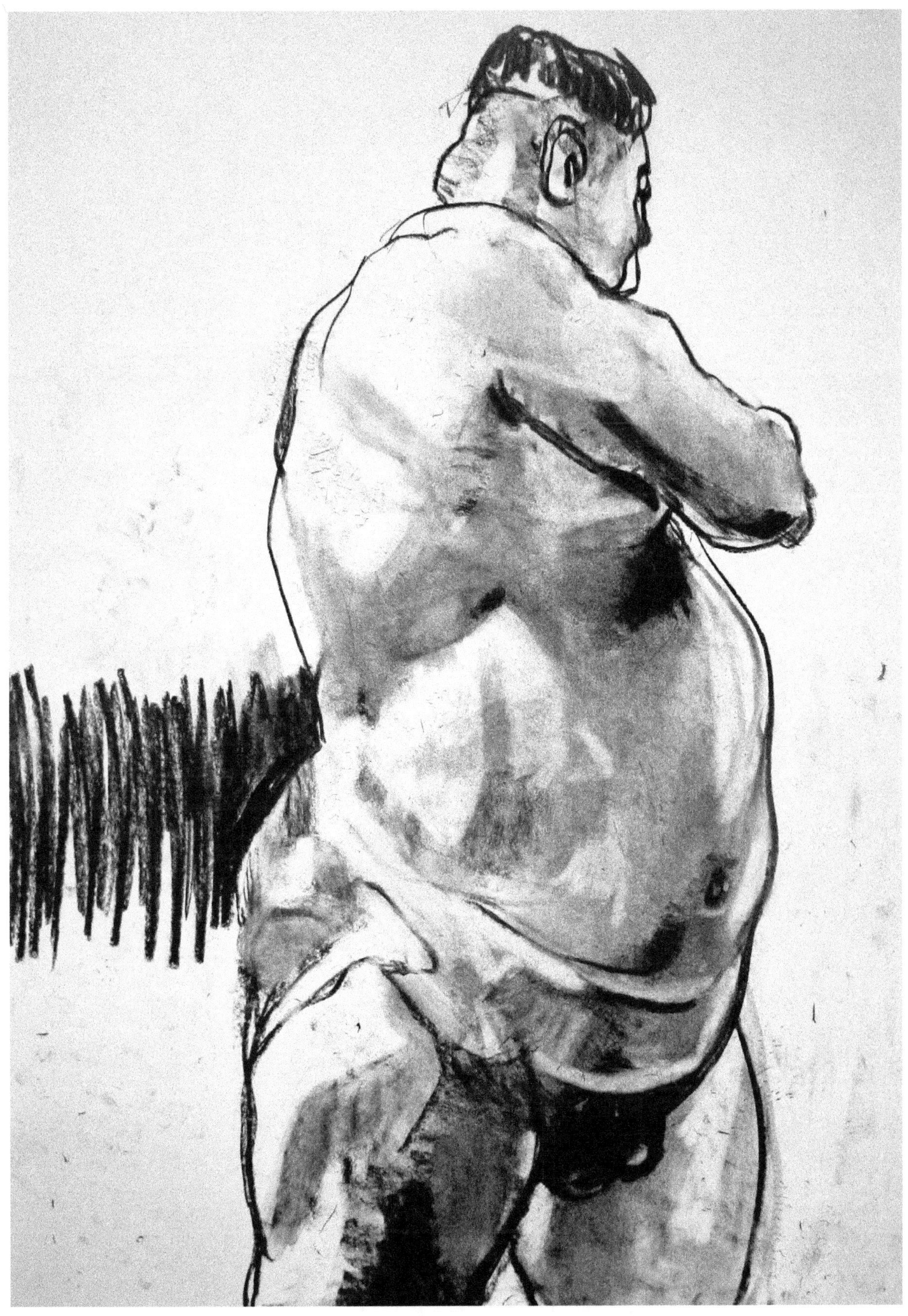

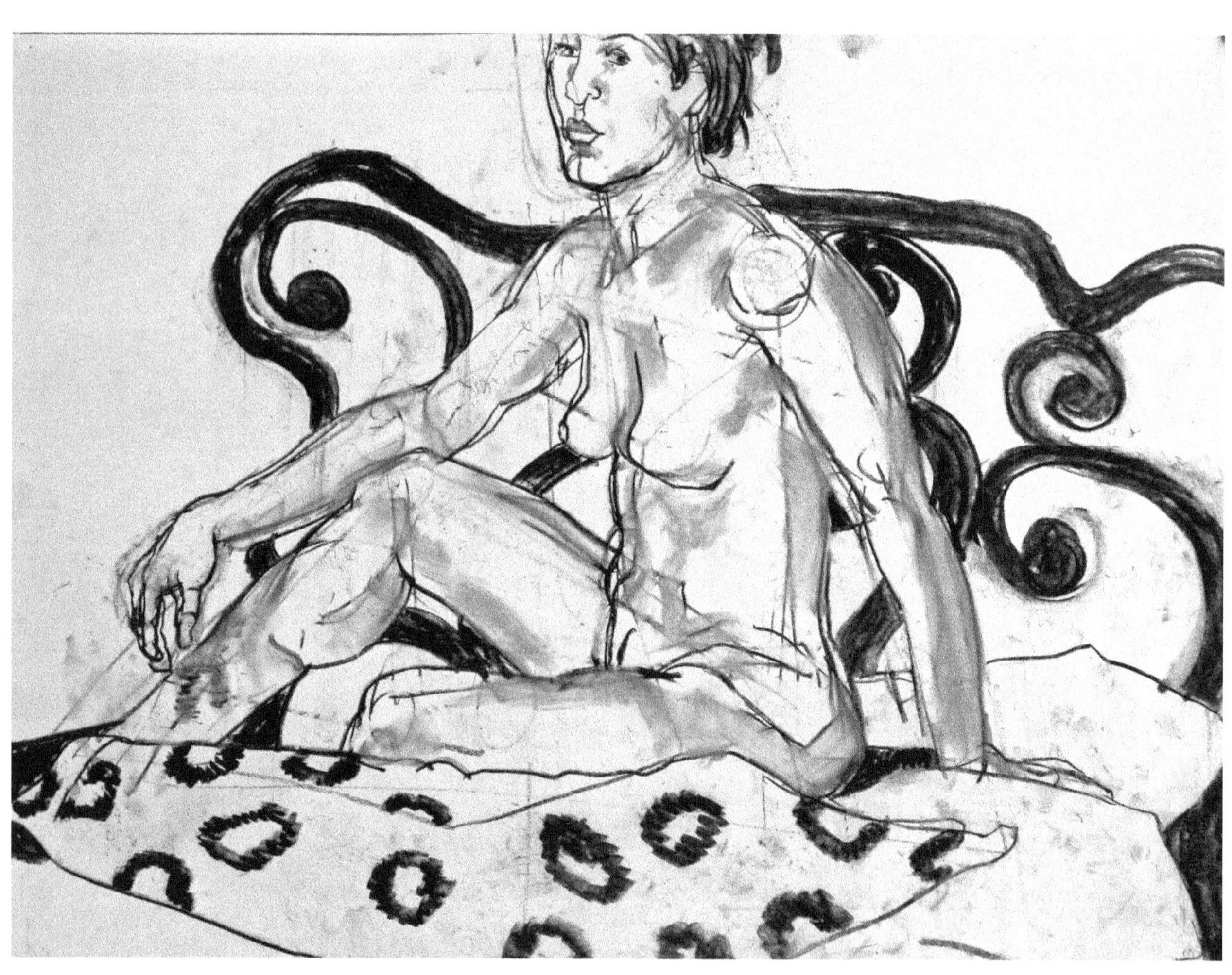

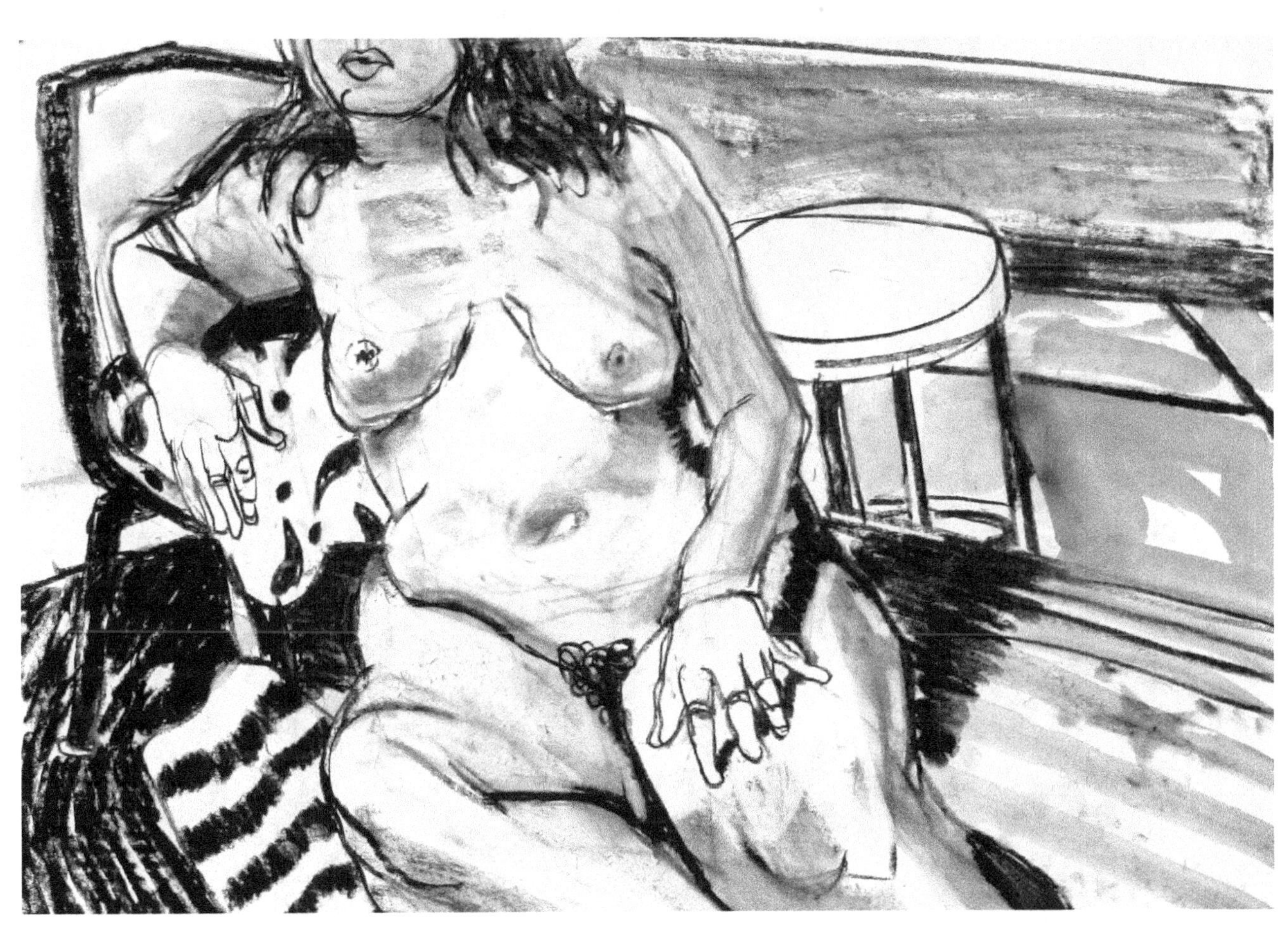

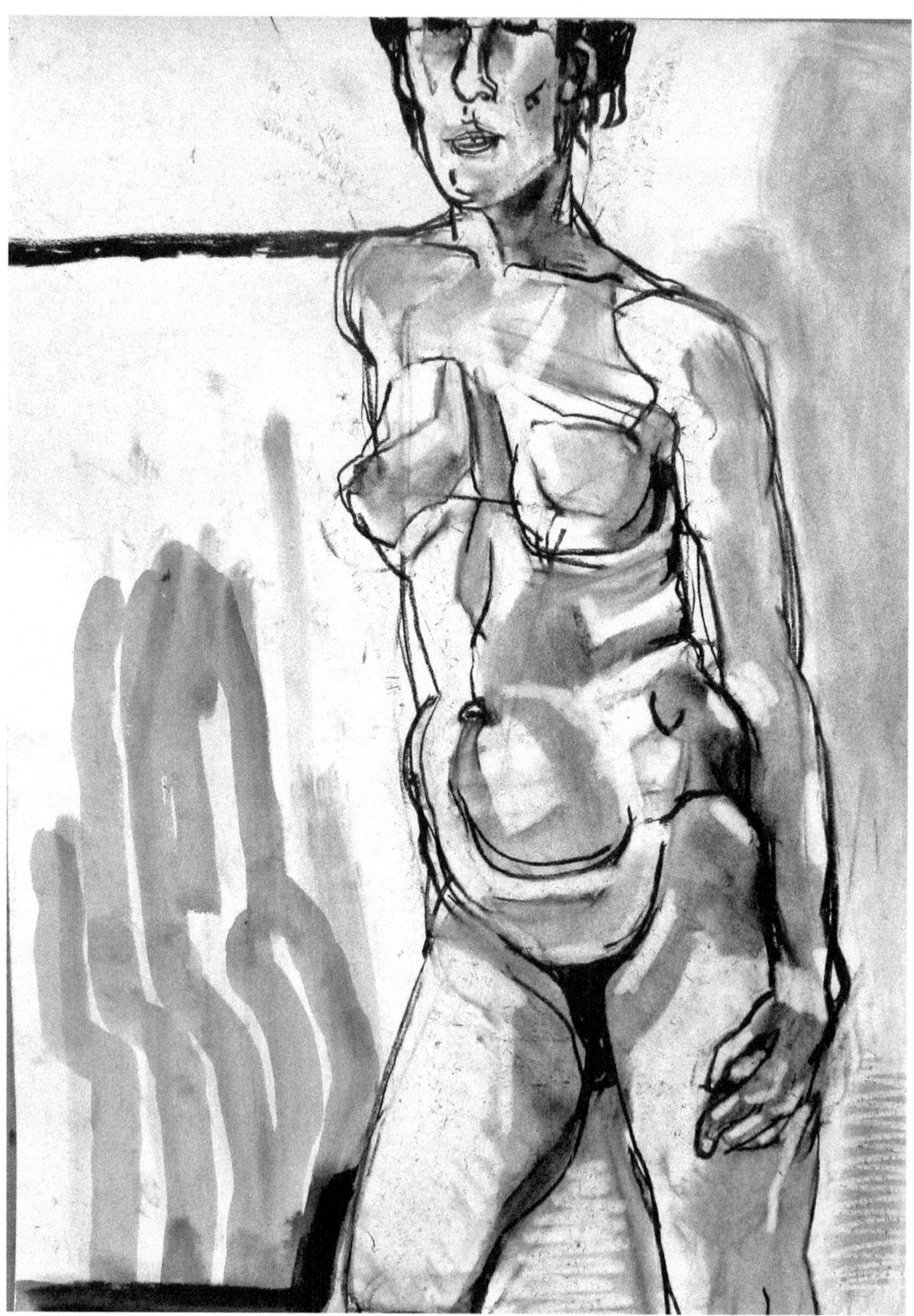

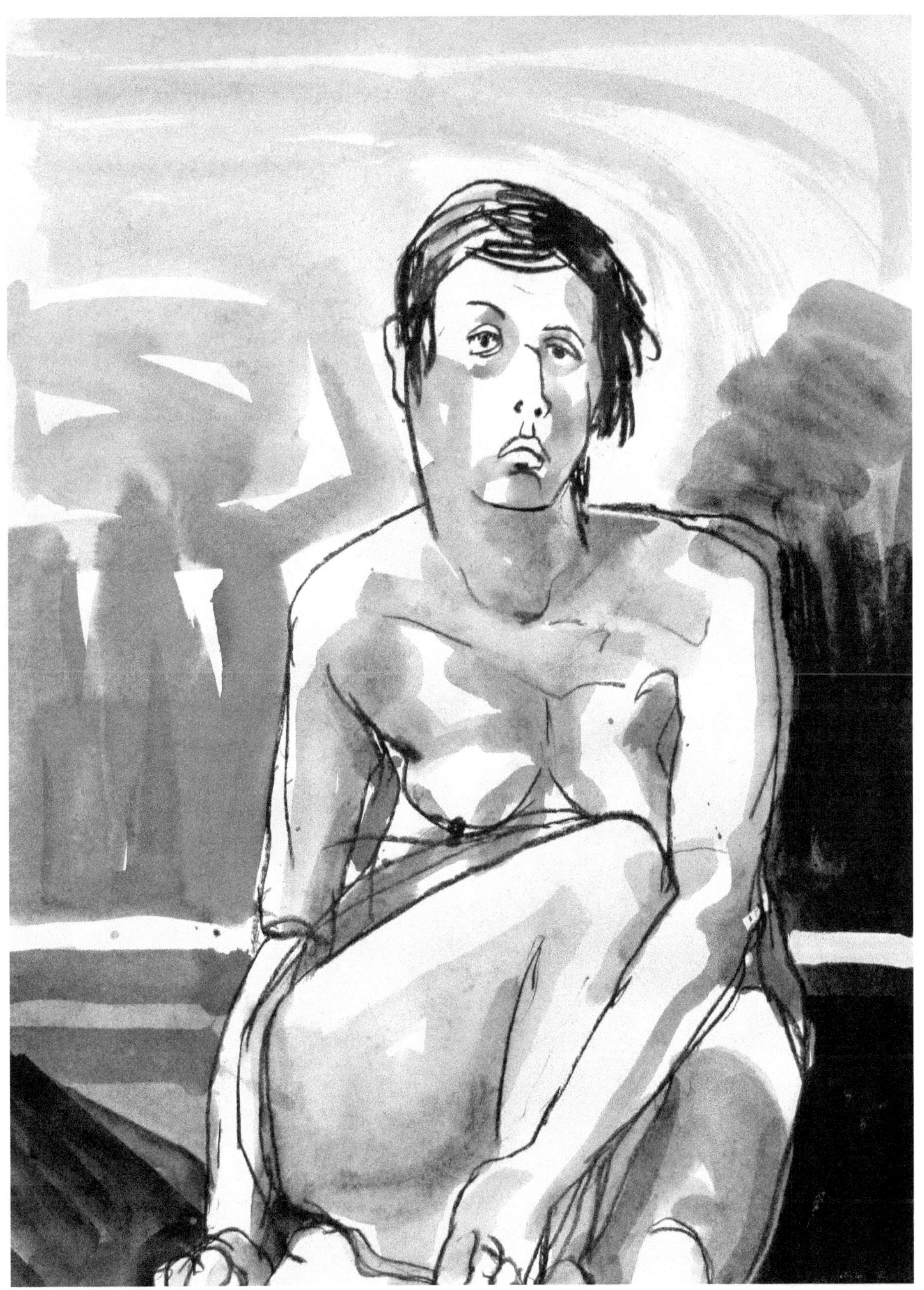

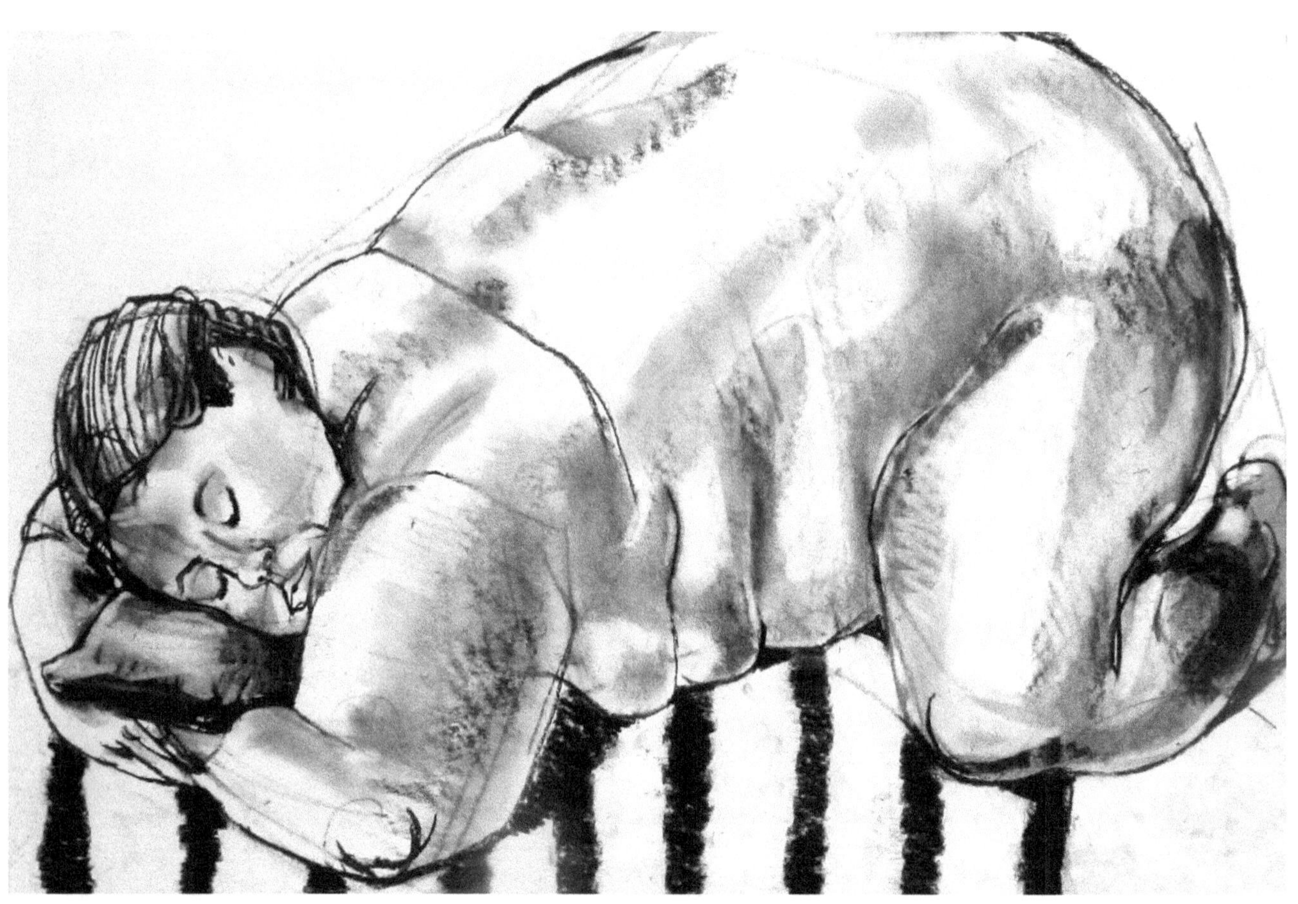

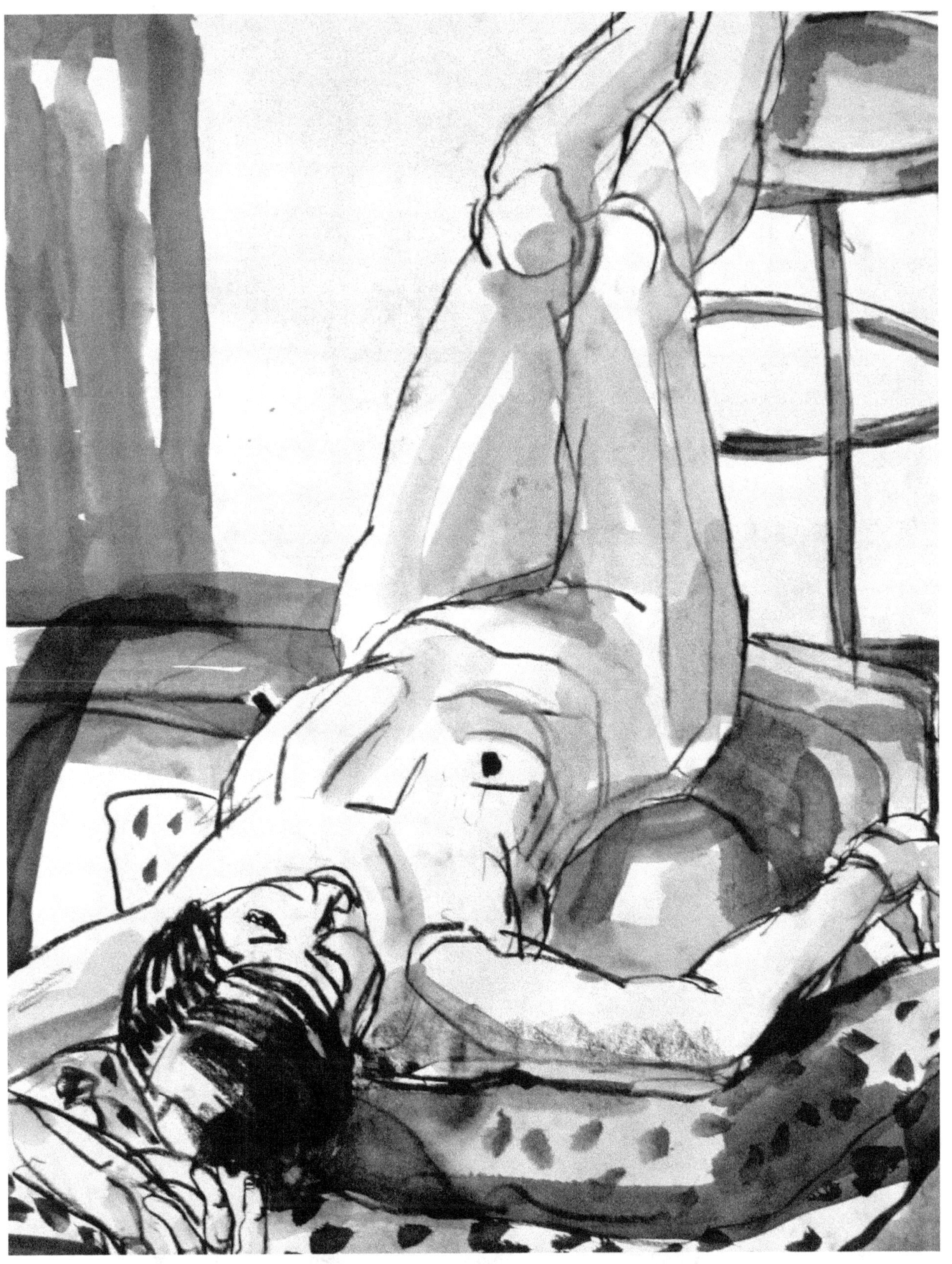

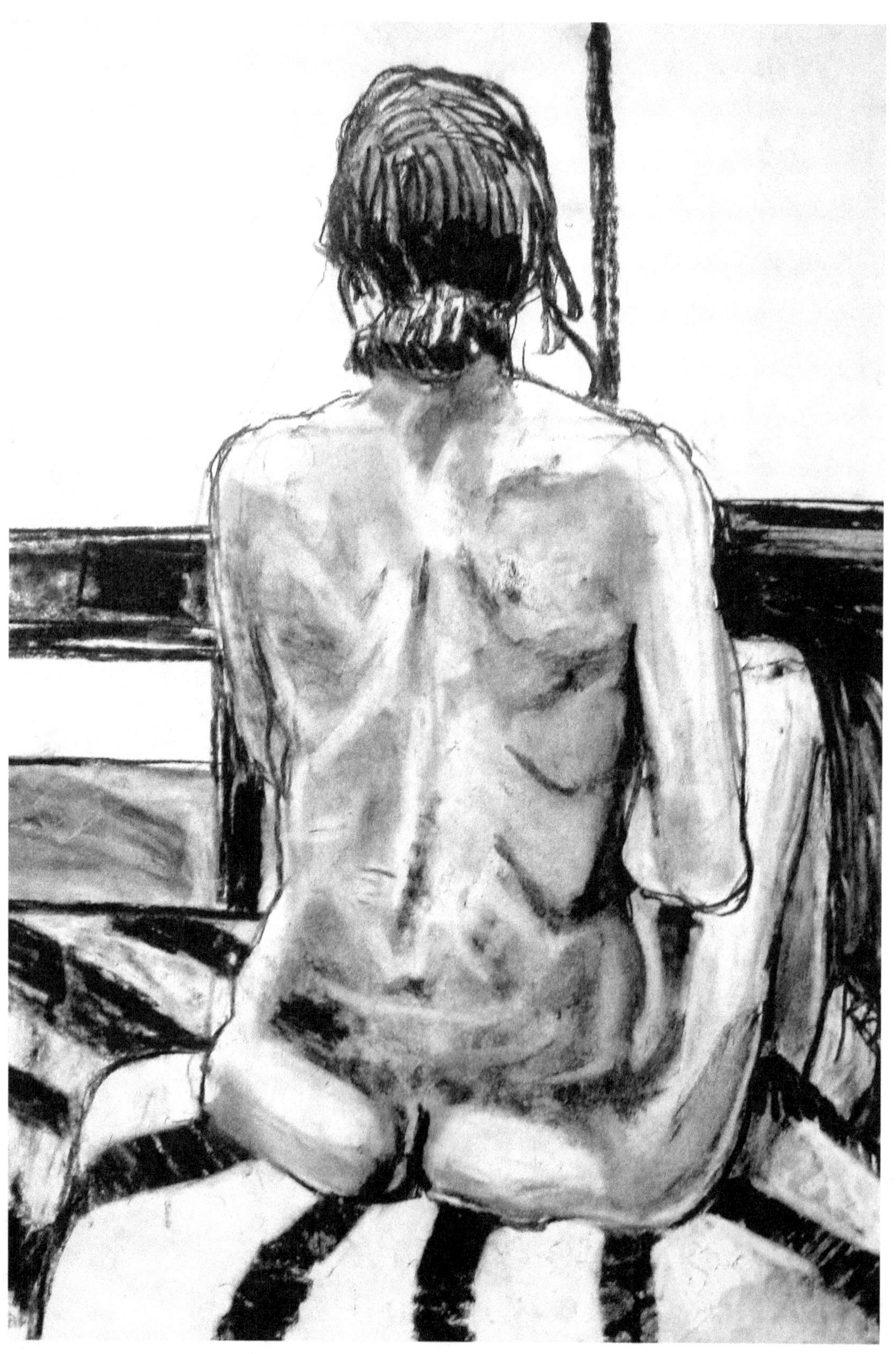

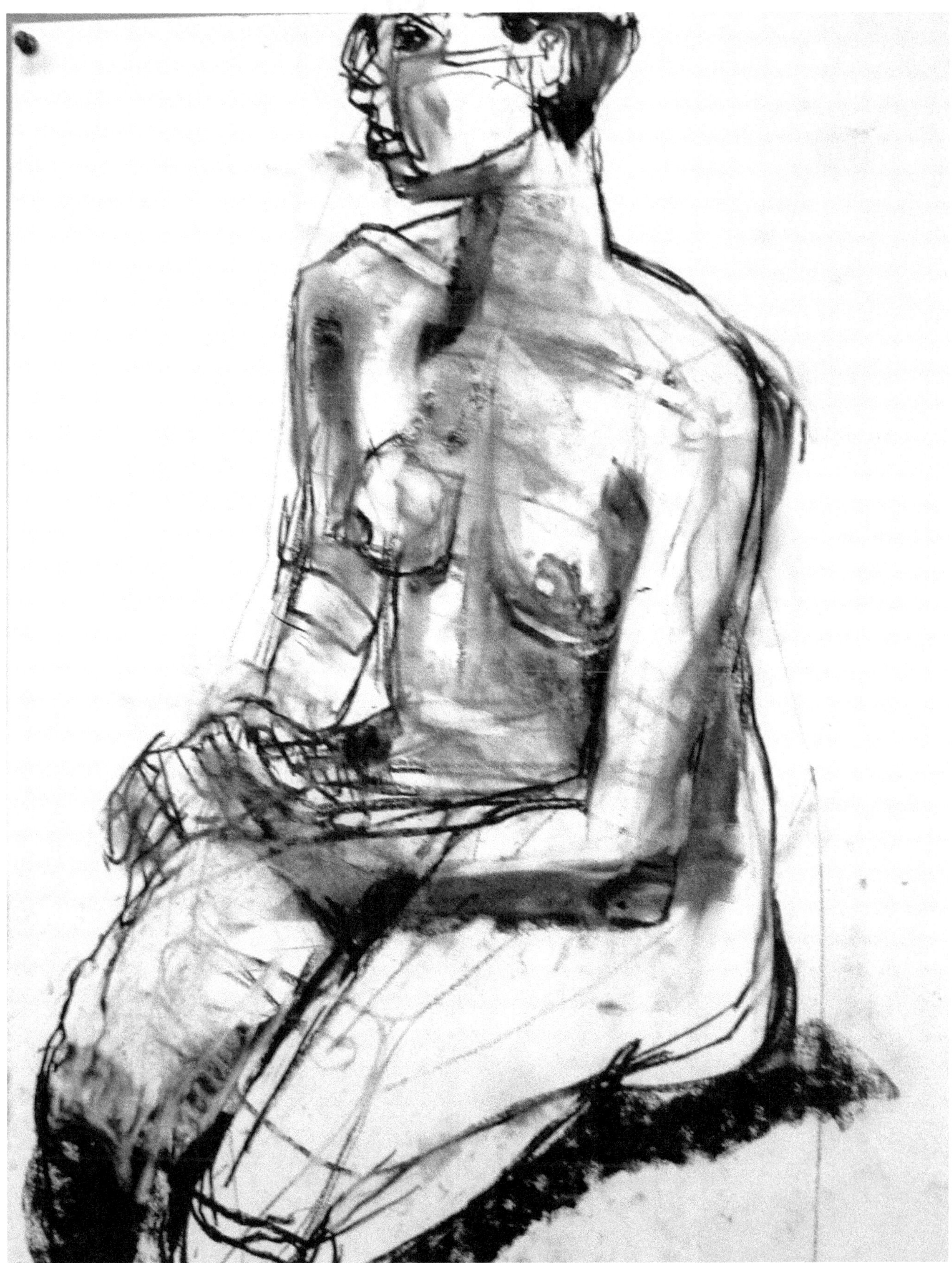

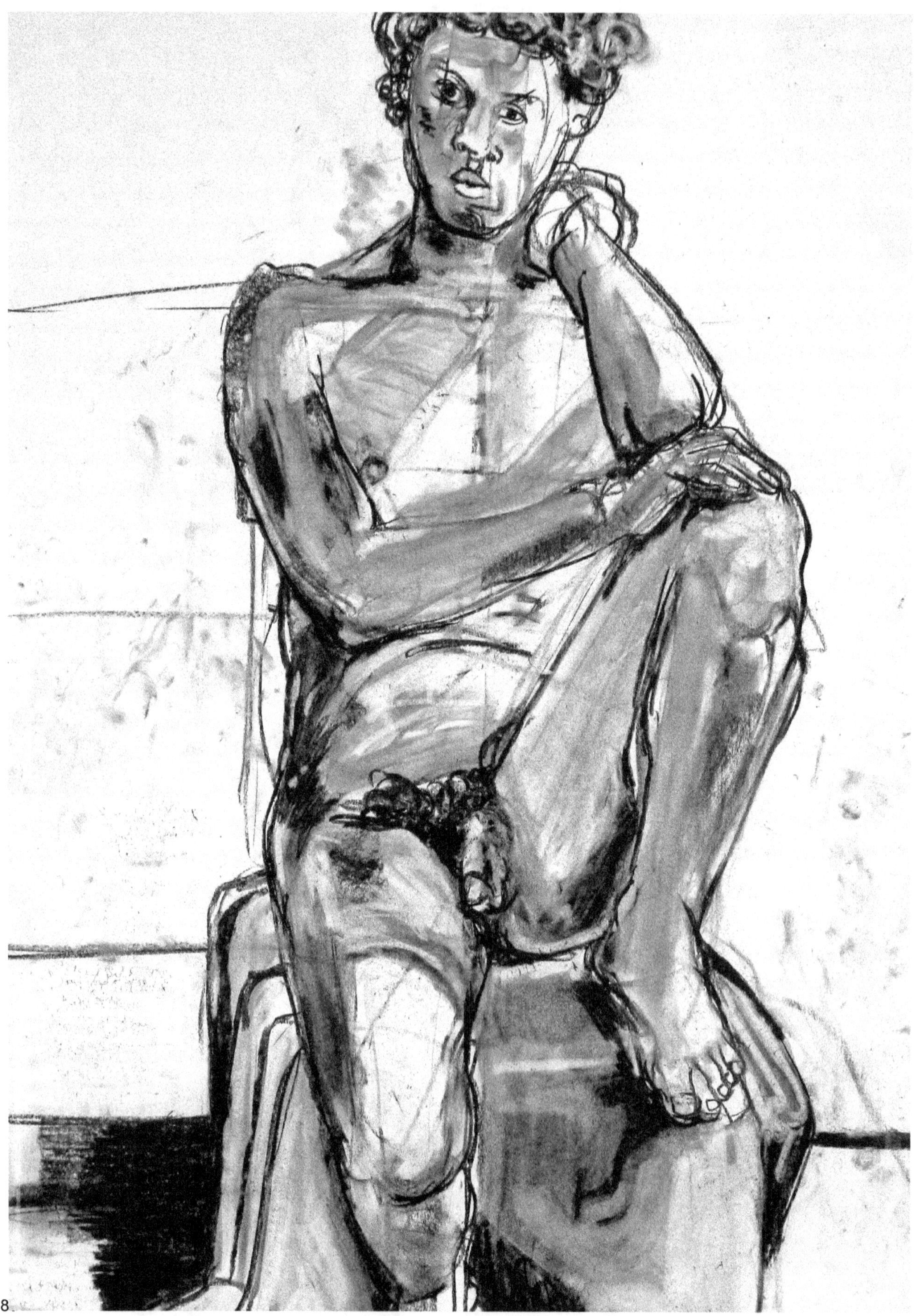

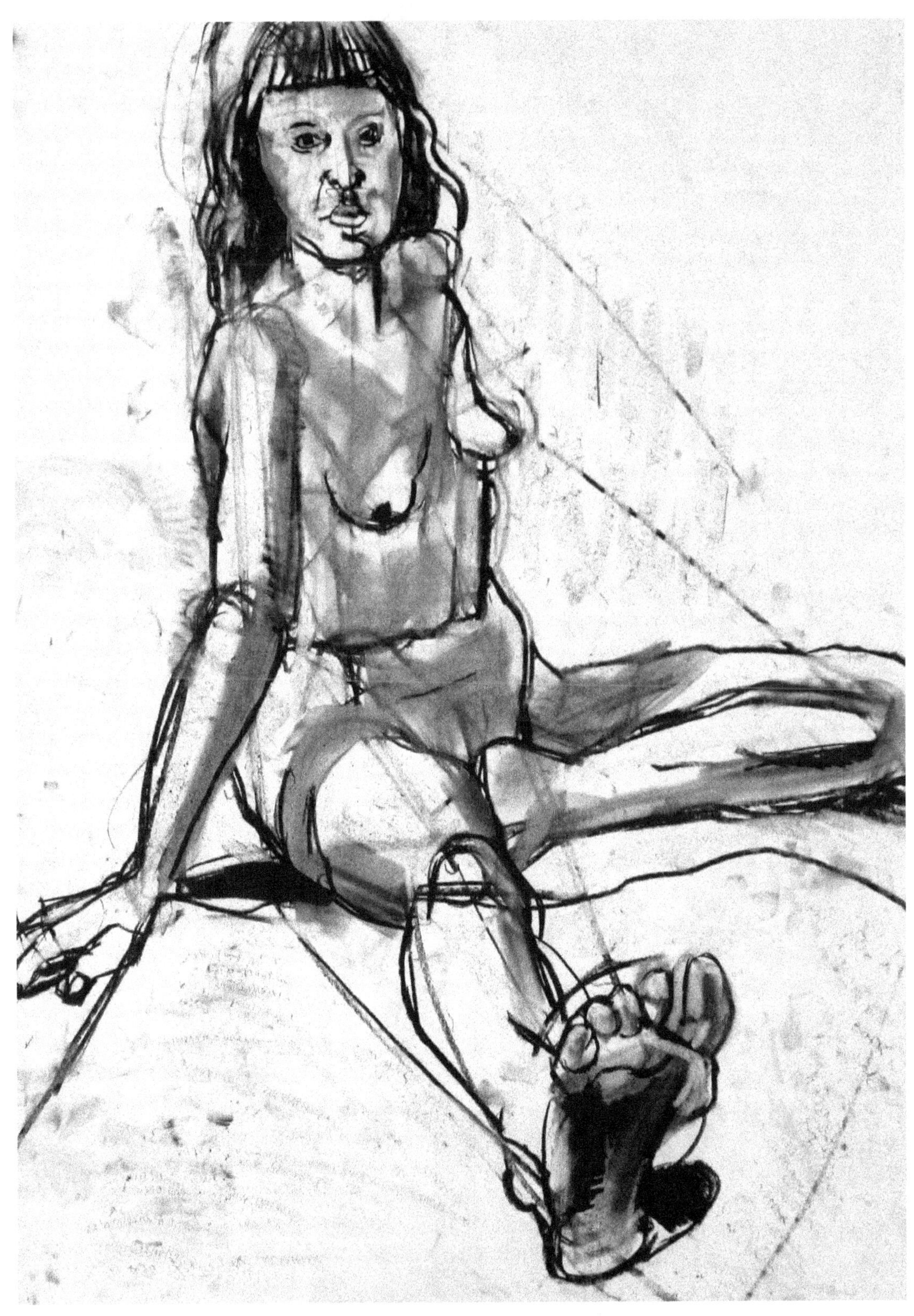

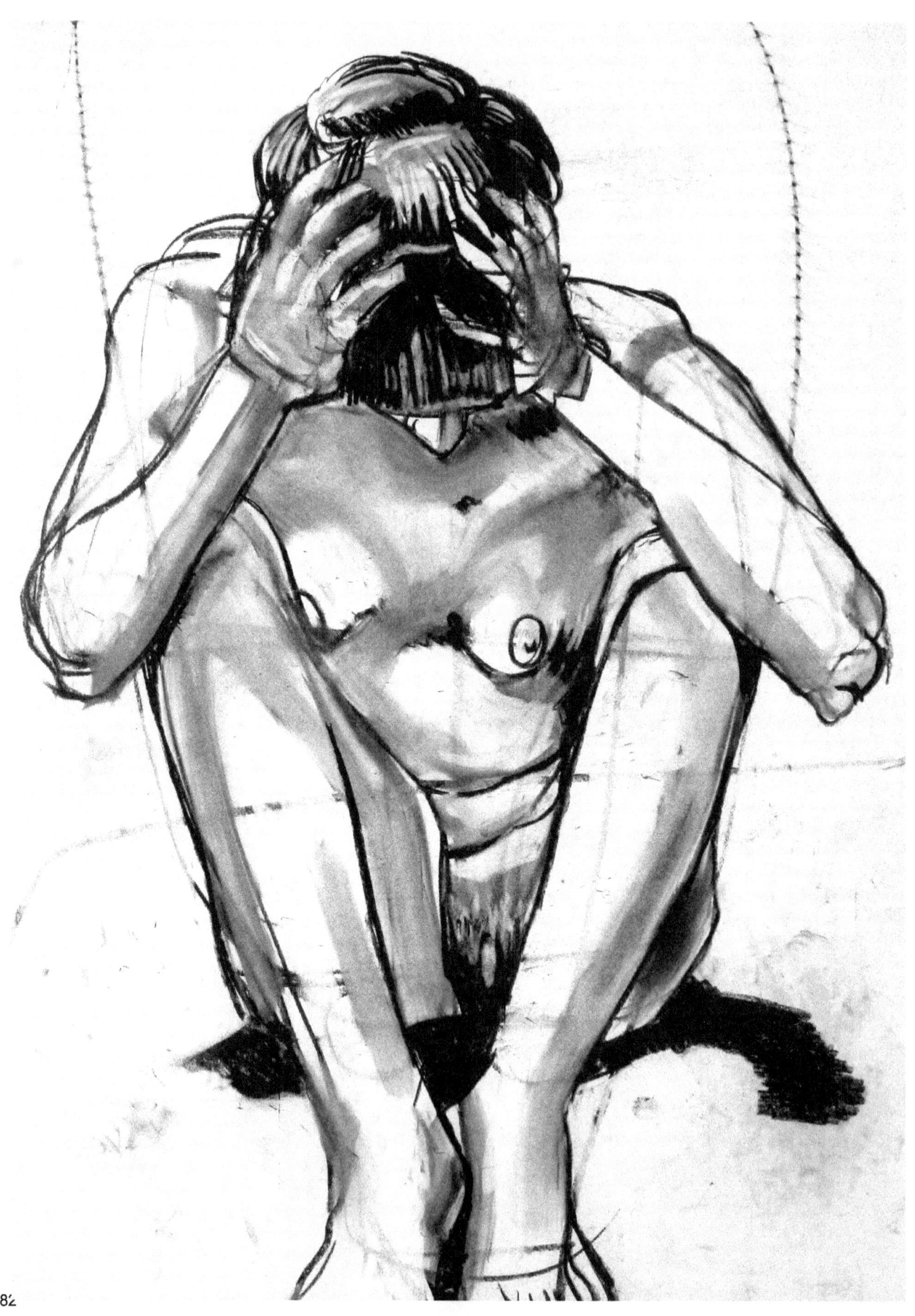

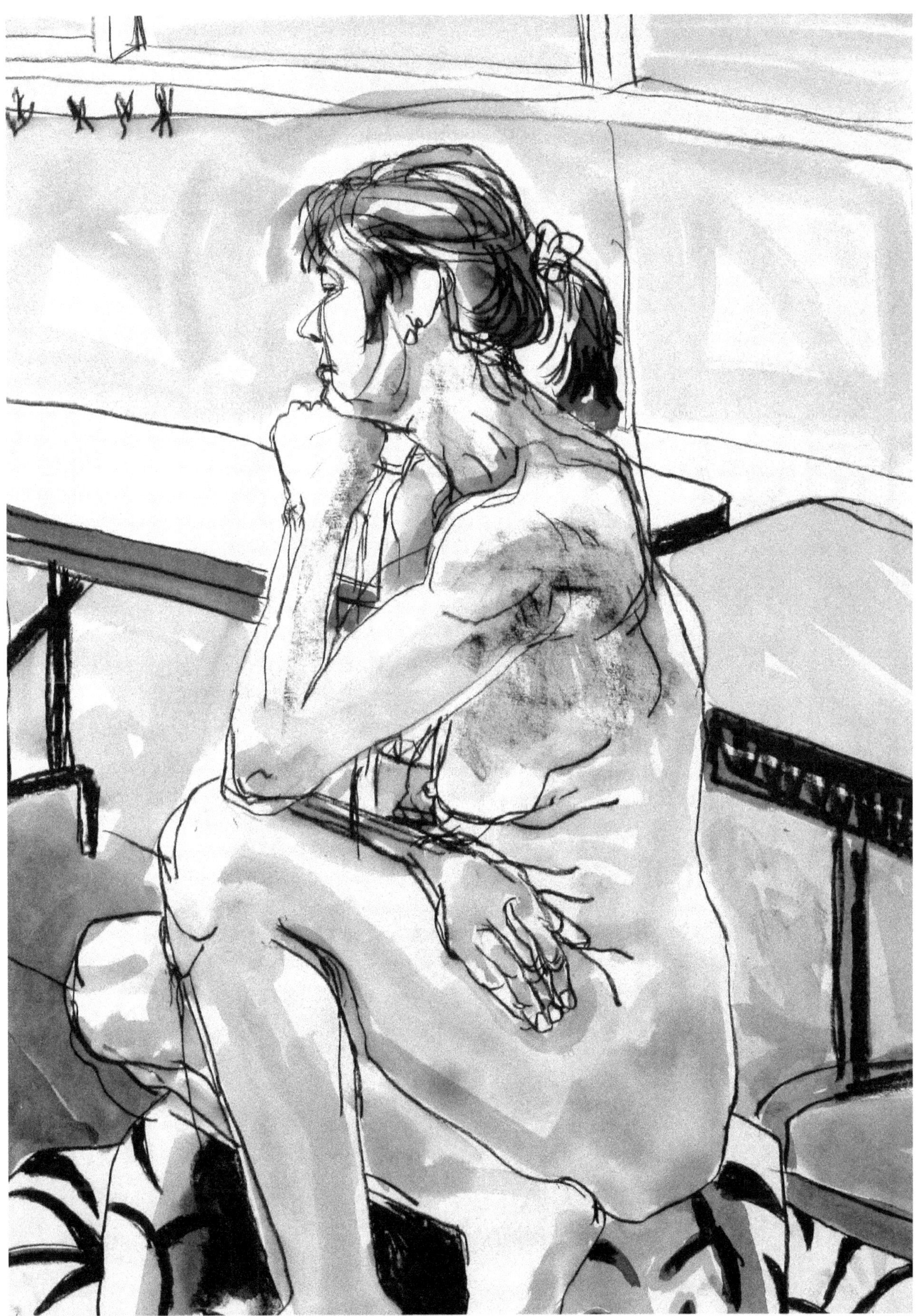

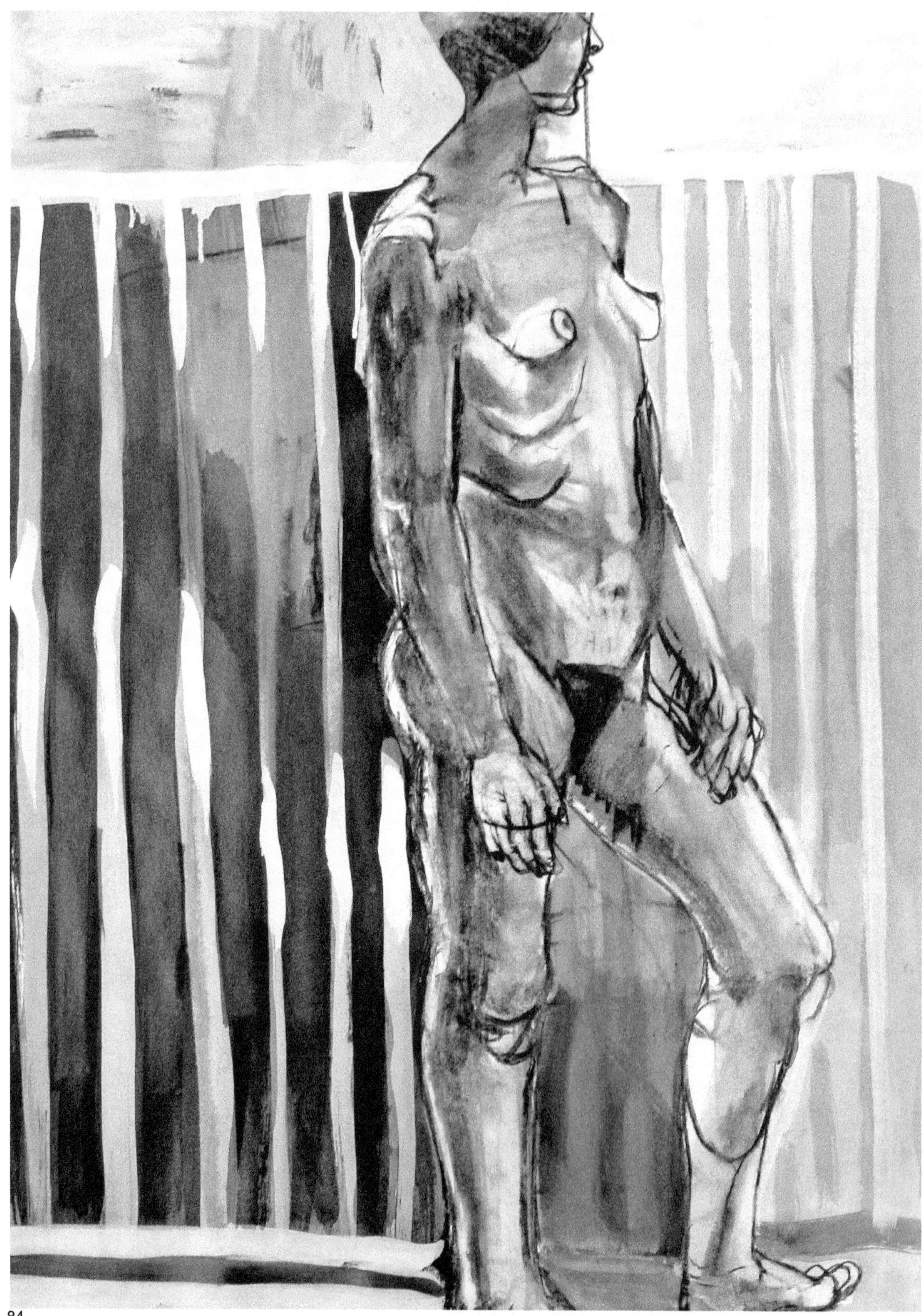

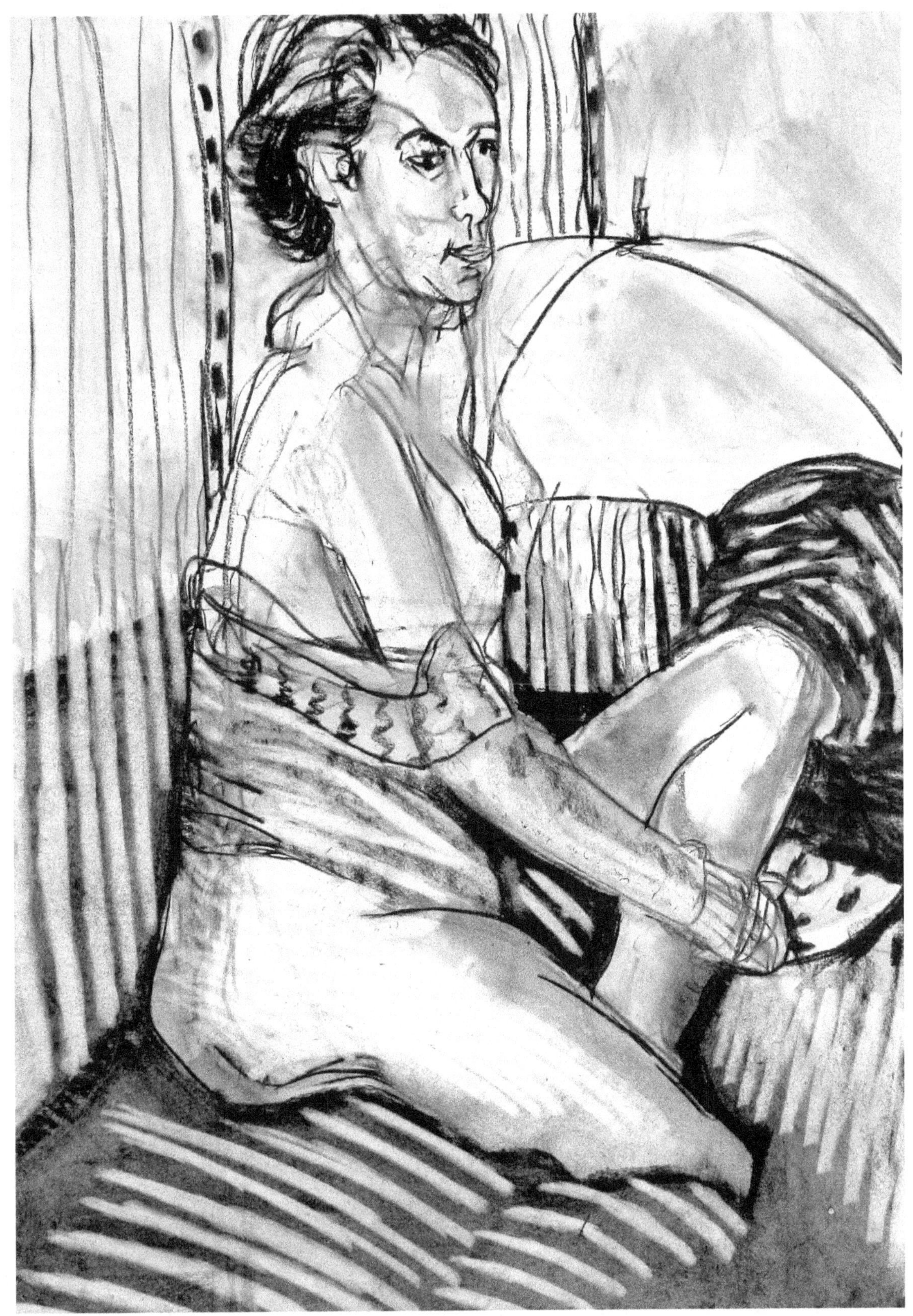

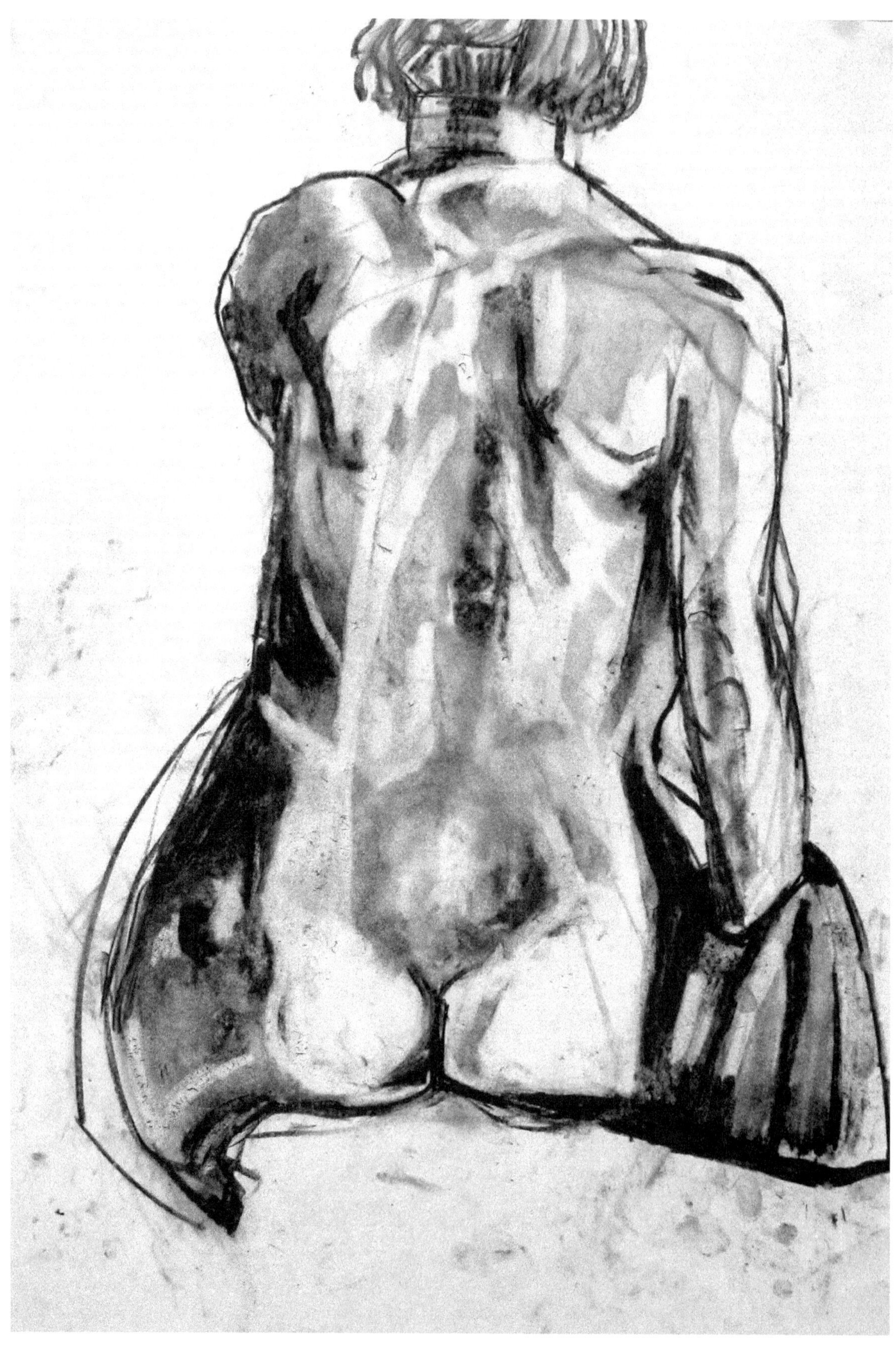

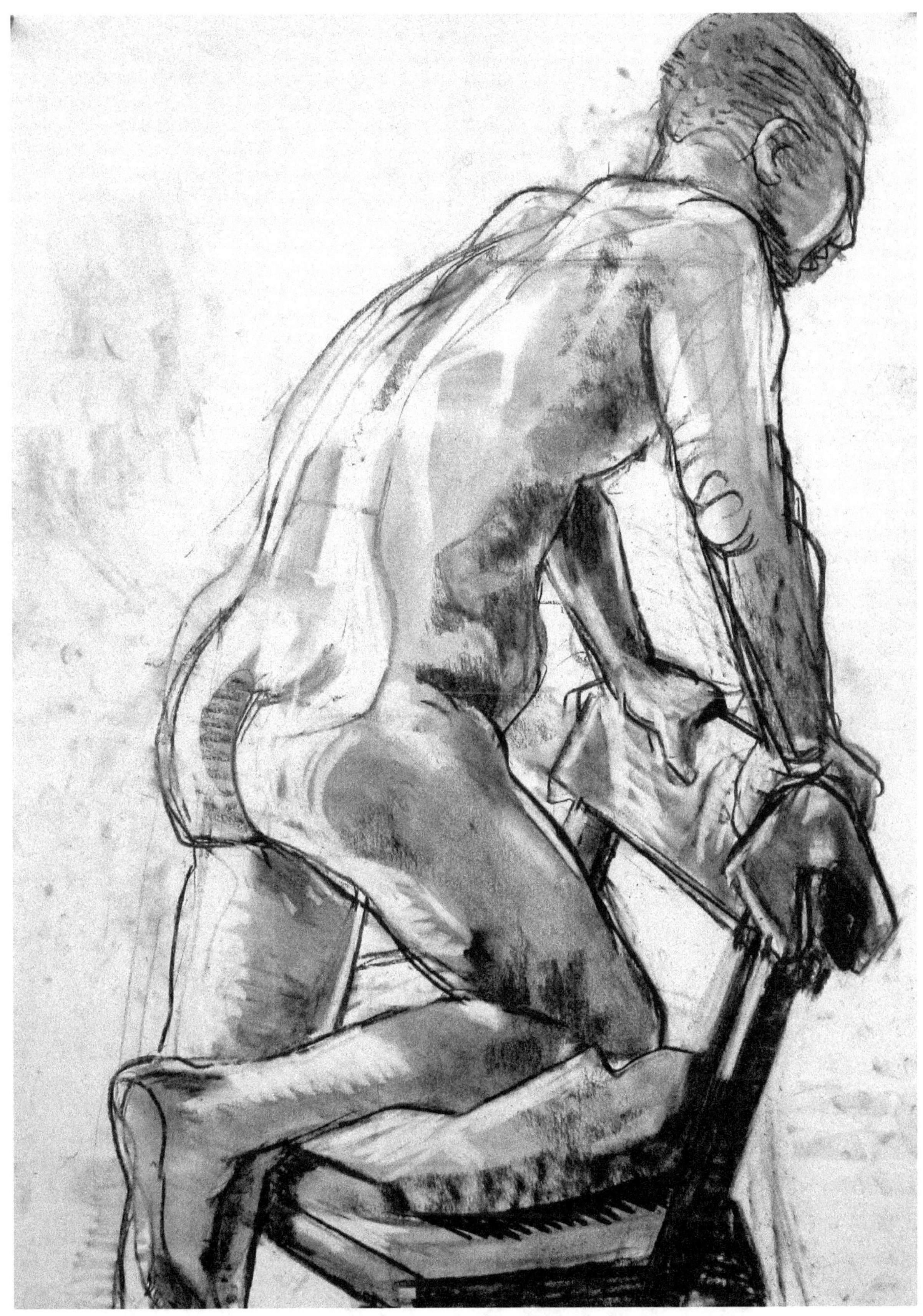

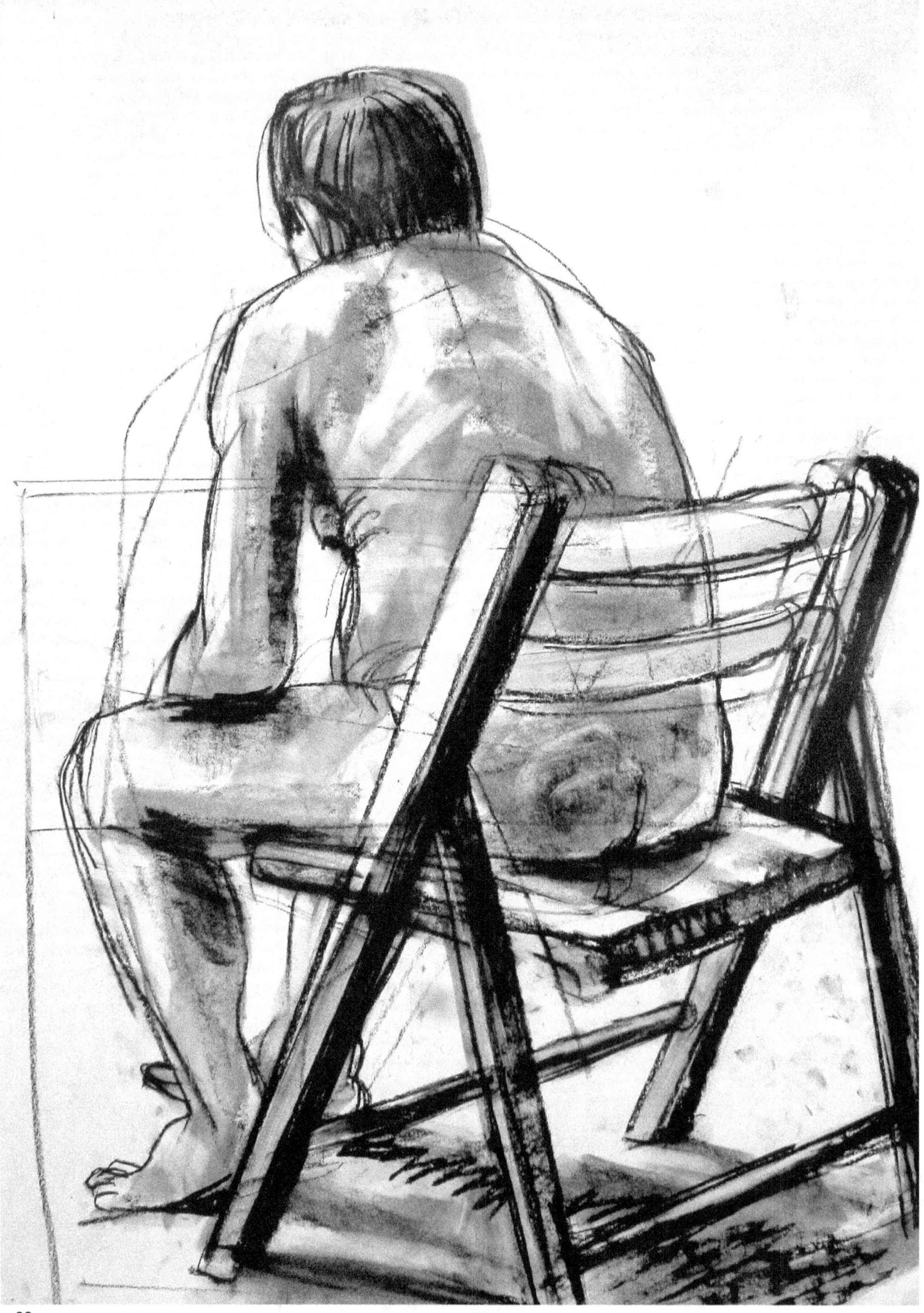

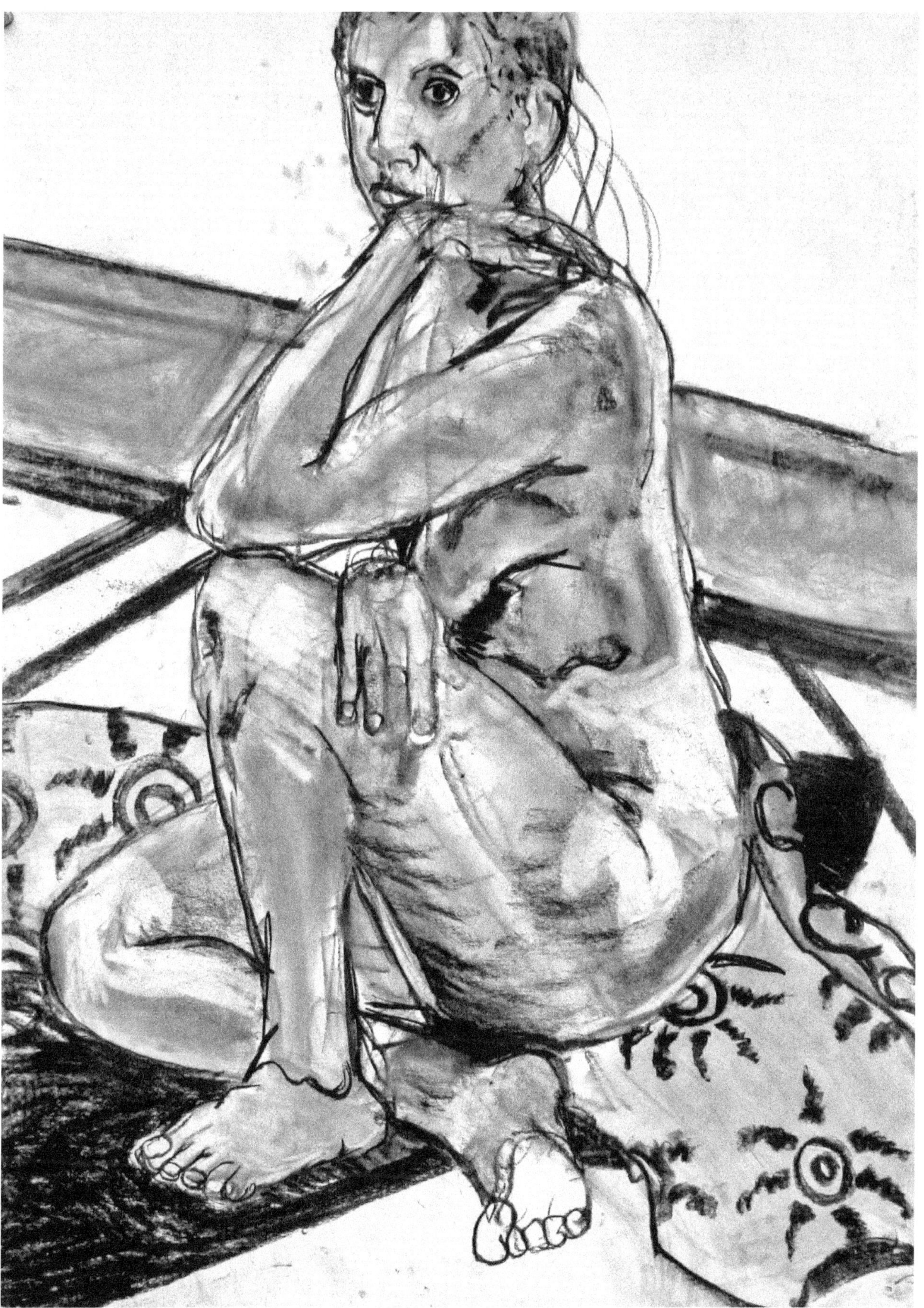

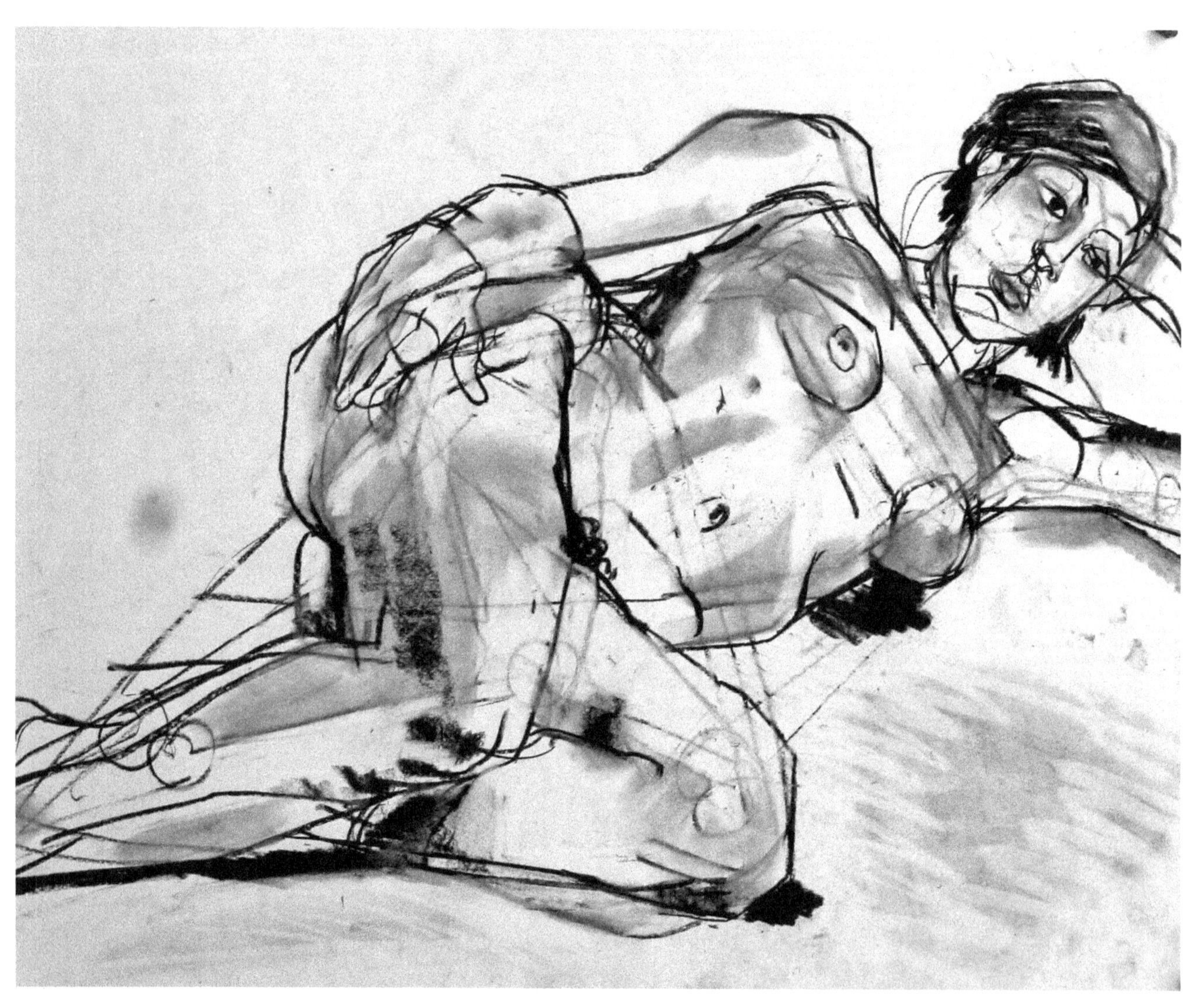

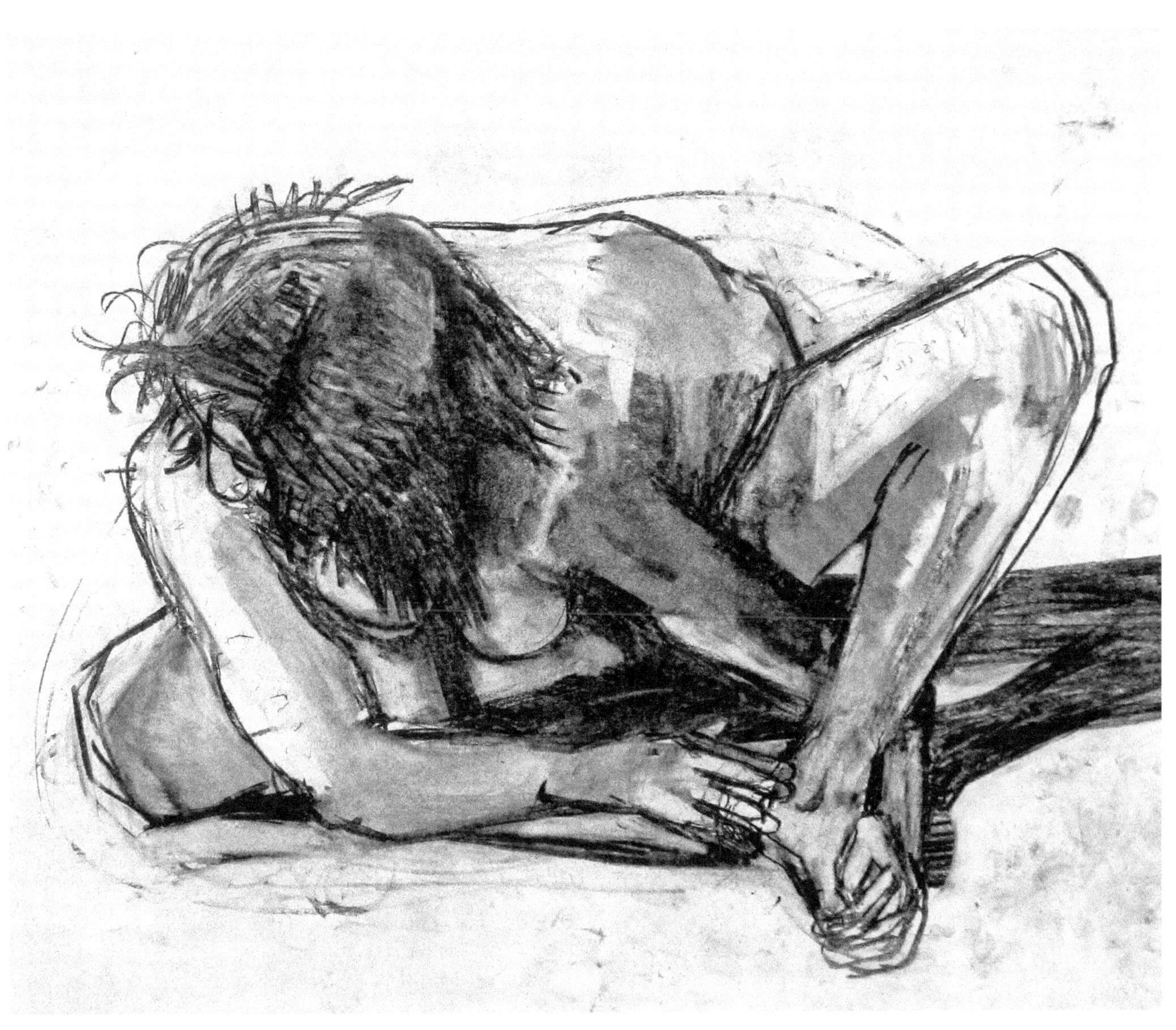

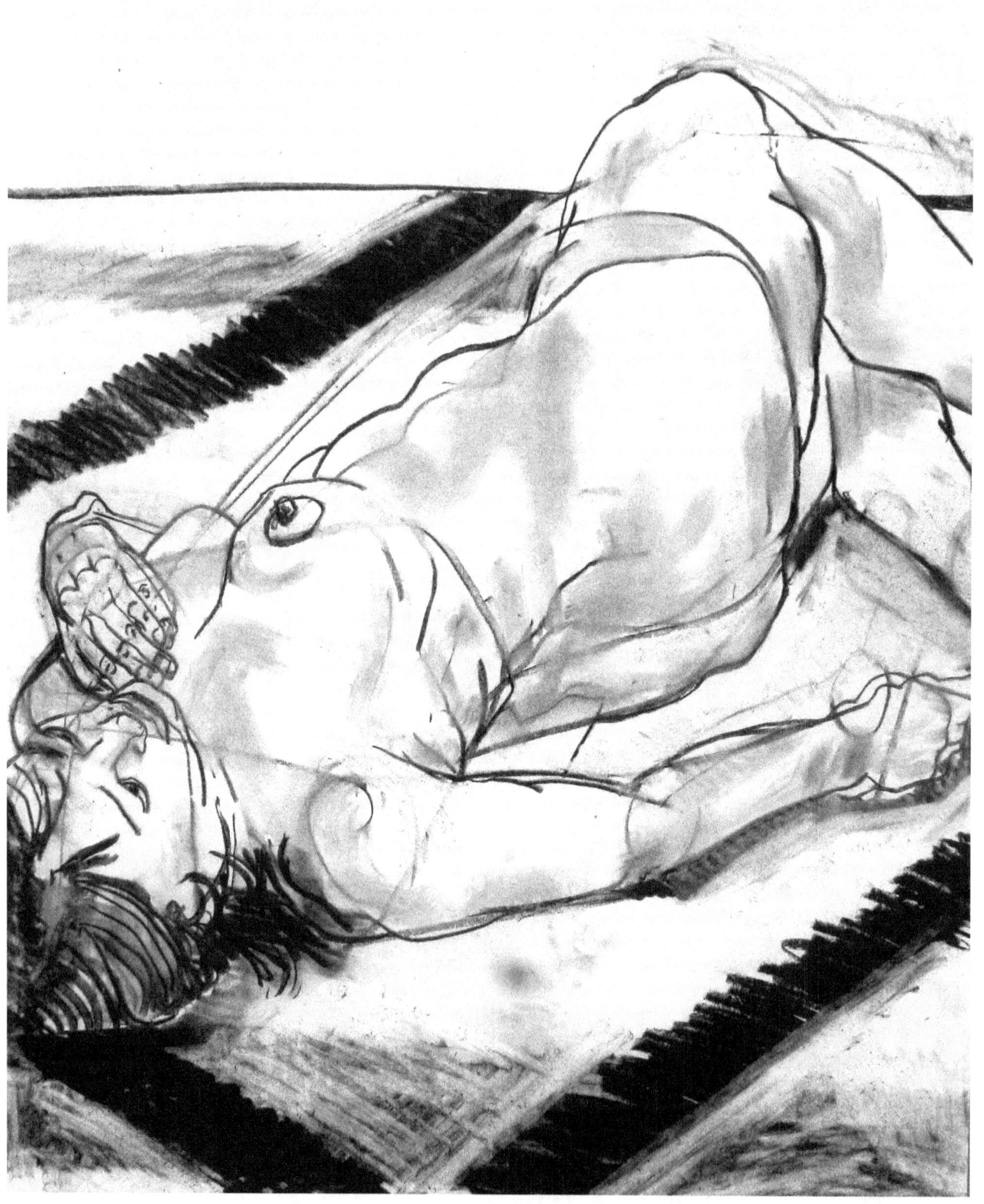

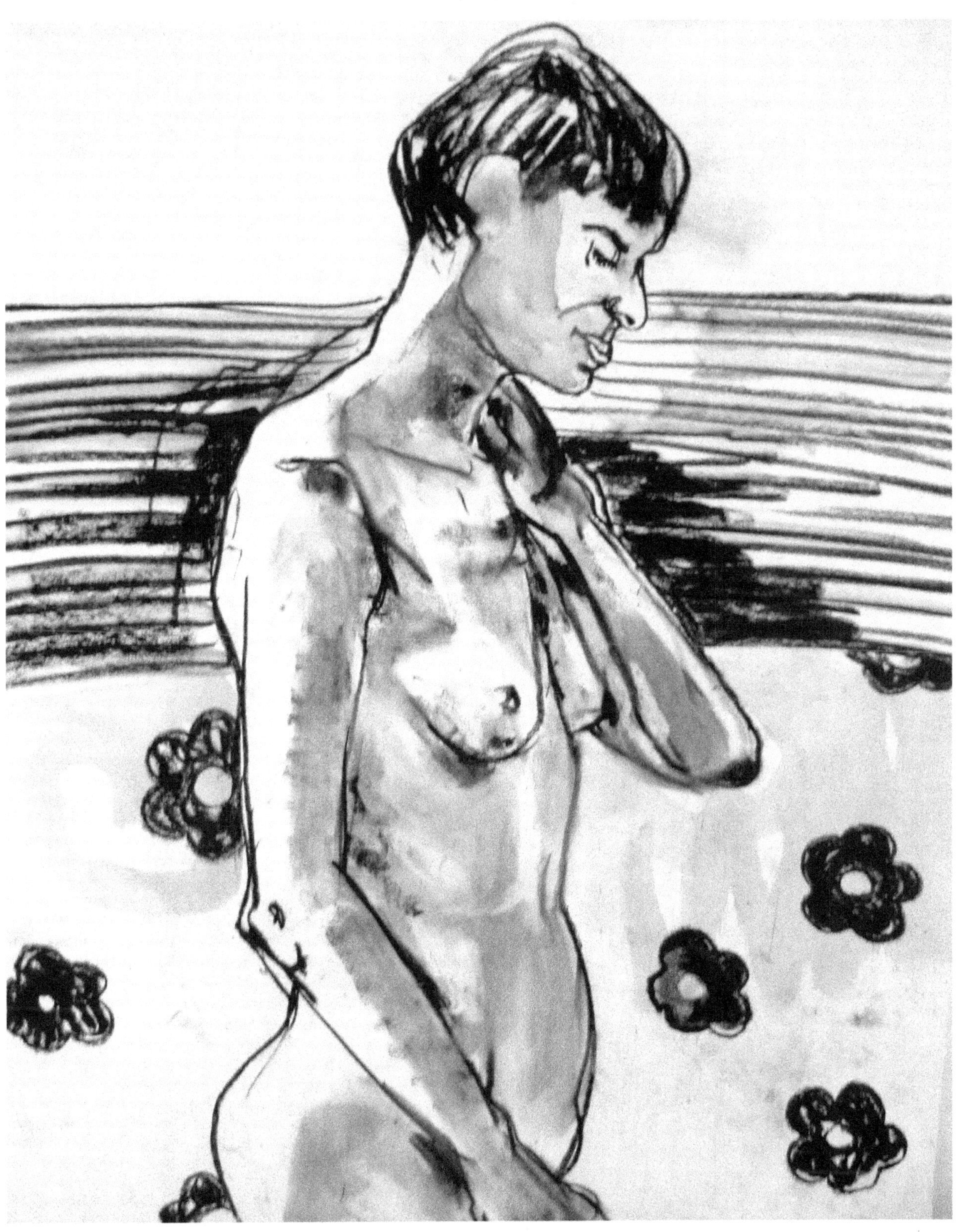

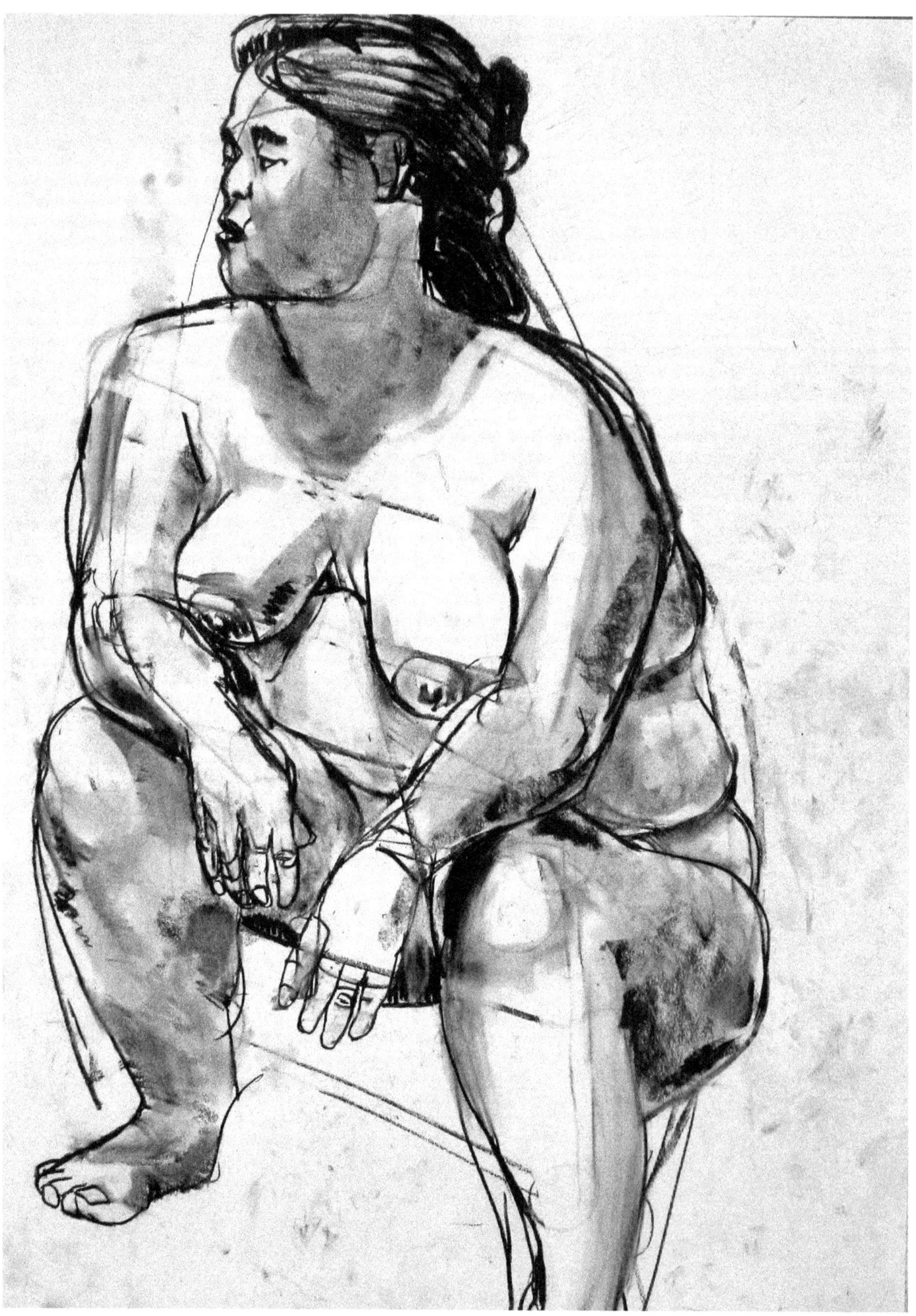

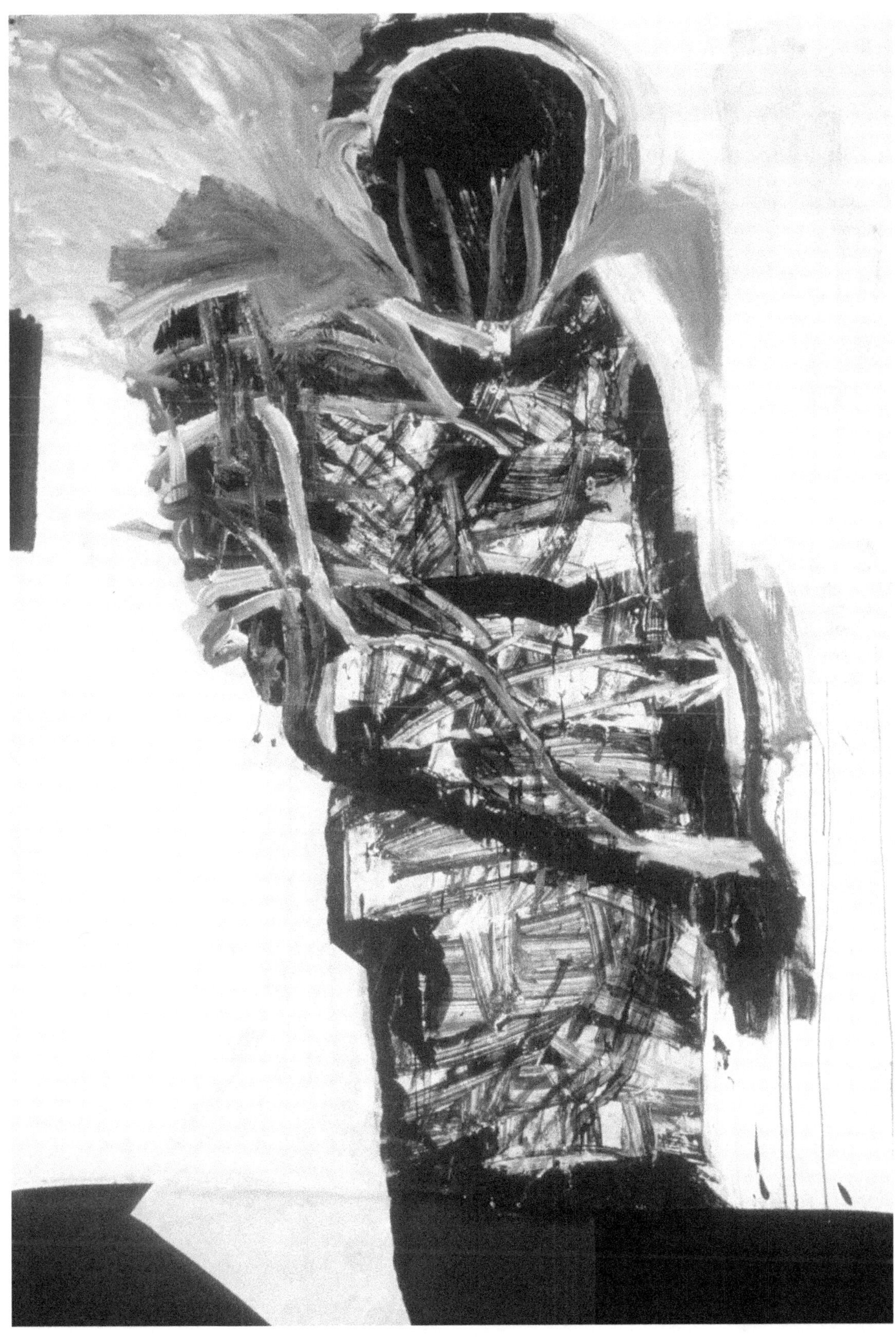

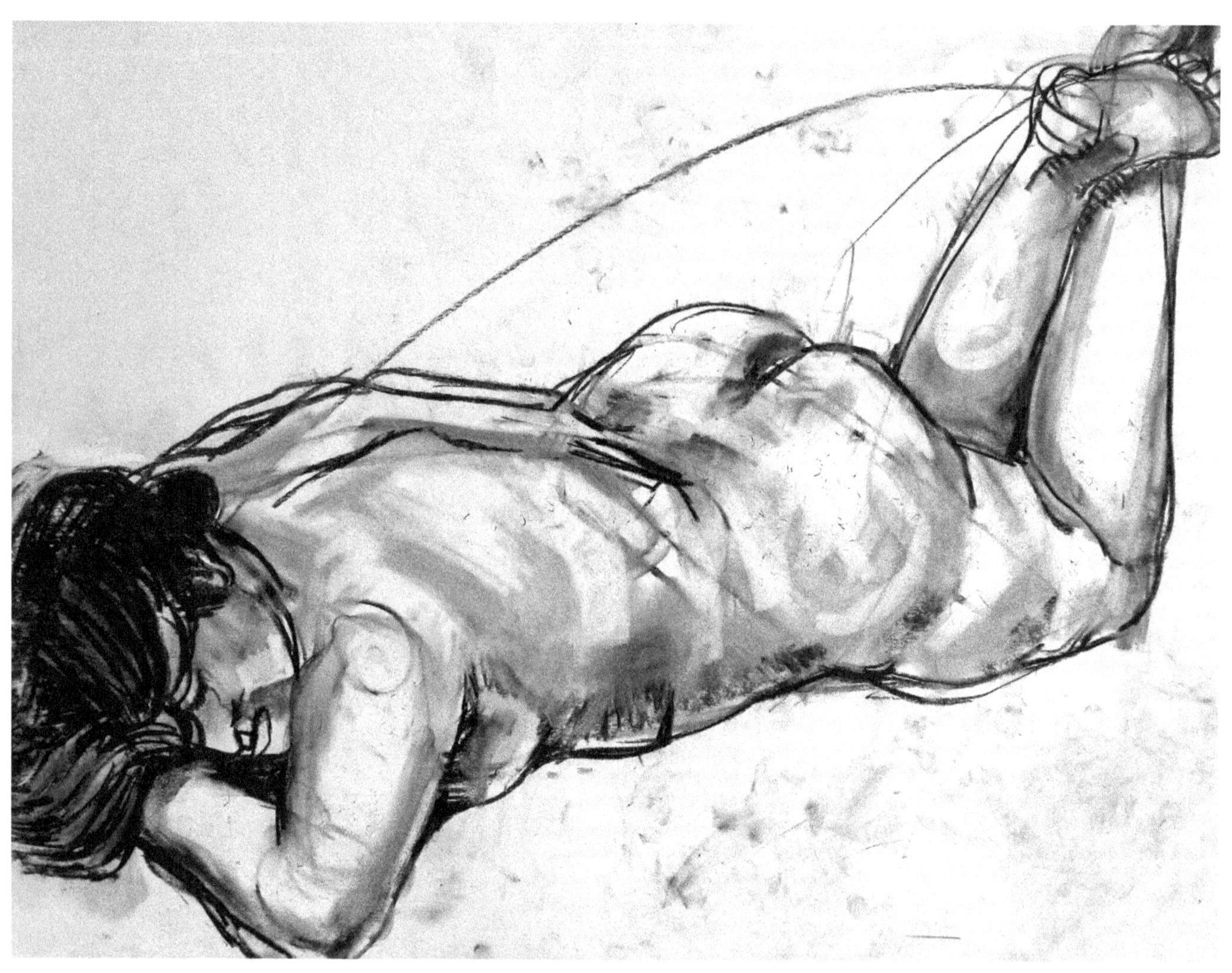

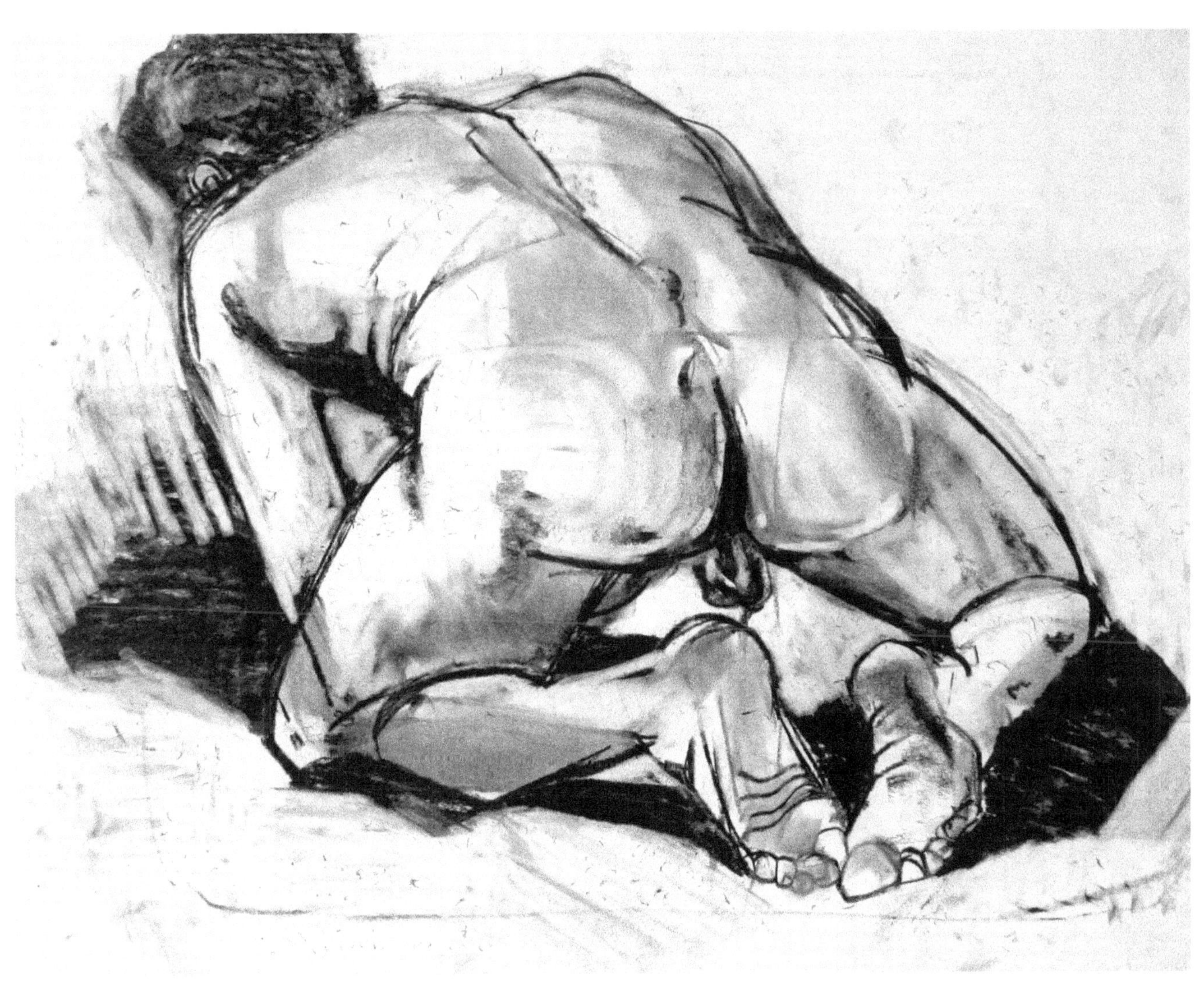

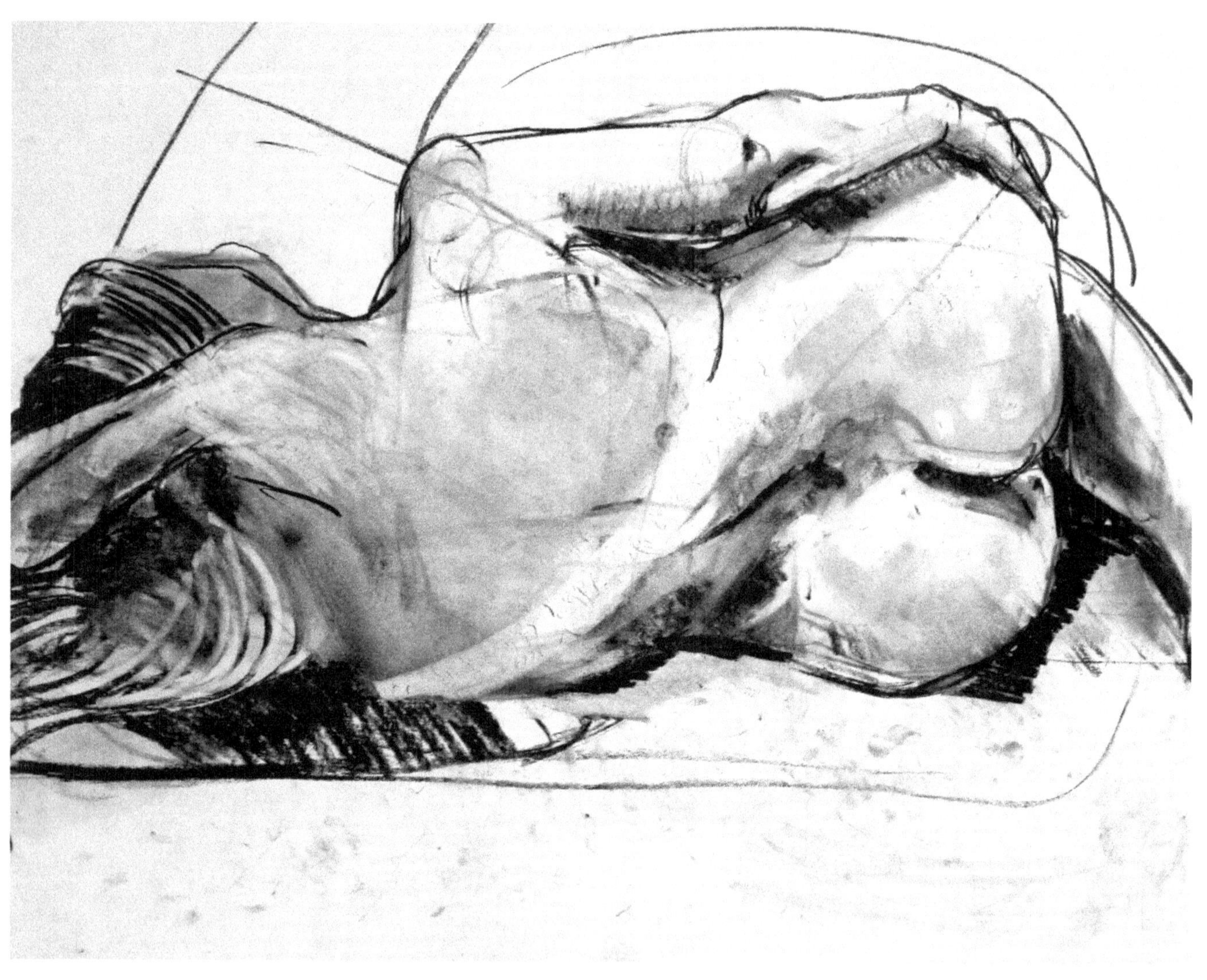

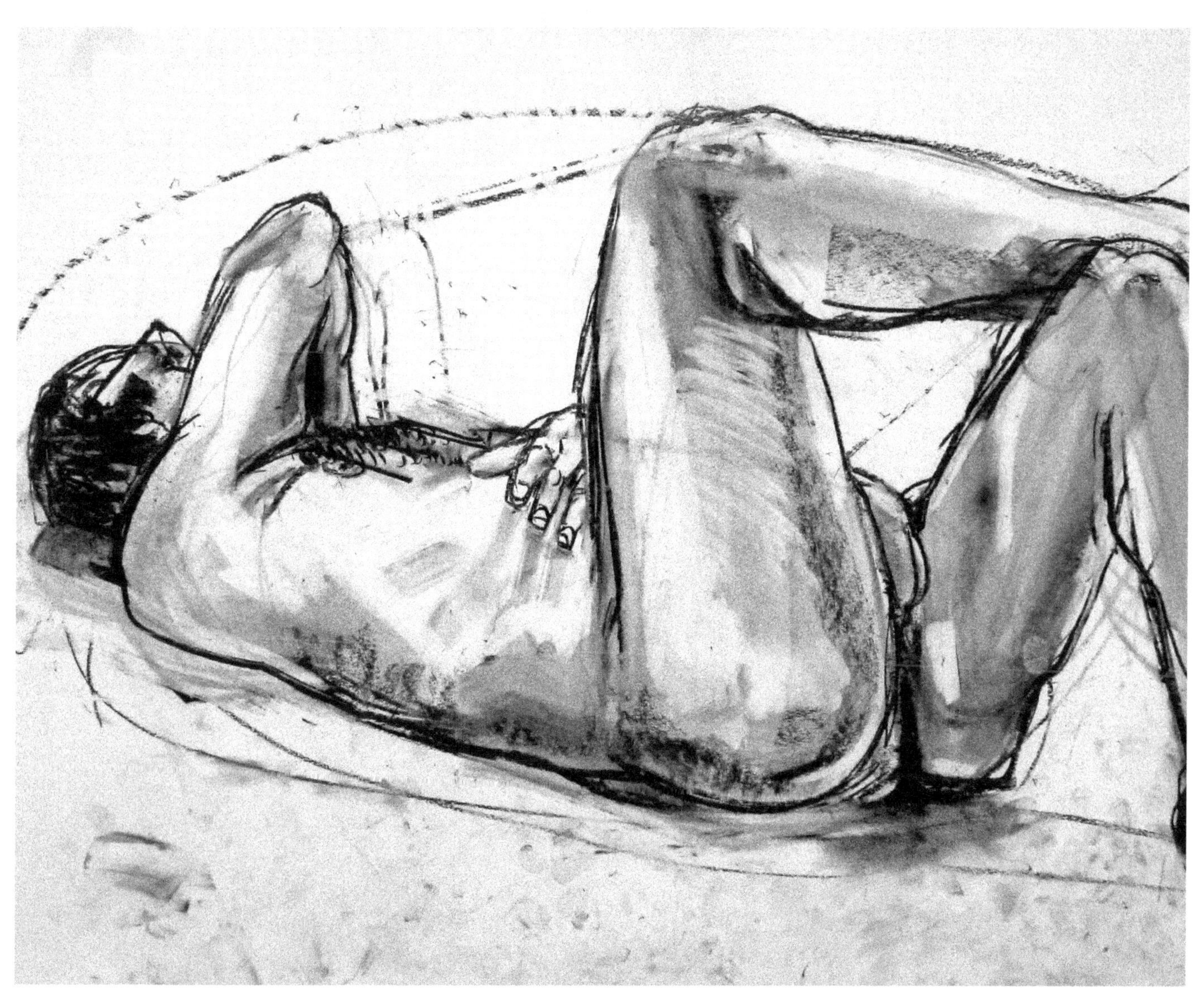

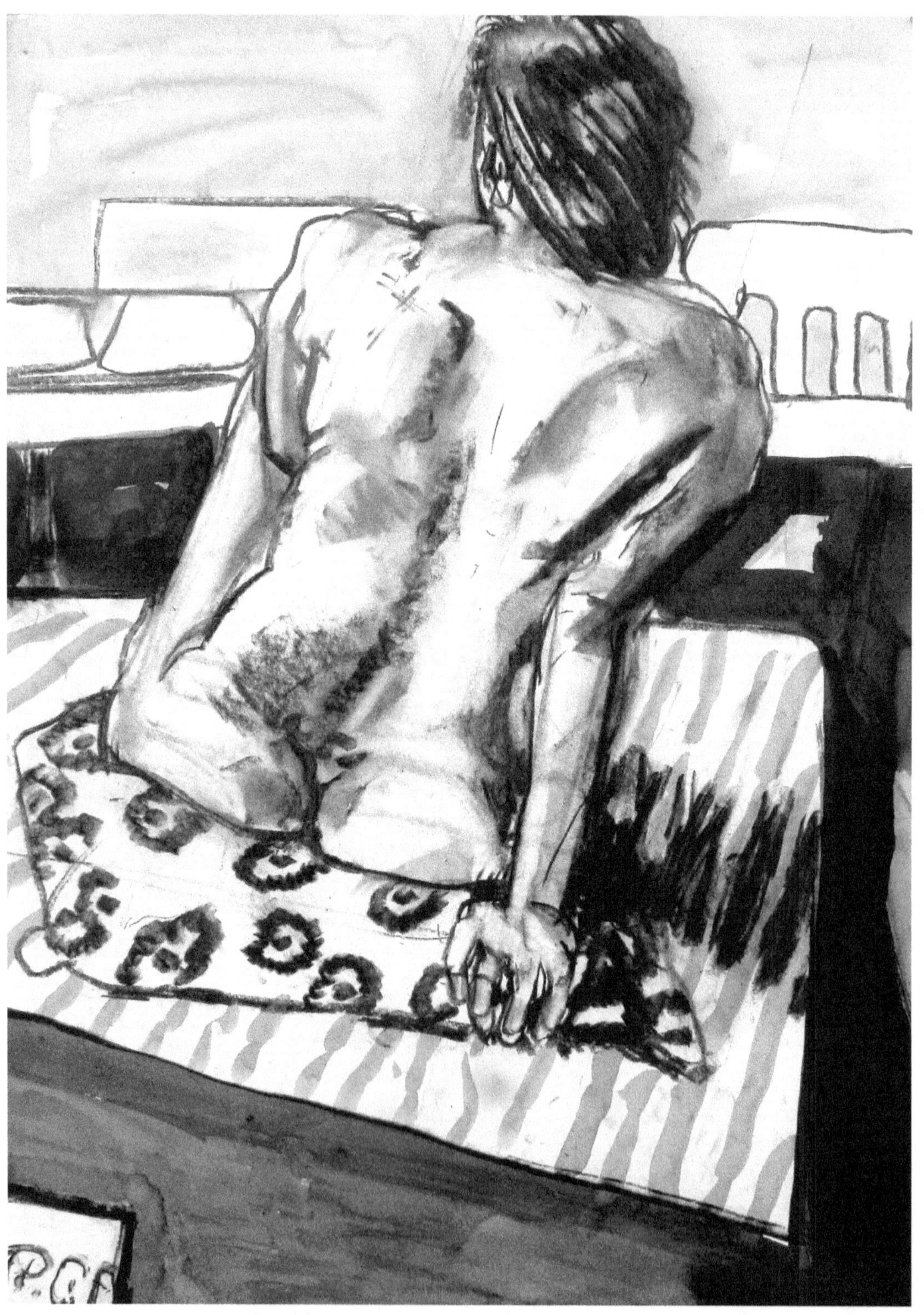

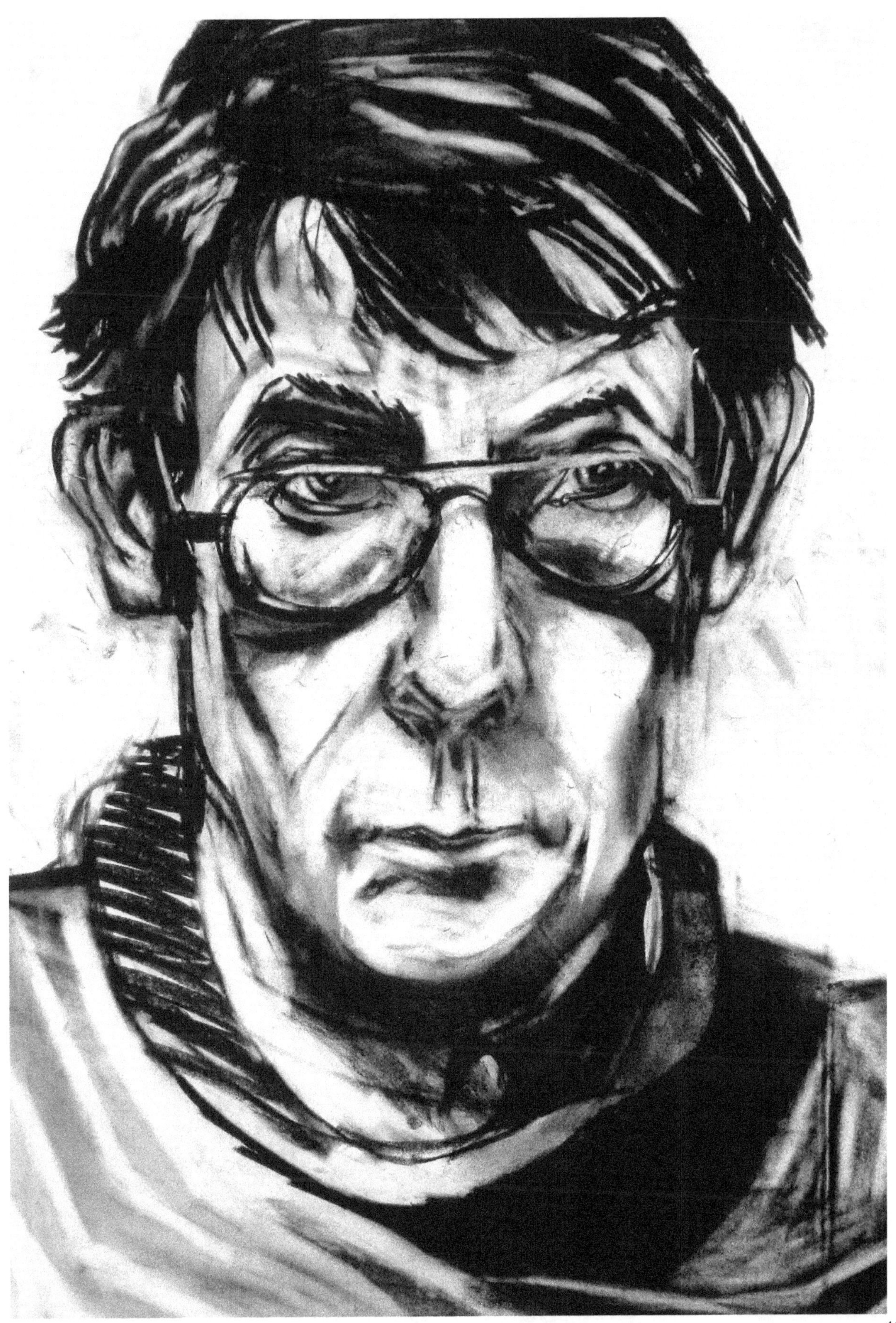

Drawing materials used are charcoal, ink, chalk and gouache on Lenox 100 paper, 22 by 30 inches.   A few images are much bigger 4 by 7 or 8 ft. on Rives paper. Images@copyrighted 2020 by Bruce Klein

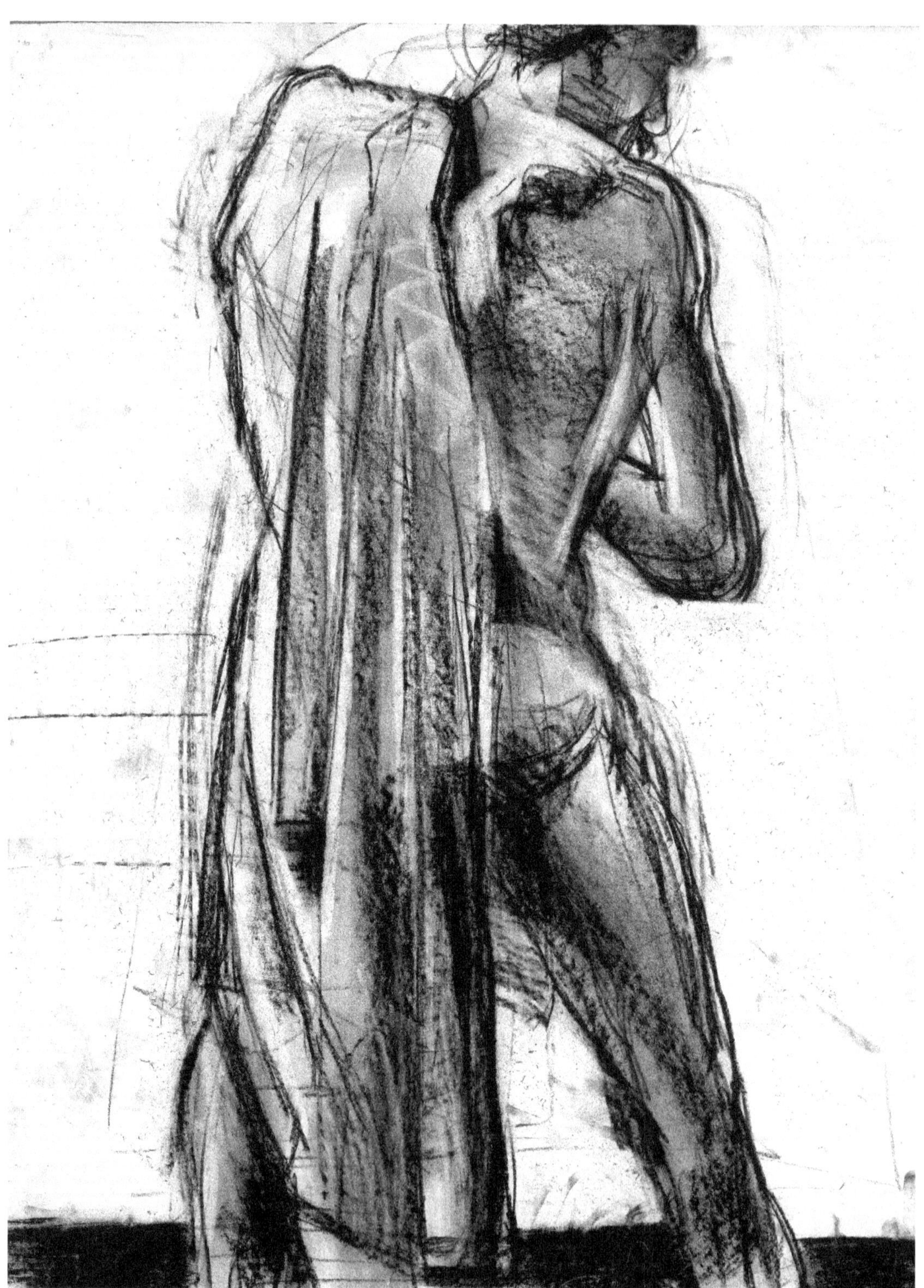